DATE DUE

NO 29'00			
E 10			

DEMCO 38-296

SPECIALTY SHOP RETAILING

National Retail Federation Series

The National Retail Federation Series comprises books on retail store management, for stores of all sizes and for all management responsibilities. The National Retail Federation is the world's largest retail trade association, with membership that includes the leading department, specialty, discount, mass merchandise, and independent stores, as well as 30 national and 50 state associations. NRF members represent an industry that encompasses more than 1.4 million U.S. retail establishments and employs nearly 20 million people—1 in 5 American workers. The NRF's international members operate stores in more than 50 nations.

The National Retail Federation Series includes the following books:

Competing with the Retail Giants: How to Survive in the New Retail Landscape, Kenneth E. Stone

Credit Card Marketing, Bill Grady

Dictionary of Retailing and Merchandising, Jerry M. Rosenberg

The Electronic Retailing Market: TV Home Shopping, Infomercials, and Interactive Retailing, Packaged Facts, Inc.

FOR 1996: Financial & Operating Results of Retail Stores in 1995, National Retail Federation

Loss Prevention Guide for Retail Businesses, Rudolf C. Kimiecik

Management of Retail Buying, 3d Edition, R. Patrick Cash, John W. Wingate, Joseph S. Friedlander

MasterMinding the Store: Advertising, Sales Promotion, and the New Marketing Reality, Donald Ziccardi with David Moin

MOR 1996: Merchandising & Operating Results of Retail Stores in 1995, National Retail Federation

Practical Merchandising Math, Leo Gafney

Retail Store Planning & Design Manual, 2d Edition, Michael Lopez

Small Store Survival: Success Strategies for Retailers, Arthur Andersen

The Software Directory for Retailers, 5th Edition, Coopers & Lybrand, L.L.P.

Specialty Shop Retailing: How to Run Your Own Store, Carol L. Schroeder

Value Retailing in the 1990s: Off-Pricers, Factory Outlets, and Closeout Stores, Packaged Facts, Inc.

SPECIALTY SHOP RETAILING

HOW TO RUN YOUR OWN STORE

CAROL L. SCHROEDER

John Wiley & Sons, Inc.

New York • Chichester • Brisbane • Toronto • Singapore • Weinheim

and my husband, friend,
and business partner, Dean

This publication is designed to provide accurate and authoritative
information in regard to the subject matter covered. It is sold with
the understanding that the publisher is not engaged in rendering legal,
accounting, or other professional services. If legal advice or other expert
assistance is required, the services of a competent professional person
should be sought.

Library of Congress Cataloging-in-Publication Data:

Schroeder, Carol L.
    Specialty shop retailing: how to run your own store/Carol L. Schroeder.
        p.   cm. — (National Retail Federation series)
    Includes bibliographical references and index.
    ISBN 0-471-14721-4 (cloth : alk. paper)
        1. Retail trade—Management.   2. Specialty stores—Management.
    I. Title.   II. Series.
    HF5429.S35566   1997
    658.8'7—DC20   96-41395

Printed in the United States of America

10 9 8 7 6 5 4 3 2

PREFACE

Twenty some years ago, I spent my junior year abroad studying Danish and English literature at the University of Copenhagen. During those long, dusky Danish winter days, the lights of Copenhagen's specialty shops cast an inviting glow over the dim sidewalks. With idle hours to fill between university literature classes, I often succumbed to the lure of fine design and friendly European service, wandering from shop to shop along Copenhagen's winding pedestrian shopping streets. As I browsed through displays of colorful handcrafts, candles, flowers, and furniture, I imagined someday creating a welcoming haven full of well-designed products back in America.

I never envisioned rivaling Sears or K-Mart. Their bottom-line-oriented style of retailing held no appeal for me. Nor was it my dream to be at the helm of a fleet of twenty-five stores, with employees I'd never met and managers who reported to the home office via computerized sales reports.

My vision was much simpler: to create a shop that would sell merchandise to enrich peoples' lives, through form, function, tradition, or amusement. I wanted to market this merchandise in an environment that would be pleasurable for customers and staff alike—a shop I would look forward to going to every morning at 10:00. (The fact that retailers don't have to report to work at 8:00 was a real plus in my mind.) If I could create meaningful employment, give back to the community, and make a living at the same time, I would consider my shop a success.

After returning to the United States to get a master's in Scandinavian Studies at the University of Wisconsin, I found myself ready to think seriously about owning a store. Unfortunately my work experience was limited to journalism and dental assisting, so I applied for a job at a Scandinavian furniture store in Madison, Wisconsin. The store had no opening in sales, but the owner was willing to hire me to tutor her in Danish until a job came up. And the perfect job appeared just a few weeks later; managing her new campus branch store. To my surprise, I was offered the position, despite an appalling lack of experience.

We opened the campus branch of Bord & Stol (Danish for "Table and Chair") in October 1974. The store carried furniture, housewares, and gifts from Scandinavia. I thought our first day of business was a great success, but on the second day, our first customer returned the expensive chair he bought the day before, resulting in a *negative* sales figure. Things could only get better!

Sales throughout the Christmas season were strong, but after the first of the year, this branch store began to compete with the main store for the limited cash available to fund its inventory. Suppliers stopped shipping to us, and it became clear that the branch would not survive for long. My husband, Dean, and I decided to make an offer to buy the business, and on May 1, 1975, we renamed it Orange Tree Imports. My dream of owning my own shop had come true.

We brought to the business world undergraduate degrees in German, English, and Danish and a graduate degree in Scandinavian Studies. Neither of us had ever taken a business course, although Dean had been working for his father selling packaging machinery. He kept this job for the first year or two of Orange Tree Imports, quitting only when it became apparent that the store could support us both. Even before that time, he would walk over to the shop with a hot lunch of grilled cheese sandwiches and soup for us both, and stay to help until he finally had to tear himself away to go back to his home office. Shopkeeping was a lot more fun than making sales calls.

Our store gradually grew from three employees to three dozen, and it tripled in size as we put on a new addition in 1980, then connected with the store next door in 1986. We expanded our merchandise mix from the basics of Scandinavian-influenced home accessories and kitchen supplies to include toys, jewelry, soaps, stationery, seasonal decorations, candles, candy, cards, gift wrap, glassware, garden gifts, porcelain, posters, and potpourri. We opened a cooking school over fifteen years ago to promote our cookware and kitchen gadgets and not long after that accepted a national award at the Plaza Hotel in New York City for promoting sticker collecting. This diversity of product mix is, I think, one of the keys to our longevity.

When we started Orange Tree Imports in the early 1970s, Madison was a hotbed of liberal thought, and capitalism was not a politically correct concept among our contemporaries. I was only twenty-three when we started the store, and I didn't know a thing about return on investment or business ratios. But that didn't matter, because profit did not interest us at all—until the year we didn't have one.

We had been lucky enough to start our store in prosperous times, and we grew steadily and had been profitable, in a modest way, almost from the start. But in the mid-1980s, things got tougher. There were too many retail stores in the Madison market, and our sales leveled off. Expenses, unfortunately, did not.

Retailing, we suddenly realized, is indeed a form of capitalism, and it requires a profit. Without a profit, the business could not continue to grow, and eventually it might cease to exist. We would no longer be able to sell wonderful products, please our customers, create a meaningful workplace for our staff, play an active part in our community, and make a living. Suddenly the bottom line became very important.

We were fortunate to have an excellent office of the Small Business Development Center (SBDC) in Madison. They helped us see that we really did know a lot about retailing—lessons we had learned through trial and error during our first years in business. They also taught us some of the things we didn't already know. We were able to turn Orange Tree Imports around, and we have been profitable ever since.

What we have learned is not complicated. Many ideas for successful retailing are actually simple, straightforward techniques that can be used in any store setting. In honor of Orange Tree Imports' twentieth anniversary in 1995, we decided to share some of the ideas we learned from the SBDC, our own years of retailing, our energetic and enthusiastic staff, and shopkeepers around the country and in Europe.

Whether you are a seasoned retailer with many years of experience or a novice just beginning to plan a store, I hope you will find yourself exclaiming, "What a great idea!" many times as you read this book. I have collected imaginative solutions to retailing challenges from a wide variety of sources for this book, which I hope you will find both helpful and entertaining. The high-energy retailing typified by the stores featured in this book is never boring, so why is it that so many books about retailing are sure cures for insomnia?

In addition to chapters touching on all the basics you need for retail success, the book features more than two dozen forms you can copy (some may need to be enlarged for ease of use), or modify, to use in your store. No special permission is needed to do so. Having designed many forms for use in my own shop, I know what a time saver it is to find one ready to use. I've also included examples of good ideas from stores around the world that you can adapt. The Glossary at the back of the book contains all the terms you need to know to sound like a long-time native in the world of retailing. And for everything I don't cover, the Bibliography contains many other excellent resources. The fact that you are reading this book shows that you are eager to find new information and ideas, so I hope you will continue that journey by reading some of the works listed in the Bibliography and by visiting specialty shops wherever you go.

If you find yourself in Madison, please visit our shop, located just down the street from the University of Wisconsin football stadium. Let me know if you're coming, and I'll try to make time to share a cup of tea and talk with you about your store. If you can't come to Madison, I'd love to get an invitation to your grand opening, or to hear about ideas and suggestions you may have for future editions of this book. Our address is Orange Tree Imports, 1721 Monroe Street, Madison, WI 53711.

ACKNOWLEDGMENTS

I'd like to sincerely thank all the retailers who shared their experiences with me so that I could pass their ideas on to you. The owners of Pegasus Games, Chris Kerwin Antiques, Oriental Specialties, Pooh Corner, the Art Mart of Urbana, Neuhauser Pharmacy, Chickadee Depot, Movin' Kids, Andrea's, Shop of the Gulls, and Cork & Bottle all took time to respond to my detailed questionnaire. Numerous other retailers and wholesale suppliers spoke to me on the telephone or in person, sharing many helpful hints. The following companies generously provided photographs and sample ads: A Southern Season, Crabtree & Evelyn, The Rouse Company, Lynne Meena & Company, Arnold Finnegan Martin, Martin Williams Advertising, Vera Bradley Designs, the retail shop at the Connecticut Audubon Center at Fairfield, and The Library Shop at The New York Public Library. Special thanks to Mari Stein for her delightful cartoons.

I thank all of my sales representatives and vendors who gave me advice over the past year about what they felt retailers need to know. I hope they'll be pleased with the sections on being nice to reps and developing positive vendor relations.

I very much appreciate the assistance of the specialists who read and critiqued individual chapters or provided professional advice on specific sections: Bill Snyder, Glen Forbes, John Anderson, Rachael Deprey, Nanci Bjorling, Connie Nadler, Pat Kellogg, Janie Nolen, Barbara Conley, Chuck Hinners, Mort Haaz, Jeffrey Greene, Jeff Schroeter, Neil Lerner, Marilyn Scholl, Tom Frost, Jeanne Anderson, and Rick Boucher.

Six people deserve special recognition for reading the first full draft of the manuscript and offering many helpful comments: Trudy Barash, Marge Tully, Malcolm Holt, Pat Groehler, Joan Maynard, and my father, Stanley Ehrlich. I appreciate the many constructive suggestions made by the copy editor, Beverly Miller, and the careful guidance given by Bernice Pettinato of Beehive Production Services. And finally, special thanks to my husband, Dean, and to my editor, Ruth Mills, for believing in the project right from the start, and to my mother, Ann Ehrlich, for helping with the manuscript every step of the way.

CONTENTS

1

GETTING STARTED

I firmly believe retailing is the most exciting and creative field of small business today. Nevertheless, when budding entrepreneurs approach me for advice about starting a store, the first thing I do is try to talk them out of it. There are, of course, many good reasons *not* to open a store: the risk of losing everything you own, the fact that discounters are beginning to dominate the marketplacc, the high percentage of new store failures. If no amount of arguing can deter a potential new retailer, I know that he or she has the determination and enthusiasm necessary to beat the odds and run a successful business.

We all start with a dream. Yours may be that you want to share merchandise you love with customers or that you've always wanted to be your own boss. Perhaps you've talked to friends about building a business together, or you've seen a wonderful storefront that inspires your creativity. Turning your dream into reality starts with a marketing study and business plan to find out if your idea is economically feasible. Once you've opened the doors to your store, the challenge is to keep your vision alive while coping with the day-to-day duties of running a business. The better your preparation is before opening, the less likely you are to let your dream be overwhelmed by the challenges you face once your store is launched.

MARKET RESEARCH

Retail chains spend thousands of research dollars before deciding on a new store location, but many novice retailers determine the location and merchandise mix of their first store without paying much attention to whether there is an adequate demand for what they will be offering in the area the store will be serving. "Market research" may sound complicated and expensive, but it is something you can do on your own simply by asking as many people as possible whether they think there is a ready market for your type of merchandise, at the prices you would need to charge. If the answer is yes, the next question to ask potential customers is where they think they would go to shop for this merchandise. Their answers will help you determine your best location.

Start informally, with family and friends. Tell everyone you know about your idea, and solicit their suggestions. Listen to what they say, and use this information to refine your concept before expanding the research to include your target customers.

Two women once came to see me about an idea they'd had for an innovative way of marketing jewelry to rural Wisconsin women. When I asked if they had actually spoken to any rural Wisconsin women to see if they were interested in a new source for jewelry, one of the potential entrepreneurs exclaimed, "Wow, this is *reality!*" Reality is a good place to begin when you are considering investing your time and money in a new retail venture.

Talking to a Focus Group

Focus groups can be very helpful in determining the direction your business should take. Invite a group of ten or twelve people with a potential interest in what you'll be selling to come together in a quiet setting and respond to a few simple questions. For example, for a quilting supply store, you might ask:

- Where do you currently buy fabric?
- Are there any types of fabric you can't find in this area?
- What price range do you look for in fabric?
- Where would you like to go to shop for quilting supplies?
- What special services would you want a quilting store to offer?
- Do you think quilting is increasing or decreasing in popularity in this area?

You might want to tape-record the discussion so that you can review every detail later. Be sure to reward those who participate in your focus groups with a small gift. If you decide to go ahead with your business plan, send focus group members a special grand opening invitation and a gift certificate.

After your store has been open for some time, a focus group of customers can help you determine how well you are meeting your shoppers' needs. We occasionally use a voluntary "customer council," made up of a dozen or so of our best customers, to help us refine our customer services and merchandise selection.

Checking Out the Competition

Competition isn't always a reason to avoid going into business in a certain area; after all, McDonald's and Burger King frequently build restaurants very near each other, though only after determining that there is enough business there for them both. Customers like having choices, and certainly having several antique stores in one block will draw more customers than one antique store will, providing there is a large enough market in antiques to support them all.

How do you determine market size? Demographics, which are statistics relating to the population of an area, can be very useful. The larger the population or number of visitors, the more shops the area can support. The higher the per capita income, the higher the price of merchandise the shoppers can afford. Check to find out whether the area's population is growing or declining. In addition to studying the statistics, look at the existing shops. What type of merchandise do they sell? Are they prospering? Talk to the shopkeepers. Explain that you are thinking of opening a store in the area and hopefully you'll get an honest answer when you ask, "How's business?"

Market size also determines how narrow your *niche*—that is, the shop's focus—can be. In a popular tourist area, such as Pier 39 in San Francisco, shops can succeed featuring nothing but magnets, or music boxes, or items with hearts on them. With thousands of potential customers walking by each day, there is a good chance that an adequate number will be interested in a certain category of merchandise. In a small town, the only viable retailer may be the general store, with as broad a mix of merchandise as you can imagine. Don't make the mistake of opening a highly specialized store in a small market. If only 5 percent of the population is likely to be interested in your merchandise, a town of 10,000 will yield a maximum of only 500 potential customers—fewer than 2 a day. Niche retailing is a viable way to compete with discount stores in prosperous areas with a large resident or tourist population, but diversity works best in more limited markets.

The Threat of Discounters

Should you open a store that will attempt to compete head-to-head with a discount giant? These stores are often referred to as *big box retailers*, in reference to their exciting architecture. But some of them are called *category killers*, and these are the ones you have to watch out for. Toys 'Я' Us, for example, is considered a category killer in the toy market, and several supersized bookstores are similarly threatening the viability of small bookshops. If you want to compete with these giants, look for a location that is not too near them but is still convenient for your potential customers. If your store is in an area with a large customer base, you might choose to focus your merchandising on a specific market segment not well served by the other stores, stocking, for example, exotic woods and special hand tools for the avid woodworker not available at the big building supply store down the street. Offer a wide selection of products in such categories, and make sure your employees are extremely knowledgeable about your merchandise. To offer services and merchandise that the big guys don't, you'll need to shop them constantly and be aware of what they are doing. Plan to cultivate a loyal customer base by stressing excellence in every aspect of your store's operation.

General discounters leave many gaps in their merchandise mix, of which a good specialty shop retailer can take advantage. Shoppers often prefer the careful merchandise selection and personalized service of a smaller shop, as long as the location and store hours are convenient. Try to find out what the shoppers in your area are looking for. Your chances of retail success are much greater if you provide something your customer base needs or wants and can't easily get anywhere else.

Starting Small

Opening a traditional retail store isn't always the best way to test the market for your store concept. Consider getting some feedback from the buying public by first leasing a pushcart (Figure 1-1) or freestanding kiosk

Figure 1-1 One way to test your retailing concept is to start with a pushcart or kiosk.

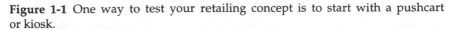

(*Courtesy of The Rouse Company.*)

at a large mall. These small retail ventures often receive special support and encouragement from mall management because they add color and variety to the shopping center, and sometimes they grow up to be full-size, permanent tenants.

You could also test your idea by renting a table at a weekend flea market. If you plan to sell crafts that you make, start by selling at an art fair or a Renaissance fair. See if there is an indoor crafters' showcase or art gallery near you that provides a year-round setting for craft sales. You may find that you prefer concentrating on your art and letting others do the selling.

Some stores allow other retailers to lease space inside an existing shop, sharing expenses and staffing responsibilities. West Palm Beach, Florida, helps new retailers get a start by renting out small *incubator shops* in a large building. The hope is that the new stores will outgrow the temporary, small space and become established, successful members of the retail community.

In addition to discovering whether there is a market in your area for the type of merchandise you plan to sell, a small venture will allow you to decide whether you like retailing. The experience of owning your own shop is, of course, quite different from having a booth at a weekend craft fair, but both experiences do involve selling and dealing with the public.

ARE YOU READY FOR RETAILING?

Once you have determined that you have a viable idea for a shop, it's time to determine whether you have the skills and capital necessary to take the plunge. Many potential shopkeepers have never worked in a store, and have no idea how to set up a bookkeeping system or even calculate retail prices. If at all possible, work in a small established shop before you invest everything you own in your retail dream, but don't work for a competitor if you plan to open a store in the same area. Look for a part-time or seasonal job at a specialty shop while you continue to work your current job. If you can't do that, you might offer to work in a store for free for a month or two so that you can learn as much as possible. Studies show, not surprisingly, that starting a business in a field you are familiar with dramatically increases your chances of success. Experience in a big corporate setting, or other past employment, may not be applicable to the challenges you'll face running a retail store.

You don't need an M.B.A. to be a shopkeeper, but a few courses in small business management will make it easier for you to get your store off to a successful start. These are often available through technical colleges or programs such as the Small Business Development Center (SBDC). Trade associations such as the American Booksellers Association offer special short courses for potential new store owners, and trade shows often feature seminars on useful topics. You may be able to audit a college-level course, although most college retailing courses seem to focus on department stores and other corporate businesses.

Use the months before you start your store to visit similar stores in other parts of the country. Subscribe to the trade magazines that cover the type of shop you'd like to open and visit wholesale trade shows to get an idea of the types of merchandise available to you and the overall range of wholesale prices you can expect to pay. Talk to the sales representatives at the shows for information about market trends and other retailing advice. Check at your local library or a bookstore for books on the various aspects of running a small business. The bibliography in the back of this book lists many excellent sources of information, and new business books are published all the time.

> When E. Diane White decided to open Blackberry, a chain of award-winning specialty stores specializing in African-inspired products adapted to the Western market, she persuaded the owner of a gift shop specializing in items from Africa to let her work for free in the evenings and on weekends to supplement her Harvard M.B.A. with practical retail experience.

The Personal Side

Are you ready emotionally and financially to open your own business? Take an honest look at your life circumstances, and evaluate whether now is the right time for you to risk this new venture. Chances are good you will put in long hours the first few years, and you may not have much take-home income. It's not uncommon for the owners of a new store to put in twelve-hour days, six or seven days a week, especially when the shop is young. There seems to be an endless amount of work to be done, and it takes some time to get staff well enough trained to delegate significant responsibilities. But if you are comfortable with the idea of putting in long hours, there is a special satisfaction that comes from working really hard for yourself rather than for someone else.

I recall a single mother with two preschool children who came to see me a few years ago about starting a store. She had a lucrative job with the state that she absolutely hated and she wanted to own a store similar to ours. She anticipated that she would be able to make as much from retailing as she currently earned at her state job, and was disappointed to learn that such earnings would be highly unlikely for at least four or five years. I also pointed out that since her children were quite young, it would be hard for her to put in the evening hours that a new store often requires. The dream of having her own shop was put on hold.

The support of family members is vital during the early years of a small business. There is a high degree of financial risk involved in starting your own store, and it is unfair to automatically expect that a spouse will want to share that risk. Talk over the pros and cons, and be realistic about the amount of time and money you plan to commit to the project. It will be a lot more fun to be in business if your spouse, siblings, and/or parents are supportive.

Don't risk more than you can afford to lose. This is a very important caveat. For some people, the idea of gambling their life savings or taking out a second or third mortgage on their home is not that threatening, but for others it is unbearable. We were in our early twenties when we launched our store, so we weren't afraid of having to start over again if the shop failed. Now that I'm in my forties, with a home and two children, I would think carefully before pledging our house and my children's college funds as collateral for a new business. As with any other gamble, you should be comfortable with the idea that you may lose what you invest. If you are married and using joint funds, be sure your spouse also understands the risks.

One way to minimize the risks in the early days of a retail venture is to work a part-time job while you open the store, or have your spouse keep his or her full-time job. It can be very reassuring to have a steady income and benefits such as health insurance from some other source during the shop's risky start-up period.

Business Partners

Should you go into business by yourself? A bad partner is worse than no partner at all, but a good partner can bring a wealth of additional experience and skills, as well as more capital, to the business. A partnership of two or more allows each owner some freedom from the day-to-day commitment of running the store. It can be a joy to have someone to share the ups and downs of a successful business. A partnership is a lot like a marriage, however. You don't really know how compatible you will be with a partner until you have been in the relationship for some time. A good partnership contract, like a prenuptial agreement, can help smooth the way for a successful relationship by spelling out all expectations.

The division of ownership in a partnership may play an important role in solving disputes while running the business, and especially if the business is ever dissolved. More ownership, or stock, means more power. My husband, Dean, and I are incorporated as fifty-fifty owners of our shop, and we alternate being president one year and vice president the next. Lawyers and accountants aren't fond of this arrangement because it means the business would be deadlocked if we ever had a major disagreement. Although it would have been impossible for us to set up our corporation any other way, we understand the advantage of having one partner or stockholder have the majority vote.

Working with Your Spouse

Should you go into business with your husband or wife? The mom-and-pop shop is such a tradition in America that the term is actually found in most dictionaries. But not every couple can handle the stress of day-to-day contact in a small shop without it taking a toll on the marriage. Try to look realistically at your relationship, your communication style, and your individual strengths and weaknesses before deciding if you would make good business partners.

It took us some time to adjust when Dean joined me in business about a year after Orange Tree Imports started. At first, I was so anxious to prove I knew how to do things correctly that I second-guessed all his decisions. We soon learned that for us, the secret to working together is to have separate areas of responsibility and to trust one another to make most decisions within those areas on our own. At Orange Tree Imports, almost everything is divided into his and hers—even the office files. Dean is in charge of merchandise relating to food, cooking, and serving. He also handles insurance, advertising, and maintenance. My merchandise is broadly described as everything else, including seasonal goods, cards, stationery, soaps, candles, toys, jewelry, and general gifts. In addition, I'm responsible for personnel, community relations, and finances. Of course, we collaborate on all major decisions, and we don't always agree. We try to work out our disagreements in private, however, and present a united front to our staff and customers.

There is a temptation to take your work home when you work with your spouse, which means you may not get any break from the worries of the business. We established a rule that we wouldn't talk about advertising after 10:00 P.M., since we both found that topic stressful.

We have also found it helpful to take one day a week off alone, plus Sunday and Monday as our "weekend" together. This means that one of us is at the store all but those two days, yet we each work only four days a week—a very humane schedule, especially for families like ours with children at home.

When our son and daughter were babies, we set up a little red crib in the office and brought them to work. We had tried an experiment earlier with an employee's bringing a baby to work and found that caring for a baby and waiting on customers were not compatible activities. It was not as hard to do buying and perform other managerial functions with a baby on board, and our customers loved seeing the children in the store. But bringing a baby to work is a compromise. You can't devote your full attention to two things at once, and Erik and Katrina never napped for long. As soon as they started crawling, we found a loving home in the neighborhood where they could go for the three days a week when we both were at work.

One of the advantages of working with your spouse is the time you get to spend with each other, working toward a common goal. There are long hours to be put in when a store is young, but we didn't mind because we were doing it together. We especially enjoyed going back to the store in the evening and working in the quiet, closed shop until the deep voice of the jazz announcer on Milwaukee's WFMR announced that it was midnight, time for us to go home.

IS A FRANCHISE RIGHT FOR YOU?

There is a higher success rate for businesses that are part of a franchise operation than for independents. When you buy into a franchise such as Play It Again Sports or Wicks 'N' Sticks, you gain the right to open a store with that name and concept. Franchise rights usually grant you exclusivity within a certain geographic area. You pay an initial fee for the franchise privilege, and an annual fee or a percentage of sales, or both, for as long as you own the business. Franchisers offer a wide arrangement of proprietary support, such as store design systems, standardized fixtures, advertising programs, personnel procedures, signage, in-store packaging, staff uniforms, and specially selected merchandise. Many franchisers supply merchandise manufactured exclusively for them; others provide buying guidelines so that the franchisee can buy from a variety of suppliers, sometimes at special pricing.

One reason for the high success rate for franchise operations is that a franchise store is a market-tested, proven retail concept. You are buying the experience and success of the franchiser instead of starting from scratch. Another reason, one less frequently mentioned, is that buying a franchise requires a large amount of capital—for example, an average of

$134,000 to $205,000 for a Play It Again Sports franchise, according to *Entrepreneur* magazine. Few retailers starting a store on their own invest or borrow that much capital. If they did, their chances of success would be closer to those of a franchise store, provided they also had some business experience and savvy.

The field of fast food restaurants is dominated by franchise operations, but this is not true of specialty shop retailing. The top ten *Entrepreneur* magazine franchises for 1996 are all restaurants, with the exception of Snap-On Tools. Name recognition, one of the primary reasons for purchasing a franchise, is not as important in specialty shop retailing as it is in the food industry, and many retail stores don't offer a concept unusual enough to make the franchise rights salable. Independent shops wishing to expand frequently do so by opening company-owned branch stores rather than by selling franchise rights.

Other companies, such as Hallmark, gain market share by granting the license to sell their products to independently owned and operated stores. These Hallmark stores are *dealerships*, not franchises, so they don't have the benefit of a protected geographic territory that comes with buying a franchise. The company does, however, set standards for licensing, such as Hallmark's requirement that a certain percentage of the store's inventory be Hallmark products. In addition to providing merchandise exclusively available to their dealers, companies such as Hallmark also make joint advertising and special signage and fixtures available to licensed stores.

There are a number of popular franchise operations in the specialty shop field. Listings of stores available by franchise can be found in magazines, including the annual Franchise 500 in the January issue of *Entrepreneur*, and also at special events, called *franchise fairs*, aimed at potential new owners. For more information about a franchise store you have visited, ask the owner to put you in touch with the home office.

If you decide to buy into a franchise, do your homework, and read *all* the fine print, before signing the contract. Research the viability of the store's concept for your area. Determine exactly what the franchise fee will cover and what other expenses are not included. Ask how much freedom you will have to make your own decisions and select your own merchandise. Consider whether you'll be happy paying the franchise fee every year for the life of the business. Talk to other franchise holders to see if they feel this is a worthwhile expense, and whether they are pleased with the level of support and communication they receive from the home office. Ideally you will find an experienced franchise operation with strong name recognition, a unique marketing concept, and enthusiastic franchisees in other geographic areas. Be sure to have your banker and a lawyer experienced in franchise work scrutinize all contracts and agreements before you sign.

BUYING AN EXISTING BUSINESS

Many of the difficulties of a new store start-up can be avoided by purchasing an existing shop. The store's owners may be ready to retire, or perhaps their interests have changed. It never hurts to ask if a store's owners would be interested in entertaining a purchase offer. Keep in mind, however, that establishing and agreeing on an asking price can be a long, drawn-out process. There are also business brokers, much like real estate agents, who can tell you which businesses are already for sale and their listed selling prices.

What do you get when you buy a business? Few retail stores own their locations, so real estate is not usually included in the deal. You therefore need to be certain the landlord will allow you to assume the seller's lease or negotiate a new one with you if you wish to stay in the same location. As with a franchise, you pay a price for the name and the reputation of the business. This part of the package is a nebulous item called "goodwill." More concretely, you usually buy the merchandise in stock, devaluing any goods that are older or shopworn, supplies on hand, and the furniture and fixtures that are part of the store's operation. Do a credit check on the business (your bank can help arrange for this) to see if there are any liens against it and whether bills have been paid in a timely manner. Find out if there are outstanding debts or receivables that you will assume with the ownership of the store.

The following factors will help you determine whether it is wiser to start on your own or to buy an existing business:

- Is the existing business profitable? Ask to see at least three to five years of its financial statements and tax records to determine whether the store is doing well. It's safer to buy a profitable business than one on the decline.
- If the business is not profitable, do you have the expertise, capital, and experience to turn it around?
- Is the business in a location you would like for your store? Will the landlord allow you to assume the lease and stay in the same location?

- Does the business have a good reputation? (If not, you can change the name or announce that it is under new management after the purchase.)
- Will you be able to retain key, experienced personnel?
- Does the current owner have a positive relationship with major suppliers? Orders from a business that has had financial problems may not be welcome, even with new owners at the helm.
- Is the merchandise in the store good-quality, salable goods?
- Are the fixtures and other supplies worth the asking price?

As with buying a home, the purchase of a business involves some negotiation. You may make an offer that does not include some items, such as older fixtures, you don't want to use. The seller may counter with an offer lowering the amount being asked for the *covenant not to compete,* a promise that for a certain number of years, the seller will not open a competing store in the same area. The valuing of an existing business is a complex and sometimes unscientific computation, taking into account the reputation of the business, the age of various segments of the inventory, the desirability of the store's location, and of course how eager the buyer and the seller are to have the transaction take place. You will need the advice of your lawyer, banker, and perhaps also a business broker who specializes in this type of transaction.

We have purchased two existing businesses. Twenty years ago, we bought the six-month-old campus branch of Bord & Stol, a Scandinavian furniture store I had managed since it opened, and ten years ago we expanded by purchasing Cabrini Gifts, the store next door to ours. In both cases, we wanted the location more than the names (which we did not keep) or the merchandise selection (which we modified to suit our needs). We paid for goodwill and a covenant not to compete, although neither business was profitable at the time of purchase. It could be argued that we paid more than we should have, but we were eager to purchase these businesses and think that the extra expenditure turned out to be worthwhile.

WRITING A BUSINESS PLAN

A *business plan* is a good way to give shape to your dream of opening your own store or to map out your plan to invest in a franchise or purchase an existing store. The purpose of writing a business plan is to create the successful business you envision. It's also an important tool in arranging necessary financing. Your plan should include:

- Your business goal: a brief description of the shop as you see it.
- Your qualifications for running this shop.
- Your plans to promote the business.
- The target customers for your shop, supported by market research.
- A proposed budget or cash flow plan.
- Financing needs and potential sources of funds.

Be sure to start with a description of your vision: what the store will look like, what type of merchandise it will feature, what customers you hope it will appeal to. When you describe how you plan to market your business, tell in what ways your store will differ from the competition. If you already have a location, include details of your lease or purchase arrangement, and perhaps photographs or sketches showing the store's exterior and interior. Give information about your background and experience, as well as the qualifications of any other owners or managers involved in the operation.

Once you have done the market study for your business plan, you can map out a budget, crucial for securing financing and for your own awareness of the many different expenses involved in running a store. The problem with the early stages of budget planning is that you must use imaginary sales figures. You can research industry standards at the library to help estimate expenditures, such as rent, utilities, payroll, and advertising, but until you've been open a few months, you won't really know what your *income* will be. Balancing the budget hinges on this key fact. Do your best to be realistic in your income and expense figures. You can then use your business plan budget as a starting point, but don't believe the figures until you've actually been in business for some time. And in projecting your sales, keep in mind that most specialty stores don't have an even distribution of sales throughout the year. Our shop, for example, brings in 40 percent of its annual income in November and December.

The goal in writing a business plan budget is to show how your business will be profitable. But you might consider adding a worst-case budget showing you have thought about what you would do if sales don't live up to your hopeful projections. This type of planning shows bankers and other potential investors that you have a realistic grasp of the challenges you face.

The business plan should show how you intend to finance the business, including the amount you hope to borrow, how and when you will repay any loans, and what you plan to use as loan collateral. Be sure to include regular payments of the interest on all business loans in your budget.

Consult some of the numerous books on the market describing how to write a business plan; several are listed in the bibliography at the back of this book. Another option is to use a computer program, such as BizPlan Builder, which will save you from having to make manual calculations. You could also set up your budget on a computer using any general spreadsheet program.

SELECTING YOUR BUSINESS FORMAT

The format of a business is its legal structure. Your store can be set up as a sole proprietorship, partnership, corporation, or cooperative. There are advantages and disadvantages to each format, primarily having to do with tax cost and personal liability. Look into which one is best for you at this stage of your business's development, and remember that you can always change the format later. We began as a sole proprietorship and incorporated a few years later when our growth, and profits, made that move advantageous from a tax planning standpoint.

The Sole Proprietorship

Most small businesses start as sole proprietorships. You decide, as an individual (or in some states, also a married couple), to create a business and pay taxes on the business income as if it were a personal salary, assuming full liability for anything that goes wrong. As a sole proprietor, you must pay self-employment tax for social security and Medicare coverage.

There is little paperwork involved in setting up a sole proprietorship, except obtaining the necessary selling permits and other licenses, and notifying city, county, or state authorities of your intention to *do business as* (DBA) an assumed name. A sole proprietorship can be changed into a corporation as the business and its profits grow.

Becoming a Corporation

Corporations have two major advantages: a lower tax rate on profits above a certain level and the limitation of liability. In many cases, the limited fiscal and legal liability is considered the more important benefit, since it prevents creditors from going after your personal assets if the business fails or if you are sued. Many business loans, however, require borrowers to pledge personal assets such as homes, cars, and savings as collateral, in which case incorporating will not protect these assets if the lender forecloses on the loan.

Another advantage of incorporating is that it allows you to apply to have a fiscal year that is not the same as the calendar year. The *fiscal year* is the accounting period used for reporting taxable income to the government. An actual count of everything in the store, called a *physical inventory*, must be taken at the end of the fiscal year. We do 40 percent of our business in November and December, so doing a physical inventory and all the other year-end tax preparations for January 1 was very difficult. Our fiscal year is now July 1 to June 30, which means we can take inventory during a quiet time of the year. It also means our staff can watch football on New Year's Day instead of spending it counting gadgets. They're quite happy about the change.

Corporations are separate legal entities, owned by one or more shareholders. States require corporations to file an application giving a business name, usually ending in "company" or "incorporated," and stating how many shares have been issued. You may need the assistance of a lawyer to incorporate, unless you feel confident filing the paperwork yourself using a kit of forms available from an office supply store, or a book on self-incorporating such as Judith McQuown's *Inc. Yourself.* Plan to set up and maintain a separate checking account and financial records for your corporation. Some states also require corporations to hold annual meetings of a board of directors elected by the shareholders and to keep records of these meetings, along with a set of bylaws, in a corporate record book.

There are several types of corporations, and your certified public accountant (CPA) or attorney can advise you as to whether you should file as a *regular*, or *C*, *corporation*, which means both your salary and the profit of the corporation are subject to taxation, or a special *subchapter S corporation*, which allows you to claim the income of the corporation on your personal tax return. The S corporation may work well if you have other income and plan to use a loss from your business occasionally to offset other taxes due, but if your store does very well, your tax bill may be higher than it would have been with a C corporation. There is also another type of corporation, the *limited liability company* (LLC), now available in most states. The LLC functions much like an S corporation, but it does not have the same restrictions on the number and types of shareholders.

Corporations can be used as a way of generating income for a new business. Those investing funds or expertise in your store can be rewarded with interest on the loan or by dividend-paying stock. The amount of the dividend, determined each year by a board of directors elected by the shareholders, is based on the company's profits. Your corporation can issue stock even though it is a *privately held,* or *closed, corporation.* The shares are not offered to the public on the stock exchange but can be sold to family or other investors. You can also be your corporation's only stockholder if you like. That certainly makes it easy to arrange for a meeting of the board.

SETTING UP A PARTNERSHIP

If you have one or more partners in your business, you can set up a corporation with each of you as a shareholder, or you can use a partnership agreement. A partnership is like a sole proprietorship in that the income of the company is taxed to the partners as if it were personal income, and the partners are all personally liable for any debts incurred by the business. It is assumed unless otherwise stated that the partners share the profits, assets, and liabilities equally.

Although not required by law, a carefully thought-out partnership contract, called the *articles of partnership,* can ease many misunderstandings that may occur at a later date. This contract should include provisions for one partner's leaving the business by choice or due to death, illness, or bankruptcy without the store having to be sold to buy out that partner's portion of the business. A clear understanding of how many hours each partner will work, how much compensation each person will receive, and how much money each partner will invest can also help avoid later problems. Consult your lawyer for assistance in drawing up articles of partnership early in the planning stages of your business.

A *limited partnership* is an investment vehicle rather than a true partnership. It allows one (or more) partners to be liable only for debts equal to the amount of equity the individual has invested. In a limited partnership, there must also be at least one party whose liability is not restricted in this manner. Limited, or silent, partners are basically investors. They don't participate in the management of the business.

Another Alternative: Cooperatives

Although cooperatives are not common in the field of specialty shop retailing, they are a viable business structure for certain types of stores. In the area of natural foods, for example, 30 percent of the market is made up of consumer *cooperatives*, stores owned and controlled by their workers, or by the customers who use them, rather than by outside investors, private owners, or partners. Members buy stock in the cooperative, which is a corporation structured somewhat like an LLC. The stockholders' liability is limited to the amount invested, and a board of directors, elected by the stockholders, hires staff and makes management decisions. "Cooperatives are in business to serve their owners," explains cooperative specialist Marilyn Scholl from the University of Wisconsin Center for Cooperatives, "and investor-owned firms are in business to give a return on investment to their shareholders. This is the difference that co-ops have to offer."

The cooperative structure is a good alternative for groups of artists or craftspeople wishing to set up a shop to market their wares. In many cases, the members contribute a set number of work hours in addition to making a financial investment. There may be some paid staff, or a paid manager, but often all the work is done by co-op members in exchange for having a viable way to market their arts or crafts.

Regulations governing the establishment of cooperatives vary by state and are usually part of the state's corporate code. For more information on setting up a cooperative, call the Cooperative Development Services office at (608) 258-4396 or the National Cooperative Business Association at (202) 638-6222.

FINANCING YOUR BUSINESS

Phyllis Sweed, editor of *Gifts and Decorative Accessories* magazine, says that when potential retailers call and ask her thoughts about opening a store with $25,000 or less, she advises them to use the money to go on a luxury cruise instead. They'll have more fun, she believes, and save themselves the pain of going out of business. Starting a store with more than $25,000 is not a magical formula for success—many stores, including ours, have been started with less, and others have started with more and still failed—but the fact remains that a well-financed business has a much better chance of surviving the difficult first years.

How much money do you need to start a store? The budget you

drew up for your business plan will give you some idea how much inventory you would like to start with and what the operating expenses may be during the first year. In addition, you'll need to pay for signage, lighting, supplies, utility and lease down payments, computer and office equipment, furniture, and display fixtures—all before you open. Renovations to your new space may be costly, especially if you are paying rent for several months while the renovations take place. You should have some money to put aside for unexpected emergencies, such as repairs to equipment. And if you have quit your other job in order to pursue this dream, you will need money to live on.

Where is all this money to come from? Perhaps you've been saving for this moment and have some funds built up in cash, securities, a retirement fund, or equity in real estate you own. It's a cold, hard fact that borrowing money without having money is difficult. Lenders want some *collateral*—an asset of yours that goes to the lender if you default on your loan—as well as proof of your commitment to the project and your financial reliability. Most lenders require you to provide something other than the store's inventory as collateral in case the business fails. Let's face it: a bank wouldn't know what to do with $10,000 worth of women's shoes.

When we first looked into financing our business, we were advised to use part of our savings as collateral rather than putting it all into the store. This proved to be excellent advice, because we were able to pledge it temporarily as collateral and know it would eventually be available to us as cash funds. When we needed money to expand our business later we had funds waiting for us so that we didn't have to try to turn $5,000 worth of toys and gifts into cash in a hurry.

Borrowing from a Bank

Banks are a traditional source of small business loans, and in recent years the Small Business Administration (SBA) has encouraged banks to make loans to entrepreneurs by assuming some of the risk. You apply for an SBA-guaranteed loan through your local bank, allowing you to develop a personal relationship with a banker who may serve as one of your store's advisers. For a new business, the SBA generally requires that a minimum of 25 percent of the start-up funds come from the applicant. You must also show that you have the knowledge and experience needed to operate a successful business. For an SBA loan information kit, call your local SBA office or the SBA Small Business Answer Desk at (800) 8-ASK-SBA.

The government sponsors a number of loan programs targeted at encouraging new businesses owned by women and minorities. Other special loans may be available if your store will aid in the economic revitalization of a depressed area or the renovation of a run-down building in an old neighborhood. Most of these programs do still require you to provide some collateral. Check with your community's economic development office or the SBA for details.

Even if you don't turn to a bank for an initial loan, you will need a bank to handle your deposits and other transactions. Working closely with the bank will help if you need to turn to it for financing in the future as your business grows. Many stores use short-term loans for specific financing needs. For example, we maintain a line of credit loan that we draw on each year to build up our inventory for the holiday season, paying it off before Christmas Eve. The line of credit arrangement, which is approved for a fixed amount and must be repaid within a short time, saves us from having to apply for a new loan each year.

Private Money for Your Business

What about private sources of capital? Many businesses begin with loans from friends and relatives, funds sometimes referred to as "love money." If you do borrow money from individuals, make sure they are aware of the risk they are taking. Set up any loans in a professional manner as promissory notes with a fixed interest rate and repayment schedule. Like any other loan, a privately held note should be secured by some collateral such as real estate. The Internal Revenue Service (IRS) may consider a private loan to be a gift if it is not properly documented. A relative or friend with a good credit standing can also help you get started by cosigning your bank loan, which means that person agrees to be liable if you default on the loan.

You may find someone who is interested in investing in your business rather than in making you a loan to be paid back at a fixed rate and by a certain date. An investor owns a part of your business and gets a return based on the store's profitability. He or she may feel justified in having something to say about how you run the business, especially when it comes to decisions such as how much salary you pay yourself. With a loan, you know that when you pay it off, you'll have full control of the business. With equity investors, this may not be the case.

Venture capitalists are professional investment groups that look for promising entrepreneurs in need of loans, although these companies are not usually interested in investments of less than $500,000. Unfortunately, some venture capitalists have earned the nickname "vulture capitalists" by withdrawing their funds swiftly from young companies that don't look as if they are going to earn the investors a sizable return on their money quickly enough. Retailing rarely shows a profit the first year or two, so impatient venture capitalists are not likely to be attracted to the field. If you work with a venture capitalist, be realistic about the time it may take to be profitable.

Occasionally a new business owner is lucky enough to attract a business "angel" who wants to help a new venture get started by investing in it. This is especially true if your business appeals to someone with money who has a special interest in your field, such as an art collector if you are opening a gallery. You may also find a businessperson who has had a successful career in your field and is willing to help you get a good start by lending you funds.

New retail store owners sometimes get into a cash crunch right from the start and yield to the temptation to pay for merchandise by credit card. More and more suppliers are willing to take credit cards in order to avoid the expense and credit risk of setting up an open account, which would allow the store to pay for the merchandise some time after receiving it. Some store owners end up using a credit card as a line of credit, paying a high interest rate to the credit card company. If you are going to use a credit card for merchandise payments, pay the balance off each month, and look for a card that gives you added features such as frequent flyer miles.

No matter where you borrow your funds, be sure to include the cost of the interest on loans in your budgeted business expenses. If you borrow a large amount of money at a high interest rate, this expense could ruin an otherwise successful retail operation. Many large department store chains have fallen victim to this problem. Look for the lowest possible interest rate, and don't borrow more than you need. Too much debt can be a crushing burden to the business and a constant worry to the business owner. At the same time, you should be realistic about the amount of money necessary to get your business to the point at which it will be profitable. Lending institutions are notoriously reluctant to make emergency loans to businesses in crisis.

PERMITS AND LICENSES

A *seller's permit*, or *resale number*, is required by all states with a sales tax. This permit allows you to buy merchandise at wholesale without paying sales tax, but commits you to paying the state sales tax on taxable merchandise when sold at retail. Normally the consumer pays the sales tax at the time of purchase, although it is your option to include sales tax in your prices. We sell T-shirts for our English friends, The King's Singers, at some of their concerts, and use a retail price that includes sales tax so that we can charge an even $17.00. The state's 5.5 percent tax comes out of our selling price. In the store, our cash registers automatically calculate and add state and local sales tax onto taxable items. Since states differ in which categories of merchandise, such as food and clothing, are exempt from sales tax, you will need to program your cash register accordingly.

In addition to a state seller's permit, the IRS requires you to obtain an employer identification number (EIN) if you will be hiring employees or if you have incorporated with yourself as an employee. The EIN is used to identify your business records relating to withholding income tax and paying Medicare and FICA, an acronym for the Federal Insurance Contributions Act, which covers the collection of social security funds. The IRS offers a packet of guidelines for new businesses that can be obtained by calling (800) 829-1040. States with income tax may require a separate identification number for the withholding of state taxes. This information may be obtained by calling your state's Department of Revenue.

FINDING THE PERFECT LOCATION

No book on retailing worth its salt can resist repeating the old adage that the three most important keys to retail success are location, location, and location. Although a great location may not guarantee success, a bad location will almost always guarantee failure. You must locate your business, at least initially, where there is a base of customers. Although your shop may be what is called a *destination store*, which means shoppers will make a special trip to buy from you, it is easier to start out in a place shoppers already frequent. Look for a location with a reasonable degree of security, access to public transportation (for your customers and your employees), and adequate parking. Check traffic patterns in the area to see how easy it will be for customers to get to your location, especially when driving home from work. Keep in mind that you'll also need a way for large trucks and other vehicles to reach you with deliveries, adequate storage space for your back stock of merchandise, and room for an office.

Most stores are located in one of four types of shopping areas: an enclosed shopping center, a strip mall (a shopping center with outside entrances for each store), a neighborhood shopping street, or an area of freestanding buildings with their own parking lots. As recently as 1990, it appeared that the enclosed mall was going to dominate the retailing scene of the future. Minnesota's Mall of America had just debuted, taking the concepts of retailing as entertainment and the mall as the modern village green to new heights. However, there is a recent trend toward a dramatic decline in the number of hours the average person spends in a shopping mall each month. Major factors influencing this change include security concerns in shopping centers and their parking lots, a decrease in free time spent shopping, and the growing dominance of freestanding discount stores such as Wal-Mart. The decision as to where to locate is complicated by these changes in consumer habits.

Your own shopping habits, and those of your potential customers, can help you decide what type of location is best for your new business. Where do shoppers in your area like to shop? Is there a need for a store like yours in a certain area? What type of store building will allow you to create the shop you envision? You want a location that already has good foot (pedestrian) or motor traffic and the potential for future growth.

The size of the merchandise you'll be carrying will have a major effect on the size of the shop you'll need. Furniture obviously requires more room than jewelry. Since you'll be paying by the square foot, don't rent a space larger than you need for the merchandise you plan to stock. Too small a space may also be a problem. Some experts feel that a store with less than 1,000 square feet is too small to stock a wide enough selection to be viable.

Keep in mind also that the store's location will determine the hours you need to keep. Most mall stores are open seven days a week and at least five evenings until 9:00 P.M.; malls require all stores to keep the same hours. In neighborhood shopping areas, stores often try to standardize their hours as a convenience to customers. The number of hours your store will be open will have an important impact on your work week and your payroll needs.

The mix of other shops is an important factor in selecting a location. On a shopping street, look for a variety of stores that appeal to the type of shopper you want to attract. In a mall, one or two large department stores have traditionally served as magnets to attract customers and are therefore referred to as "anchors." An anchor store today might be a discounter or even a large grocery store, but an enclosed mall without any anchor store may not be a viable location. If the leasing agent promises that an important anchor is going to locate in the mall in the future, ask for lower rent until the big store opens, and an escape clause in your lease should the anchor back out.

To Rent or to Buy

Most new retailers lease space rather than purchase a building; of course, in a shopping center or mall, leasing is the only option. Cash flow is a consideration in deciding whether to lease or buy, as is the amount of experience you have with the type of business you'll be running. If you are a novice shopkeeper, my advice is to concentrate your energy and funds on building your business rather than buying a building. If your store doesn't succeed, you can usually sublet a leased space. If it succeeds beyond your wildest dreams, you can move to a larger location.

We were able to buy our seventy-five-year-old freestanding building a few years after we started Orange Tree Imports, and ten years ago we also purchased the hundred-year-old store next door and connected it to ours. Both buildings have been good investments, despite the headaches involved in being our own landlord (we own the buildings as individuals and lease the space back to our corporation).

If you decide to purchase a building for your store, check with local authorities about any zoning restrictions. Retail stores require commercial zoning, so you cannot open a store in most residential areas. Because cities also have building codes for commercial buildings that must be followed carefully, be certain you have the necessary building permits before beginning any construction or major remodeling. In buying or building real estate for your store, remember that should your business fail, you will have to sell or lease the property. When making changes to the building, try to keep the space flexible in case you need to sell or rent it to someone else someday.

Negotiating a Lease

If you have ever rented an apartment, you are familiar with some of the basic concepts of leases: a lease covers a specific period of time, with a penalty for breaking the lease, and a security deposit is usually required. But commercial leases often have added features, adding up to a total referred to as the *occupancy cost*. In addition to monthly base rent, your lease may specify that you pay *percentage rent*, a share of all your sales, or possibly profits, above a certain level. Or you might be offered a *net lease*, which states that you are responsible for expenses such as utilities, maintenance, and insurance in addition to rent. There are even *net net net leases* (I wonder who invented *that* term?), which require the tenant to pay all expenses, including structural repairs to the building. The landlord may offer to pay for carpeting, painting, or some of the other preparation of the space, but often these leasehold improvements are the responsibility of the tenant—even though they will remain behind when you leave.

If your shop is successful, a long-term lease will allow you to stay in that location as long as you want. A commercial lease is usually written for several years, with an option to renew at the end of the lease period, albeit often at a higher rate. But you also need to limit your liability should your shop fail. Ask for a provision allowing you to surrender the lease after giving a certain amount of notice and perhaps paying a penalty, or to sublet the space to someone else.

You may be able to find a location for your store by subletting a space from a store that is moving or going out of business. Find out whether the location, or the landlord, had anything to do with the previous shop not wanting to stay. Meet with the property owner or leasing agent yourself before taking on the remainder of someone else's lease.

Retail space is usually priced by the square foot, per year. A 2,000-square-foot store renting for $15 per square foot would cost $30,000 per year, or $2,500 per month. In theory, the higher the cost per square foot, the more desirable the space. This presents a real dilemma for the new retailer: should you commit to a high rent in an area with more potential customers or try to save money by renting in a less popular area? How do you know if the rental rate is fair?

The chamber of commerce or library should be able to provide you with a chart showing comparative rental rates for different retail locations in your community. In trying to determine the level of rent you should pay, check to see what types of businesses are prospering in each area. Since shopping center management sets the rent for all the spaces in a mall, you can talk to current mall retailers about how their businesses are faring at their rental rate. On a shopping street with many different landlords, ask around to find out whether the rate you are being charged is comparable to other rents in the area, and whether the merchants feel there is an adequate level of customer traffic.

Commercial leases are usually subject to negotiation. You can always ask for concessions from the landlord, such as a lower rate, a few months free rent, or a setup allowance, if you feel these requests can be justified. Go over all the details carefully with the assistance of a lawyer or accountant experienced with this type of transaction before agreeing to a lease. There are also real estate companies with expertise in site selection and lease negotiations, and you may wish to engage the services of one of these site selection consultants to help you select the best possible location.

A Merchants' Association

Shopping centers and malls usually require all tenants to participate in joint advertising and special events. The mall's management organizes promotions, such as special crafts and antique shows, charity fund-raisers, or a visit-with-Santa booth, to bring more traffic to the center. When considering a mall location, find out what types of promotions the center usually features and whether tenant input is encouraged. Ask how much you should allow in your budget for merchant participation fees in your business plan.

If you are considering a neighborhood location, look for an area with an active merchants' association or chamber of commerce. Cooperation among retailers makes the promotion of a shopping area more efficient and helps ease the isolation new business owners sometimes feel. A well-established merchants' group is the sign of a retail neighborhood that cares about its future. If there is no organization in the area you choose, consider starting one once you've gotten your business off the ground.

NAMING YOUR STORE

Naming a store is rather like naming a baby. You come up with lots of ideas and reject most of them for one reason or another. There are many poor choices of names for babies, and for shops. The store we bought when we went into business was called Bord & Stol, which an insignificant percentage of the Madison population knew was Danish for "table and chair." A charming children's clothing store down the street from us back then was named Crudbar's after the owner's teddy bear. A store in a nearby town bore the unpoetic name Christmas Stuff.

Try for a store name that is easy to pronounce, spell, and remember. If you are going to run a niche store, committed to carrying basically one category of merchandise, look for a name that readily identifies what the store sells. If you want to be able to carry a wider range of merchandise, you'll need a name that doesn't limit you to one category. Even the name Orange Tree Imports, based on my nickname, Orange, and the fact that we sell mostly imported merchandise ("tree" was thrown in to give it some consonance) occasionally causes customers to ask whether we actually import orange trees. You might consider using your first or last name as part of the business name, or perhaps an imaginary name that appeals to you. You might choose a name that reflects the style of merchandise you plan to carry, such as art deco or country, or perhaps an attitude, such as whimsical or traditional. Some stores are named after a location, although this can limit your options if you decide to relocate. Two businesses in our town were stuck with "upstairs" in their names long after they moved to the ground floor.

In the television show *Ellen*, the main character runs a shop called Buy the Book. The name is memorable for its cleverness and instantly conveys the fact that the store sells books.

When you have narrowed your list of name choices, check with your library through the reference desk to be certain the name, or one very much like it, is not already in use in your area. You can also find out if the name is in use anywhere in the country by checking a national Internet directory, such as the one at www3.switchboard.com. Most states (through the secretary of state), and some cities, allow you to register a trade name and logo. This registration does not provide name protection beyond that of common law, but it does serve as official notice to anyone who inquires whether the name is already taken, and how long it has been in use. Obtaining national trademark registration is a more expensive and time-consuming process, but it is the only way to stake out legal rights to a name or logo. Avoid choosing a name similar to one that is already trademark protected by a large corporation, such as Disney. No matter how small your operation, Mickey's lawyers will find you and force you to change your name.

DEVELOPING A LOGO

Once you have selected a name for your business, you'll want to determine a typestyle, or font, in which to print it. Look for a legible typestyle in keeping with the image you have of your store and its merchandise. There are hundreds of distinctive fonts available for computer use today, and it will be easier to design your own ads and graphics if you select a font you have access to on your computer. If you choose to have the name of the business done by hand in a calligraphy style, or custom designed by a professional, arrange to have the name scanned onto a disk for use on the store's computer.

In addition to a logo font, you may wish to have a logo symbol to represent your store. The logo can be used on store packaging and signage and in print advertising. A good logo should be easily recognized and should be in some way representative of your store and what it sells. You may want a full color logo to use on your signs and packaging, but be sure it will also work well in black and white for newspaper, Yellow Pages, and magazine ads.

How do you begin to design a logo symbol? If you want to create your own, look into books and CD-ROM disks of copyright-free art. You may be able to take an image you see there and simplify it to be your logo. Local art students are also a good source of logo designs. You might be fortunate enough to have a commercial art program design your logo as a class project, providing you with a number of options to choose from. Be sure to provide fair compensation for the student whose art you select.

There are many commercial artists talented at designing logos, but you may find that you cannot afford a professional. Check with several advertising or design agencies to get an idea of their fees before authorizing proposals for a logo. Large corporations spend thousands of dollars on logo design, but a fledgling retail shop should probably not spend more than $1,000. Remember that you can always start out with a typestyle logo of your business name and add a symbol logo later, when you are successful enough to have money to spare.

WHERE TO GET HELP

As you begin to plan your new venture, look for mentors who can help answer some of your questions. Other retailers are often a great source of information; provided your store will not be a direct competitor, experienced merchants are often very willing to share their expertise. Come prepared with a short list of specific questions. To avoid the constant interruptions of customers and telephone calls, you might treat the retailer to lunch at a nearby restaurant.

The start-up period is a good time to form an advisory team for your business. You need the services of an accountant and a lawyer experienced in retail business. Once you have established which bank you'll be dealing with, bring your banker on to the advisory team. Be sure these individuals know and respect each other, because they will all be working to help you create a successful business. You should also establish a comfortable relationship with an insurance agent who can help you with the variety of insurance needs you will have (see Chapter 11). In addition to these paid professional advisers, invite a few customers and experienced business-people to serve on a voluntary advisory team. Most people are pleased to be asked to share their opinions and expertise.

Another valuable source of assistance is the Service Corps of Retired Executives (SCORE), a free program of business assistance sponsored by the SBA and staffed by retired volunteer businessmen and -women, including retailers. The SBA also maintains a national toll-free answer desk for small business at (800) 8-ASK-SBA and several on-line assistance programs. Publications and videotapes by the SBA, including a checklist for going into business, are available for a nominal charge by calling your local SBA office (in the U.S. Government section of the telephone book), or by writing to SBA Publications, P.O. Box 46521, Denver, CO 80201-0030.

The SBDC, a collaborative effort between local colleges and universities and the SBA, provides excellent seminars and counseling services for retail businesses. If there is one in your area, be sure to contact the office immediately to find out how they can assist you. Your local chamber of commerce may also have specialists whose job it is to encourage new businesses. Why try to go it alone when so much help and expertise is available?

2

MANAGING YOUR STORE'S FINANCES

You've chosen your business name; designed a logo; gotten the financing you need; set up your corporation, partnership, or sole proprietorship; and signed a lease. In addition to ordering merchandise and designing the shop, topics covered in Chapters 3 and 4, you now need to set up a system of financial record keeping. Your business should have its bookkeeping system in place before the store opens, with a *sales and cash receipts journal* to record the money coming in and another journal for *disbursements*, or money going out. The expenses you begin to track now will hopefully soon be joined by sales income, and if all goes well, the income eventually will outweigh the expenditures.

SETTING UP THE CASH REGISTERS

Most of your income will come through cash register sales, so it is important to select a cash register system that can do much of the capturing of sales data for you. Sales are usually broken down as *taxable* and *nontaxable*, information you will need for sales tax reporting. In addition, the cash register will separate cash, check, and credit card sales so that you can balance each account when you close at the end of the day. A cash register can also be used to track sales by category. We use the twenty-six letters of the alphabet to code our merchandise by category on price tags and ring each item being purchased on one of the twenty-six letter keys on the register. The keys for our only nontaxable category, food, and for nontaxable services, such as gift wrapping, are programmed not to add sales tax. There are other nontaxable transactions as well, such as sales to nonprofit organizations and merchandise to be shipped out of state. A tax shift key is used to remove the sales tax from taxable items when the purchase is nontaxable.

More sophisticated cash register systems can track many more categories or even individual items based on numerical or bar codes on the merchandise. Cash registers can record which sales assistant rings up a sale, essential data for stores paying commissions. This information can also be useful if you are concerned about employee accuracy and efficiency, or suspect an employee of dishonesty.

A *point-of-sale* (POS) system is a computerized cash register system, usually used to read the *Universal Price Code* (UPC), or bar code, on each product and match it to the price, or PLU (price look up) assigned to the item. It also feeds information about each sale directly into the computer's data bank. A POS system can be used with a bar code scanner or by entering the numeric codes from price tags into the system manually.

POS systems can track customers and their purchases, building a detailed database and mailing list for the store. Shops with more than one location can easily combine data from their POS systems for centralized reordering. A POS system can be set up to generate a reorder automatically when stock on an item falls below a certain level—especially useful if much of your stock remains the same from one order to the next and if you have multiple locations so it is difficult to keep an eye on inventory levels.

POS systems tend to be expensive, and the expense may be hard to justify in small, single-location stores. Not all of the items we sell come bar code labeled yet, so we do not use POS or bar code technology, although if we wanted to, we could print our own bar code labels for items arriving unlabeled using the store computer and special bar code software and a label printer. Some POS systems come with this software and equipment as part of the program.

Bar code labeling is becoming increasingly common, even on imported goods, and the day may come when price tags are not really necessary. But for shoppers to know how much an untagged item costs, every item has to be displayed by a price sign at all times. Customers generally find it much more convenient to see price tags on the merchandise, which means that even precoded items need to be priced upon arrival. For grocery and discount stores that no longer use price tags, having the merchandise arrive already bar coded results in a huge savings in stock handling costs. The majority of specialty stores, however, will continue to price each piece of merchandise for the convenience of the customer, so handling costs will not decrease.

Most cash registers have a plate that prints the store name on each receipt. There is sometimes also room for additional information such as the store's hours, return policy, or tag line (motto). Order your printing plate when you purchase your cash register, so that it will arrive before you open. Don't forget to order extra rolls of paper receipt tape and ink ribbons. When the cash register arrives, hold several practice sessions for staff members to get them comfortable with ringing up sales and returns and changing the tape and ribbon.

Filling the Till

The cash register fund, or *till*, needs some coins and bills to start each day. Decide on an even amount, such as $50, to have on hand when you open, and put aside that amount in a variety of small bills and coins when you close every night. We also keep a stock of rolls of coins near the checkout counter, and "buy" a roll of quarters or pennies from this fund with bills from the register. As part of our daily cash reconciliation, we count the money in the change fund to be sure it totals the correct amount. For special events, very busy weekends, and holidays when the banks are closed, we plan ahead to have extra change on hand.

Take a cue from the bank and have all the bills in your register face in the same direction. This makes it easier to count out a customer's change neatly. Cash registers now calculate the amount of change owed to a customer, but sales staff should still count out the money as they give change, showing customers that the amount is correct.

At the end of the day, the cash register will provide the day's sales figures broken down into cash, check, and credit card sales. If an employee mistakenly hits the wrong key for a transaction, he or she should leave a note so the figures can be adjusted. We have made up a customized reconciliation form to use each day to assure that the amount deposited into the store's bank account matches the register's figures for the day. The cash, check, and credit card figures from the register's daily report are listed across the top of the form. These figures are matched up with the total amount of cash in the till, minus the daily start-up fund of $50; an adding machine total of the checks; and the data capture unit's total of credit card transactions. Any discrepancies in the totals are noted on the reconciliation form for the bookkeeper to investigate before making the deposit the next day. Checks are stamped with a cancellation stamp, and the credit card sales data is transmitted electronically before we leave.

The bookkeeper compiles the sales data from the cash registers into a daily sales journal, either using a manual sales record book or entering the data into the store's computer. (Sophisticated POS systems transmit data directly into the computer.) In addition to bank reconciliation, accurate sales records are essential for sales tax reporting. Sales tax forms will often ask for a description of all nontaxable sales, such as shipments out-of-state or the sale of food items, so taxable and nontaxable sales need to be recorded separately by category.

WILL THAT BE CASH, CHECK, OR CHARGE?

Cash is still the universally accepted method of paying for any purchase. Nevertheless, the dangers of carrying large amounts of cash, especially when traveling, combined with the easy record keeping and free grace period on many credit cards are making "plastic" a convenient and cost-effective way for customers to pay for a purchase. The credit card service charge to the merchant, however, can be as high as 5 percent. It would be unwise not to accept the most common credit cards, but it does pay to shop around for the best rate on this service charge. Most banks offer credit card services, as do several national processing companies. Some trade associations, such as the National Retail Federation, offer group rates. If you don't want to deal with an out-of-state service, you might ask your local bank if it can match the competitor's rate. Credit card service charges are based to some extent on volume, so you may be able to negotiate a better rate as your business grows. The speed with which funds are transferred from the service into your checking account is also an important factor to consider, and it may vary significantly from one company to the next.

One of the costs of starting up a business is buying the electronic data capture terminals that allow you to scan a credit card and automatically transfer the sales information to the company that will service the transaction. Fortunately, the major credit card companies now cooperate, so one terminal will allow you to accept Master Card, Visa, American Express, and Discover. The commission rate, however, may vary, as will the process by which the funds are transmitted into the store's checking account. Some credit cards deduct their service charge from the daily deposit; others debit your checking account for their fee once a month.

The data capture system automatically procures an authorization number for all transactions. If a card had been reported lost or stolen, or if the customer is over his or her credit limit, authorization will be denied. Although most businesses now use an electronic system, it is still possible to imprint credit card receipts manually and to call a toll-free number to request an authorization number. This is usually only required for purchases above a certain amount, such as $75.00, which is referred to as the store's *floor limit*.

Each data capture terminal requires its own telephone line, which can add up to considerable expense if you have several checkout areas. Be sure to have a manual imprinter, with a plate showing your store name and merchant number, for when the electronic system is not functioning. You won't want to lose sales if the power goes out, the electronic printer jams, or the system gets tied up with a problem.

Some customers may wish to pay with a *debit card*, a credit card that automatically deducts the amount of the purchase from the customer's bank account. Debit cards have no advantage over regular credit cards to the retailer, but they do allow those with no credit history to take advantage of the convenience of a credit card. And when they are used as an alternative to a personal check, they eliminate the problem of a check being returned unpaid for insufficient funds.

Accepting Checks

Bounced checks can be a real headache for retailers. A person shoplifting a $10 item will usually be prosecuted to the full extent of the law, but someone making a $100 purchase with a worthless check is often considered to be the shopkeeper's problem.

When a check is returned by the bank marked NSF ("not sufficient funds"), you usually have the option of waiting a few days and redepositing it. In many cases, the check will clear the second time, because the customer has made an innocent error. But if the check bounces a second time, it usually cannot be redeposited. Your only choice now is to call the customer and ask the person to bring in the cash. Failing this, you can call the police or hire a collection agency. Some stores discourage bad checks by posting a policy of fining customers as much as $20 for each returned check. This fine helps cover the fee that banks sometimes assess for handling an NSF check, but is helpful only if you are able to collect for the check—and the charge.

If bad checks are a real problem for your store, consider using a service such as CheckWrite or TeleCheck. These services electronically read the account data encoded on the check and reject any check reported lost or stolen, or from an account that shows up in their database as having past problems such as overdrafts. The fee for this service sometimes includes a guarantee to reimburse you for any approved check that later turns out to be invalid.

Asking to see a picture identification, such as a driver's license, will help discourage the use of stolen checks and can help you verify information such as address and phone number in case you later need to track down a customer who has written a bad check. But if bad checks are not much of a problem, consider risking the occasional bad one as a cost of doing business, and accept your customers' checks with a smile and a thank you.

Stores that accept checks—and most should—need to have a policy regarding checks written for more than the amount of purchase, cashing third-party checks made out to someone other than your store, and accepting out-of-state checks. Help your staff treat all customers fairly by spelling out your check acceptance policies in writing.

Store Accounts

There was a time when most specialty shops allowed their best customers to have a "house account," signing for their purchases and paying for them when they received a bill from the shop at the end of the month. With the advent of credit cards, many stores decided it wasn't worth dealing with sending out their own billings and possibly having to collect interest on past-due payments. But in some situations, this type of service for preferred customers may make them loyal and frequent shoppers, and the added effort may result in a solid increase in sales.

A store charge account is also an easy way to track purchases in order to reward the shop's best customers with incentives such as a gift or

One hospital gift shop in Ohio found a unique way to offer in-house accounts to the staff that makes up 75 percent of its customer base: payroll deduction. Employees of the hospital are welcome to sign for their purchases, which are later listed as debits on their payroll statements.

discount when they reach a certain dollar volume. Sending out monthly statements to these customers provides an added opportunity to enclose a note or newsletter highlighting new merchandise. An outside credit service can often be hired to check references, set up the accounts, handle the billing, and take care of any financing necessary for delinquent payments. It may even be able to provide your store with customized plastic credit cards, called *proprietary cards*, if you have a large volume of accounts. But be sure that the credit agency will provide the same friendly and competent level of customer service as your store.

Proprietary credit cards allow stores to finance customer purchases by offering promotions such as "six months same as cash" or "no payment for sixty days." Depending on the store's cash flow needs, the store may need to borrow money to cover these accounts receivable, and if so, the store's interest costs are usually covered in the selling price.

BOOKKEEPING 101

The goal of bookkeeping, in a nutshell, is to keep a record of expenses and income and to track assets and liabilities. If the expenses outweigh the sales income, you are *in the red*, or losing money. This is a natural situation the first year, or even two, but if you don't make money in five years, the Internal Revenue Service (IRS) considers your business a hobby, which may have serious tax consequences. When your sales outweigh your expenses, you are *in the black*, or making a profit.

The amount you take out to pay yourself has an enormous effect on whether there is any profit left. The IRS will consider any profit on a sole proprietorship or partnership to be your income, whether you have taken it home as a salary or not. But if your business is going well, there should be money left as a profit even after you've been paid a reasonable salary. Taking an excessively large salary, on the other hand, may drain the store's cash reserves, hindering its ability to invest in inventory and prosper. You should leave some of the store's profits in the business each year as seed money, to help it grow.

Most businesses use a form of double-entry bookkeeping, a system of checks and balances that must have been designed by Alice after stepping through the looking glass. Everything that should be a positive number, such as sales, is negative, and everything that should be a negative number, such as expenses, is positive. The reason the system is called *double entry* is that every item is posted twice. Sales income is posted to both the cash/checking account and to total sales. A check for merchandise is posted to cash/checking and to inventory purchases, usually by product category. For every debit, there must be a corresponding credit entry. The goal is to

It seems like everything that should be positive is negative, and everything that should be negative is positive. . . .

have all the accounts come out balanced when a *trial balance* of debits and credits is done at the end of each month. The accounts must balance before the income statement and balance sheet can be considered accurate.

Few novice retailers have much of a grasp of accounting, but even with a computer system to do the actual record keeping, or a full-time bookkeeper, you need to understand the basic principles. One of the goals of a good bookkeeping system is to produce figures that can help guide your business decisions, but these figures are useless if you don't understand where they come from and how to interpret them. I know, because it took me years to be able to make sense out of a balance sheet and income statement. They just don't teach those skills in Scandinavian Studies.

Tracking Disbursements

Every time your business spends money, by cash or check, it should be recorded in a *disbursement account*. Setting up these accounts is one of the first tasks before you when you start your bookkeeping system. Some of the category titles will be obvious, such as rent, advertising, and payroll. Others may be specific to your store, such as mall participation fees. You can make as many categories as you like. For example, you may wish to have telephone expense as a separate category rather than including it with heating and lighting under utilities. Merchandise purchases can be a single category, or separate categories for each department of the store. Separate categories will be helpful as you track inventory purchases and budget future buying.

It may be worthwhile to seek the guidance of an accountant in setting up your disbursement categories, because you should try not to change them once you have gotten the system underway. The data you have collected become difficult to track if you make changes in the categories.

In addition to disbursement categories, you will probably want to create vendor ledgers or accounts to track the purchases you make from each supplier. We buy from over 850 companies (undoubtedly more than we should) and need to be able to tell at a glance what our standing is with each vendor.

Money should never be taken out of the cash register to pay for even a small purchase, because the till will not balance with the sales report at the end of the day. Set up a petty cash fund for small purchases with a fixed amount of money, such as $25. Keep receipts for any purchases made from this fund. When petty cash is depleted, write a check to bring the bal-

Figure 2-1 Sample petty cash slip.

```
┌─────────────────────────────────────────────────────────┐
│                     PETTY CASH                          │
│                                                         │
│     Date:_____ Received  by:_____     │
│                                                         │
│     Item:_____       │
│                                                         │
│            Amount:_____Account:_____       │
│                                                         │
│     Item:_____       │
│                                                         │
│            Amount:_____Account:_____       │
│                                                         │
│                            TOTAL:_____              │
│                                                         │
│     Please staple sales receipt to back of petty cash form. │
└─────────────────────────────────────────────────────────┘
```

ance back up to $25, posting the disbursements to the various accounts listed on the petty cash slips. Figure 2-1 shows a sample petty cash slip.

A business credit card can be an effective way to track incidental purchases for the store, as well as buying trip travel expenses. Keep all receipts, and when the credit card invoice is paid, disburse each expense to the appropriate account.

Computers and Alternatives

If you are not ready for a computer, disbursements can be tracked through a check writing system, such as the one from Safeguard (800-523-2422), which we used for almost twenty years. This "one-write" system allows you to write a check and disburse it to the proper account on a single form. Invoices and payments are posted to individual vendor ledger cards for each manufacturer you buy from, tracking your activity with that company over the years. A sales journal and general ledger book are also necessary for manual bookkeeping.

How do you know if you should computerize? Five years ago, I would have recommended waiting until you got your business going before investing in any expensive computer equipment and bookkeeping software. Now that the price of both has dropped, my advice is to start computerizing bookkeeping records right away. We discovered that converting from a manual system to a computerized one (especially after almost two decades of handwritten records!) can be very disruptive, and you might as well capture your data in the same format from the start. But don't buy a more elaborate computer or POS cash register system than you need. There are several inexpensive software programs specifically designed for the bookkeeping needs of small businesses. Select a well-established program with good software support, so that you can get answers to the many questions you will have as you get started. (It may be useful to have your computer hooked up to a modem so that you can get "online" software support. Without this feature, you have to try to describe your problem over the telephone.) Ask your accountant for a software recommendation, and select a program he or she will be able to help you with. If you are not knowledgeable about computers or bookkeeping, bite the bullet and pay a consultant to help you get the system up and running. By all means, back up your data frequently, keeping a copy somewhere other than your store in case of fire.

ACCOUNTING REPORTS

Once you have set up a system of recording the money coming into your business and going out, you can develop a monthly or quarterly summary from this information called an *income*, or *profit and loss*, *statement*. The wholesale cost of the merchandise is subtracted from the total, or *net*, sales figure to produce the *gross margin*. Operating costs and other expenses such as depreciation are subtracted from the gross margin, resulting in a net profit or loss.

The wholesale cost of the merchandise is also referred to as the *cost of goods sold* (COGS). It is calculated by taking the beginning inventory, adding merchandise purchases (including freight costs), and subtracting the ending inventory. Most stores do a physical count of the inventory only once a year, so the COGS is usually determined at that time and applied as a percentage the rest of the year. Our current COGS, for example, is 59 percent. A slightly lower percentage would be better.

The COGS figure reflects not only the cost of the goods sold, but also any goods stolen, disposed of, purchased at an employee discount, or given to charity. Even if your margin on every item is 50 percent, your COGS will be a higher percentage because of these factors, as well as markdowns taken on slow-moving merchandise.

The other standard accounting report you will need to produce is a *balance sheet*. Unlike the income statement, which changes every day as money comes in and out of the business, the balance sheet is a "big picture" report, showing a comparison of the business's assets and short- and long-term liabilities. Any increase in the value of the inventory or cash in the bank adds to the assets. A new loan, or taxes owed but not yet paid, increases the liabilities. A healthy business has more assets than liabilities.

The balance sheet also shows the capital invested in the business, such as the owners' equity, plus retained profits and less any money that has been taken out by the owners. For a sole proprietorship or partnership, the capital is attributed to the proprietor(s). In a corporation, the assets are considered capital stock, and new profit is added to retained earnings. Funds paid out to stockholders are listed as dividends.

Ratios and Comparisons

Financial statements allow you to analyze how the store is doing by comparing the figures. These comparisons, called *financial* and *operating* ratios, are one way to take the pulse of the business. The *current ratio*, for example, is the current assets divided by the current liabilities. A ratio of two or higher is considered healthy. The ratio of net sales to net profit shows the percentage of profit your business is earning and is useful in comparing one year with the next as the business grows. If this percentage gets too low, consider what action to take to increase sales or decrease expenses.

Return on investment (ROI) is calculated by dividing the net profit by the amount of money invested in the business. This ratio can be a painful one for small retailers, because it often shows that one would earn a higher rate of return on the investment by putting it in the bank instead of the business. But ROI doesn't reflect the satisfaction of creating an imaginative, well-run specialty shop. Nor does it take into account the fact that before the profit is calculated, you and all your employees (or if you are a sole proprietorship, just the employees) have been paid a good wage. The money you have generated for your own salary is part of the return you are getting on your investment, and the money you generate to pay your staff is a positive contribution to the economy.

WORKING WITH AN ACCOUNTANT

You may be able to produce balance sheets and income statements with the store's computer system, but you still should have the work checked by an accountant. You probably will want to have an accountant help you with all the tax filings required of a small business. The penalties for missing a tax deadline can be severe, and as with other areas of the law, ignorance is no defense. A certified public accountant who works with other retailers can also advise you about some of the difficult financial decisions you will need to make as a business owner.

The bank or other investors helping to finance your business will want to see periodic financial statements, and these documents carry more weight if they have been prepared or reviewed by an accountant. Keep a binder of your statements where you can find them easily to compare past and present performance.

BUDGETS AND FUTURE PLANNING

The business plan provides a road map for the first year or two of a business; many retailers find it useful to continue to set financial goals and plans as the business matures. The store's monthly financial statements can be very useful in setting realistic financial goals for the future. You can do a budget projection for all aspects of your operation, including sales and operating expenses, or you can use a budget specifically for planning the best way to spend the dollars in a certain category such as advertising or payroll. Open-to-buy budgeting, discussed in Chapter 4, helps you plan inventory purchases by month and by category, maximizing the effectiveness of the money invested in merchandise.

One important budget planning process, especially for new businesses, is *cash flow forecasting*. Never spend money you don't have. To order merchandise, hire carpenters to do remodeling, or commit to an advertising campaign without having any idea how you are going to pay the bills is unethical. Estimate what your income will be each month, and know what your cash reserves are in advance. Then budget your expenditures based on these two factors. If there won't be enough cash to cover your needs, you will have to choose between cutting back on purchases and expenses, or finding additional outside funding and increasing the store's debt.

Most computer bookkeeping programs allow you to enter budget figures, as well as any previous year's figures, and print out variance reports comparing actual results with previous and budgeted amounts. These reports can help you see where you need to make adjustments throughout the year to bring you closer to reaching your goals.

TIPS FOR TAKING INVENTORY

Once a year, you are required to take a complete physical inventory of all the merchandise on hand. This is usually done on the last day of your fiscal year, although you may wish to select the closest Sunday, or another slow day of the week, if you need to be closed to do the count.

Stores using a bar code scanning system can use hand-held scanners to "read" the shelves of merchandise, but most stores still take inventory manually. We have our entire staff of thirty-six on hand to count inventory, and get it done in one day. If you don't have enough employees, invite family and friends to help. Some stores even use members of a nonprofit group for inventory assistance, making a donation to the cause in exchange for a few hours of work. No advance training is required if your inventory system is well planned.

Divide the store into sections based on product categories. Assign a pair of inventory counters to each section, armed with a clipboard and a calculator. One person counts the items while the other records the figures. You can use the memory function of a small printing calculator to multiply as you go, or enter the number of items at each price point and extend the totals later. For those who choose to record the number of items at each price, instead of just totals, *OTB Book* author Mort Haaz suggests making copies of a list of your most common price points ($1.00, $1.25, $1.50, $1.75, $2.00, etc.) and putting hash marks next to each price for every item you count at that price.

We get a head start on inventory day by counting merchandise in back stock during the week before. Once an area has been counted, a note is posted by it so that anyone removing merchandise will record what is taken and the inventory will be adjusted. We also count seasonal merchandise as we pack it away at the end of the season and keep those figures on file for inventory day.

All of our inventory is counted at retail. We then go back through the figures and try to calculate the wholesale value, based on what we know of the markup taken on each merchandise category.

The physical inventory figure is an important tool in calculating the store's financial status. Inventory taking is also a good opportunity to account for every piece of merchandise in stock and to make sure that every item is on display or stored where it is easily accessible. We try to neaten and dust shelves as we count, and when we are done, the store looks ready for the new year.

SETTING UP YOUR BUSINESS OFFICE

Your store's office, which should be handicapped accessible, needs electrical and telephone wiring for computers, a copier, and a fax machine, as well as space for vendor files, financial records, desks, and storage of office supplies. It is helpful to have a table for meetings with sales representatives, who often need room to spread out their bulky catalogs and cases of samples. Our bookkeeping office also doubles as a gift wrap area, and at busy times both of our bookkeepers have been known to pitch in with the wrapping.

The computer and its printer may be the central features of your store's office. We also have a typewriter that we use, albeit infrequently, for government forms that require certain information on certain lines. One of the most useful pieces of equipment in the office is the fax machine, which we use daily to send out purchase orders. We also receive some product literature via fax from our suppliers, but this is surprisingly rare. In the future, product updates will probably come via e-mail.

We rewarded ourselves with a copier when our sales hit the million-dollar mark for the first time a few years ago, and now we'd be hard pressed to live without it. We use it to copy the newsletter that goes to our employees with their paychecks and to copy the many forms we use in our daily operations. We keep a supply of various colors of paper on hand and make many of our own signs and customer handouts.

Records and Files

There is a lot of paperwork involved in running a retail store. We file vendor catalogs and paid invoices from the previous twelve months in alphabetical file folders in the store office. Paid invoices, stapled to their purchase orders and packing lists, are filed in chronological order in the front of the files, with catalogs and price lists in the back. Periodically weed your files of duplicate and outdated product literature. One of my pet peeves is that vendors often don't clearly date their price lists and catalogs, making it difficult to know which ones to discard. Before filing product literature, jot down the date received in an upper corner.

Invoices yet to be paid are in alphabetical order in the bookkeeper's file, together with the purchase order and any other paperwork relating to the pending invoice. When we used a manual bookkeeping system, we kept unpaid invoices behind a ledger card for each vendor. Invoices and payments were recorded on the ledger card, giving us a clear history of our status with the account. Color-coded Post-it tape flags on the ledger cards indicated when invoices were due (a red flag, for example, indicated there was a December invoice behind that card). With our computerized system, we separate the invoices by company using horizontal pieces of bright blue paper with each vendor's name in large type. The invoice data is entered in a vendor ledger in the bookkeeping system on the computer.

We also maintain a file of sales representatives' business cards and a small card file of all our vendors listing the names of the current sales representatives. In the gift industry, companies seem to change their minds capriciously about who is representing their line in an area. I note all sales rep changes on the suppliers' file cards in an attempt to make sure the current rep gets credit for every order.

One filing cabinet in our office contains employee records, and this is the only cabinet that is kept locked. Employees have access to their own file but not to the personnel files of others. We also have files for the various types of taxes we pay and for nonvendor expenditures, such as insurance, store supplies, trade shows, and advertising.

The government requires that businesses retain many documents for years in case of an audit, but these do not need to be kept close at hand in the business office. Payroll records, invoices, tax forms, financial statements, and canceled checks all need a place to be stored. Check with the IRS for the current regulations about how long each record should be kept. We store past records in inexpensive cardboard files, called *bankers' boxes*, available at office supply stores. They are clearly dated on the outside, and when we put in the current year's documents, the expired year's papers go into the recycling bin.

THE BOTTOM LINE

One book on small shop retailing suggests that readers think of their stores as cash machines, but the vast majority of us would be very unhappy with our shops if we viewed them that way. A recent study, in fact, shows that most retailers would enjoy a greater return on investment from well-managed mutual funds than they do from their stores. Many retailers are satisfied with the accomplishments of their business despite the absence of a large profit. They enjoy the freedom of owning their own business, the challenge of creative retailing, and the opportunity to provide a steady income to themselves and their staff.

Of course, a profit *is* a good thing to have. Being profitable provides a sense of security, and when you don't have to worry constantly about your business, you have more freedom to experiment with new ideas, products, and services. Being profitable also allows you to do more for your community and your employees, and it allows your store to grow. But profitability is only one measure of the pulse of a successful business. Keep the bottom line at the bottom, where it belongs.

3

STORE DESIGN

Think of a customer walking through the front door of your shop for the very first time. What do you want that person to see, hear, and sense? Creating an exciting retail environment for your customers involves much more than putting up shelves to display the merchandise. A good specialty shop integrates such diverse elements as lighting, flooring, displays, windows, signage, music, and even aroma to create the perfect setting for merchandising its product selection.

The Rain Forest Cafe's gift shop at the Mall of America stops traffic with its entry filled with the colorful spectacle of live exotic parrots on hoops and then keeps shoppers enthralled with a wall of tropical fish once they enter the store. A new era of imaginative retailing is upon us, and many customers are looking for shopping experiences that are entertaining, aesthetically pleasing, or relaxing. You may not want a talking tree, a wall of TV screens, or a two-story waterfall in your shop, but you need to let your imagination roam beyond the traditional rows of shelves and hooks. Your shop design should make your merchandise look special and your customers feel special.

ESTABLISHING A DESIGN BUDGET

The size of your store and the amount of remodeling required to convert the space you've leased into the store of your dreams will dictate whether you need to hire an architect, store designer, or other professionals to assist you. If the shop is small and you have good design sense, along with some basic construction skills, you may be able to do much of the work yourself. In planning, it is important to include key factors specific to store design: traffic flow, lighting, security, product display, storage, and checkout functions. A design professional with retail experience should be able to help you incorporate these elements into the store design while still maintaining your vision of what the store should be. If you cannot afford a store designer, check to see if any of the suppliers of store fixtures in your area offer knowledgeable design assistance.

> Select a designer who is adept at translating *your* personal store concept into reality. According to Frank Lloyd Wright expert Richard Cleary, when Wright designed the V. C. Morris Gift Shop in San Francisco in 1949, he took such a proprietary interest in the project that he would visit the shop after its completion and "correct" any displays or arrangements of furnishings that conflicted with his vision of the store.

Keep in mind that there are requirements that must be met regarding handicapped access (both state codes and the national standards set by the Americans with Disabilities Act), fire regulations, building codes, zoning regulations, and possibly also Occupational Safety and Health Administration standards. The requirements often vary depending on whether you are taking over an existing store without making changes, doing extensive remodeling to an existing space, or building a new structure. It is best to find out about all the requirements that will apply to your store when you are still in the planning stage. Contact your local planning department immediately, unless you will be working with an architect or store designer who is already knowledgeable about applicable regulations in your area.

Be realistic in what you decide to spend on store renovations, including design services. It is a mistake to cut corners so much that the store looks amateurish or unfinished, but many new retailers err in the opposite direction. In an attempt to look successful and well established from the start, novice retailers sometimes spend so much on fixtures and other furnishings that there is not enough money left for merchandise and the first year's operating expenses. Be aware that most professional store designers are used to working with chain stores with deep pockets. Establish a realistic budget early in the design process, and assume you will go over it by 10 or 20 percent. You can stretch your budget by purchasing some fixtures used from a store going out of business. You may also be able to get some displays at no charge from your suppliers. Companies sometimes create special shelving units, wire spinners, or racks for their products and offer these fixtures to stores for free, or at a price offset by free merchandise. Old furniture and storage containers can be refurbished and transformed into displays. Crate & Barrel, which now has a number of breathtakingly beautiful retail stores, started out as a small shop displaying merchandise in the crates and barrels it arrived in.

Flexibility should be a key element in the design of a new store. If you have never owned a shop before, chances are good that your store will go through several major changes in the first year or two. You will refine your merchandise selection as you learn what customers want. The checkout and storage areas, and perhaps even the store layout, will change as you see what works best for you and your staff. Look for shelves that are adjustable, fixtures that are movable, lighting that is flexible, and flooring that allows you to make layout changes easily.

REMODELING YOUR STORE

Few store designs are timeless. Even when your store is well established, you will need to redesign sections of it every few years to keep up with the times. A stagnant, dated store has a difficult time competing with new arrivals. Your merchandise mix will probably change over the years, and perhaps you will need to expand. Remodeling can be done as a total makeover, which may require being closed for some time, or piecemeal. Remodeling offers the opportunity to correct mistakes made when the store first opened and to bring in new retail technology.

Be sure to involve your staff in remodeling plans, asking them what they think could be improved. Check sales by department to see if some product categories deserve more floor space. Look for display fixtures and ideas that you like as you attend trade shows and visit stores in other areas. Your increasing experience in retailing should make design decisions easier each time you decide to make a change.

THE DESIGN CONCEPT

The store's merchandise focus will largely dictate the design direction you will choose to follow. Expensive jewelry, for example, requires a more subdued and elegant setting than art supplies. Traditionally, the more luxurious the merchandise, the more spacious the store. A narrow doorway, subtle lighting, and soft carpeting also create a feeling of exclusivity. Expensive items are usually featured in displays that highlight individual pieces rather than being "massed" on a shelf.

The color range of the merchandise to be featured may inspire a store design concept. One of the most beautiful new stores in New York is Origins, a tiny shop featuring natural soaps and cosmetics. The simple packaging and ingredients of Origins' products inspired a store with a modern, environmental look incorporating blonde wood fixtures accented by a dark green wall. Floor-to-ceiling windows on two sides bring in lots of natural light during the day, and miniature halogen fixtures fall like stars from the ceiling to illuminate the store by night.

Crabtree & Evelyn's stores also sell soap, but their approach to store design is completely different. Inspired by the English origin of many of the company's products, Crabtree & Evelyn creates elegant stores with a traditional Victorian look, featuring dark wood fixtures and floral wallpaper. Some stores use different design concepts within the same store. The Library Shop at The New York Public Library, for example, features a bright yellow, stepped pyramid display unit in the children's area (see Figure 3-1) and antique furniture and statuary in the section featuring readers' gifts.

Some types of merchandise require special facilities, such as fitting rooms, mirrors, seating, or easy access to back stock. You may want to design a flexible space that can be used for merchandise as well as occasional classes and lectures, or a display counter that can double as a place to hold demonstrations and samplings. Visiting other stores selling the same types of goods can give you a sense of what works best for them. Make a list of special layout needs before you begin the design process. Keep in mind that fitting rooms and other special facilities need to be handicapped ac-

Figure 3-1 Brightly colored fixtures displaying merchandise at various levels appeal to young shoppers in The Library Shop at The New York Public Library.

51

cessible. The regulations for the height of the fitting room mirror, the size of the door, and other factors important to the comfort of customers in wheelchairs are very precise.

In addition to the merchandise mix, it is important to base your store design on the types of customers you hope the store will attract. A toy store with a colorful and playful design will appeal to children and their parents. A shop selling clothes for teenagers might want to go with a high-tech look, with TV screens showing music and fashion videos. The store design concept should encompass a color scheme and a "look" that can be carried through in all the elements of the store: the storefront, signage, fixtures, lighting, and merchandising. The design concept will also influence the store's advertising, product selection, and even the way employees dress. The more clearly defined the design concept is, the stronger the shop's identity will be.

THE STOREFRONT AND ENTRANCE

Perhaps live parrots are not the best way to draw shoppers to your store, but your storefront should be as engaging and attractive as possible in whatever way is appropriate to your retailing vision. The location and architecture of your store are key elements in determining the type of storefront you can consider. Stores located on shopping streets need to keep the nature of the streetscape in mind, and those in malls must conform to management's standards for storefront design. Within these parameters, it is important to create a distinctive and attractive look for your shop, because the storefront is the first impression you make on passersby—and will often determine whether they come through the door.

Few stores can survive without display windows, and for many the window display is their most successful advertising. Older buildings or homes being renovated into retail space should create some windows for merchandise display in order to announce that a retail store is within. To create dynamic displays, you will need storefront windows with adequate space, easy access, several electrical outlets, a ceiling grid for suspending things, and flexible lighting. The back of these show windows can be open, with a view of the store, or closed off with a glass or wood panel. A closed back allows more creative use of backdrops and prevents customers from reaching into the display, but an open-backed window is considered better for security purposes, since it allows passersby to see what is happening in the store.

Stores selling small items, such as jewelry, will find it easier to display their merchandise in smaller windows—either independent shadowbox windows, allowing for separate themed displays, or one long, narrow window at a good viewing level for pedestrians. If valuables will need to be removed from the window at night for security purposes, the backs of the displays should provide easy access for staff, but not customers.

The location and accessibility of the door may influence whether people decide to enter the store. Some mall stores have wide, open entrances that span almost the entire storefront, in contrast to the locked and guarded doors of exclusive jewelry or antique stores. The nature of the doorway can communicate a great deal about the store's range of merchandise and prices. In an area without a large base of wealthy shoppers, creating a store entrance that intimidates the average customer would be a real mistake. Most people judge a store's level of exclusivity from its exterior, and won't go inside to see whether the shop's merchandise actually happens to be within their price range.

Stores with parking lots or even sidewalk space have an added opportunity to create a pleasing first impression. Build a low wood or brick fence around your parking area, and landscape it with small trees and bushes. Place pots of flowering plants by the store entrance, or hang flower boxes under the display windows. In the winter, remove unused planters and wind small white Christmas lights through the trees and bushes by your store. In planning your landscaping, be sure to allow for enough electrical outlets for seasonal lighting.

Signs and Awnings

Good signage is an essential part of any store's advertising program, communicating a quick message about the store to all those who drive or walk by. An effective sign, well lit, is an important part of the store image, especially for stores that are not in a mall. The store's signage or awnings, and the design of the logo and graphics, should complement the overall design concept to make a clear statement of the store's identity. Determine whether your community has specific codes about what types of signs and awnings are permissible before commissioning this work or any other exterior changes. We were surprised to learn that technically we are not even allowed to take down our sign to clean it without getting a permit.

A free-hanging sign or banner, hung perpendicular to the store, can be an effective way to catch the attention of pedestrians. Most stores also need a sign across the front of the store, or by the entrance, that gives the name of the store and perhaps a brief tag line describing what it sells. The material and type style used for the main sign should be in keeping with the image you are trying to develop for the shop. You might paint the name on wood, or purchase an illuminated box sign, with the name or logo applied to a sheet of opaque plastic that is lit from behind. Another way of writing the store name is to use individual letters, like the gold ones we found for our storefronts. These sturdy letters look as if they are made of painted wood, but they are actually durable plastic. The manufacturer of our letters is Gemini, Inc. (800-538-8377), but they are also available through local sign companies throughout the country. Other signs use separate letters that are illuminated from behind, giving good visibility at night and an attractive appearance during the day.

One popular trend is to feature the name of the store on an awning—either a retractable one intended for rain and sun protection or a permanent architectural feature used to add character to a storefront. Permanent awnings can be quite effective as a facelift for an older building and can be lit from inside or above. All awnings detract somewhat from the visibility of the store windows, which should be taken into account when deciding whether to use them.

Neon logo and name signs can be an effective design element on a storefront or in a window if the bright look of neon is in keeping with your store image. Neon is visible from some distance and comes in a wide variety of colors that can echo the color scheme used in the store. Neon in the window should be hung high enough that it will not interfere with window displays, since it is not easy to move once it is in place. Some store design specialists claim that a neon "open" sign can be one of the most important features in a store's window. Certainly freestanding stores open evening and weekend hours may want to promote this fact with a neon sign. Be sure to keep all sections of any neon sign functioning at all times; a burned-out letter or two makes a poor first impression.

Can your store be seen from the side as well as the front? This presents an added opportunity for signage, or perhaps an attractive mural that incorporates the store name. Schmitt Music Center in Minneapolis is easily recognized by the huge painting of sheet music on the side of its building.

If your shop is located on a neighborhood street, check sign ordinances to see if you are allowed to place a sandwich-board sign between the sidewalk and the curb. This sign can state the name of the shop and the fact that you are open, or can include a chalkboard area to announce daily specials. Stores set back from the street, or on an upper level, may be able to arrange for a signpost near the sidewalk with information about the store. A small vertical showcase built onto the sign, with a few samples of merchandise, may help lure customers into the shop.

Stores not located in a mall need to feature their street number in large letters on the storefront, or on or above the door. Customers often have difficulty finding a certain address, because many stores don't use numbers large enough to be seen from a car. There should also be a sign on the door saying "welcome" and giving the store hours. Make your own hours sign if those that are commercially available are not in keeping with the image you are trying to create.

LAYOUT

Once the customer walks through the door, the layout of the displays and other fixtures will influence the path he or she takes through the store. Traditional wisdom has it that most people naturally turn to the right, so many stores are laid out like an oval racetrack, leading the customer around the loop. Others place the fixtures in a random pattern, hoping that shoppers will explore every area on their own.

If your retail space is rectangular, you may be tempted to line up displays parallel to the walls, forming orderly, straight aisles. This grid layout is fine for grocery or convenience stores but it is too boring for specialty shops concerned with creating an interesting atmosphere. Try putting up partial partitions perpendicular to the walls, forming small display alcoves, or setting up new walls extending out from the existing walls in a zigzag pattern. Freestanding displays can be used to break up a rectangle into smaller spaces that invite shoppers to explore. Although you don't want to create totally hidden nooks and crannies that are tempting to shoplifters, you do want to give the impression that the store has more to it than can be seen at a quick glance. In a mall, it is especially important to create an eye-catching display against the back wall in order to draw shoppers all the way into your store.

When laying out the floor plan, keep in mind that customers in wheelchairs or pushing strollers need to be able to negotiate the aisles and the spaces between displays. Apparel stores especially tend to pack too many fixtures into a small space, making it difficult for anyone to get through, let alone browse comfortably. Plan for 36 inches of clearance on all sides of your displays, keeping in mind that clothing hangers and merchandise often extend out from the display unit itself. Adequate open space shows respect for customers' comfort—and highlights the merchandise to its best advantage. Check to be sure that you conform with the minimum aisle width dictated by building codes, for fire safety and handicapped access regulations.

The location of amenities, such as the checkout counter (also called a *cash wrap*), should be determined early in the layout process. There are many factors to take into account in deciding what shape to make this counter and where to put it. Some security-minded stores build central, elevated round checkout "fortresses." These allow staff to view shoppers throughout the store, but are a barrier to staff interaction with customers. Ideally, sales associates should be able to get out from behind the counter easily to assist customers. A checkout counter placed in the back of a small store allows staff to see customers entering the store, but may allow shoplifters to make a quick retreat with merchandise stolen from displays near the entrance. A checkout counter located too close to the entrance, on the other hand, does not invite shoppers to come in and browse. For most stores, the best solution is to locate one or more checkouts partway into the store, but not so far back that the sales associates at the counter cannot greet customers soon after they enter.

FLOORING MATERIALS

The path the customer takes through the store can be influenced by the flooring you choose. Vinyl, rubber, wood, or linoleum is often used in entranceways and checkout areas. When used to highlight heavily trafficked paths through the store, this hard flooring delineates the route the shopper is expected to take. These types of flooring are easier to maintain than carpeting and can be covered with rented mats in inclement weather. Rental mat service costs more than owning your own floor mats, but we love having our service pick up our wet and muddy mats on Friday and replace them with clean, dry ones—almost like diaper service, and every bit as welcome.

Carpeting creates a feeling of luxury, and may be used throughout the store or just in display areas. Nylon carpets with a low pile are durable and will last many years if cleaned regularly. Solution-dyed nylon carpet allows for the removal of stains using bleach and other very strong cleaners. Be sure to buy high-quality, commercial-grade carpeting, and select a shade and blend or pattern (not a solid color) that will not readily show dirt. We chose too light a color when we last carpeted, and it showed stains almost immediately. Putting in new carpeting requires dismantling most of the fixtures in the store, so we've been putting off replacement as long as we can.

Keep handicapped and low-vision customers in mind when selecting your flooring. Dense, short-pile carpeting is easier than other types of carpeting for those in wheelchairs. And changes in surface texture help signal a step up or a ramp for those with vision problems. Avoid materials that may be slippery, such as marble that has not been treated with a nonslip finish.

WALL TREATMENTS

The walls of a shop usually are used to form a neutral backdrop for the merchandise and fixtures. Some merchandise, however, needs a bright background to liven it up. Dramatic wall treatments, including murals, can also be used to draw attention to displays of small items such as shoes. Walls of different colors can be used to distinguish one area of the store from another, but, of course, these colors must be well coordinated.

Most recently built stores have uninteresting white walls made of wallboard, a surface that fortunately takes well to paint or wallpaper. The latest fashion in some stores on the coasts is to paint the walls in a strong color and then to create a textured feeling by sponging on a second shade of the same color. Other stores leave the walls a light, neutral color that does not overpower the merchandise. A compromise is to have one accent wall, or areas around the top of the walls painted in a distinctive color, while the rest of the walls are neutral. These accent areas can be repainted or wallpapered periodically to reflect changes in the seasons or in color trends of merchandise, giving the store a fresh look.

Brick or block walls, usually found in older buildings, add warmth and character to a store but are difficult to drill into. Freestanding display fixtures work best in this situation, along with a rail along the top of the wall that allows you to attach wires for hanging pictures, posters, and banners. Wood paneling is a warm, comfortable wall surface but does not allow for easy change and can overpower rather than complement some merchandise. Fabric panels that can be taken down and recovered are more versatile, and can give the store a whole new look each time the color scheme is changed.

LIGHTING

The correct choice of lighting is essential to setting the store's mood and displaying merchandise to its best advantage. Visiting a variety of stores in order to see what type of lighting is used can be very helpful, since most of us don't normally pay conscious attention to this detail. You will notice that most grocery and discount stores use economical, bright fluorescent or high-density discharge lighting. Specialty shops are more likely to use incandescent, tungsten, or halogen lights and sometimes also natural daylight.

A combination of lighting types often works best. Fluorescent lights, especially full-spectrum bulbs designed to resemble daylight, work well in areas needing overall lighting. Fluorescents are energy efficient and require less maintenance than other types of bulbs. Some stores use fluorescents in a valance around the perimeter walls, and also overhead to give general lighting, with nonfluorescent spotlights to highlight merchandise and show the true color of the goods.

Many smaller shops avoid fluorescents altogether, except in storage and work areas, finding that subdued lighting is one factor that helps distinguish a specialty shop from the glaring, impersonal feeling of a big box discounter. A few, however, go too far in trying to appear intimate or exclusive, and create a dark, uninviting space. A store needs to look as if it is open for business. Excessively dim lightly is intimidating and makes it difficult for customers to see the merchandise.

Incandescent or halogen track lighting, attached to fixed rails on the ceiling or wall, or on hanging parallel wires, offers versatile lighting that can be adjusted to focus on various displays. We use incandescent reflector flood, or spot, lights in inexpensive clamp-on lamps attached to the ceiling grids throughout the store. For certain merchandise, such as glassware and silver, we use special halogen floodlights that enhance the sparkle of these items. Low-voltage, narrow spotlights are also excellent for true color rendering and adding sparkle to displays. When focusing lighting on a display, be sure to provide enough light for the customer to see details such as the price and description and avoid shadows and glare.

In addition to ambient and merchandise illumination, lighting can be used as a design feature in the store. Attractive wall sconces in the entranceway, for example, help create a welcoming environment. Dramatic lighting can lead customers from one area of the store to another. Drop lights, either tiny halogens or traditional incandescent, can demarcate and illuminate checkout counters. Be sure that lights in work areas such as this do not shine in anyone's eyes or force a standing customer or seated employee to look at an exposed bulb.

Ideally, natural light should be used some of the time, saving energy and showing merchandise exactly as it will look outside the store. But natural light can be a challenge to work with unless you live in a dependably sunny climate. Supplementary lighting needs to be available for rainy days and for after sunset, preferably set up so that it is triggered to come on only when needed. We use a timer on the lights in our display windows so they are only illuminated from dusk to early morning, but we have not yet managed to adjust our interior lighting to the ever-changing Wisconsin weather.

Consider emergency lighting at the same time that your lighting system is installed. Exit lights are available with battery backups so that they will remain illuminated during a power outage. You may also want to install self-charging, battery-operated lights that will maintain at least a minimal amount of lighting in an emergency. All shops should have a few working flashlights on hand, along with a battery-operated radio.

Store designers are usually very knowledgeable about the special lighting needs of a retail environment. Other sources of information include display fixture companies, wholesale suppliers of light bulbs, and your local electric utility. Lumber yards and stores selling light fixtures for homes may have many types of lighting that you can use, but you cannot count on the sales staff knowing much about retail lighting. Several books on store planning in the bibliography may provide useful ideas for designing your store's lighting.

Some localities require commercial users to submit calculations of their proposed energy usage, which will affect your lighting options. Be sure to check with these regulations before purchasing light fixtures.

CEILINGS

The type of lighting you choose will strongly influence the ceiling treatment that works best in your store. We painted our ceilings black, with a wood grid hanging a few feet below to hold our inexpensive metal reflector clamp lights. Track lighting, which comes in a wide variety of styles, looks best attached to a solid ceiling painted a light or dark neutral color. Acoustic tile with built-in fluorescent fixtures is not an exciting look, but may work well in areas where it is not necessary to focus lighting on merchandise displays. Special hooks available for the metal grid used to hold acoustic ceiling tiles allow signs, banners, and even merchandise to be hung easily from the ceiling.

Older buildings with high ceilings offer a special challenge. If the ceiling is attractive—for example, an antique tin ceiling—consider leaving it exposed, but focus customers' attention on merchandise at eye level by using lots of small halogen drop lights, a wood grid, or a wire system with track lighting. Pipes, wiring, and other exposed utilities on the ceiling can be painted black so they disappear, or they can be decorated as part of the store decor. Very high ceilings may create the feeling of an impersonal, unfriendly space, so it is important to keep lighting and displays at a height that is comfortable for the average shopper.

SELLING ON SEVERAL LEVELS

Stores with a balcony, mezzanine, or upper level face a special challenge. Customers are much more likely to browse on the main floor on impulse, but in order to get anyone to go up a flight of stairs, there must be special motivation. Upper levels are best used for merchandise that customers have specifically come in for, and for which they are willing to make an extra effort. Good signage is essential to draw customers to an upper level, and it is important that sales assistance be available once the customer has climbed the stairs. We have a work station on the second floor so we can make good use of the time between customers, but shoppers are sometimes reluctant to ask us for help if we are working there, despite the large "customer assistance" sign on the desk.

Using a second-floor retail space poses two main drawbacks. The first is that customers who are physically challenged find it difficult or impossible to come upstairs unless there is an elevator. New stores under construction and those undergoing major renovations should check the requirements for ramps, a wheelchair lift, or an elevator. The second drawback is that shoplifting is a greater problem upstairs because there are usually fewer customers and sales assistants present. We must have very neatly dressed thieves in Madison, because someone keeps stealing the irons we display in our second-floor area.

Stores merchandising on just one level sometimes use slight elevations to break up a large space or to highlight one area of merchandise by making it a few steps higher than the rest of the store. This arrangement may be visually appealing, but great care needs to be taken to keep customers from tripping on steps they may not notice. Ramps for wheelchairs to go up even the slightest elevation can take considerable floor space, since the ramp must be 1 foot in length for every 1 inch of rise.

DECIDING WHAT MERCHANDISE GOES WHERE

Some view retailing as an exact science, with the location and number of square feet allotted to each merchandise department determined by the dollar volume and profitability of that area. Others like store design to be a bit more spontaneous. You don't know from the outset which merchandise categories will be the most popular anyway, and customers often enjoy an element of serendipity. The store that develops somewhat organically can easily adapt to trends in merchandising and decide at any time to allot more space to a department showing a major increase in sales.

A good store layout and exciting displays will lead customers through the entire shop, so the only really key decision is what to place in the front of the store in order to draw shoppers in. Front displays should make a statement about the store and what it has to offer. Never put clearance merchandise in the front part of the store, unless you are promoting price above selection or quality.

Display Fixtures: Highlighting Special Merchandise

There are two basic approaches to displaying merchandise: showcasing a few examples of each item, with more in back stock, or massing the items out for self-service. We live in an era of mass merchandising, and most retail stores put as much merchandise as possible on the selling floor. This cuts down on storage costs and customer service expense, but it is not the best way for all stores to show all merchandise. In general, the more expensive the item, the fewer you should have on display. Highlighting a single sample of an item makes it seem special. This exclusivity is a positive selling point for jewelry, art, crafts items, collectibles, designer clothing, antiques, and other high-end merchandise.

The types of fixtures used for single-item display are different from those designed to hold as much as possible. Locked showcases are necessary for the security of very expensive items. Keep the keys to these showcases in a place accessible only to staff, and be sure to have a second set in case they are misplaced. A large, unusual key ring can help keep a thief from pocketing the showcase keys and prevent staff members from inadvertently leaving them where they don't belong.

> Søstrene Grene, an innovate Copenhagen shop selling an eclectic mix of gifts, closeouts, and environmentally friendly products, makes humorous use of locked glass display cases by playfully spotlighting a single sample of two or three $1.00 items as if they were precious gems.

For unique products that do not need to be under lock and key, glass shelving may work best. It allows light to focus on the item from all four sides and can be attached to the wall or built-in shelf units, or used in freestanding standards made of wood or metal. Display systems made up of glass cubes are generally adjustable and versatile in their display uses. The one disadvantage to using glass is that it shows dust and fingerprints easily and needs constant attention to prevent customers from seeing telltale outlines when they pick up items to examine them.

Many stores use furniture to display their products, creating settings that help customers imagine how the merchandise might look in their own homes. The warm color of wooden furniture makes an excellent background for many items, and tables and bookshelves can be accessorized with runners, tablecloths, or other fabric to change their look throughout the year. The main drawbacks to using furniture are that most etagères and hutches lack the adjustability that one looks for in a display fixture, and large tables can take up a lot of floor space without allowing for merchandise to be displayed above or below the tabletop level. Some stores offer the furniture they display merchandise on for sale, getting double duty out of their display space (though you may face a display crisis if a customer decides to buy a key fixture).

Maximizing Mass Merchandise Fixtures

Mass merchandising need not be unattractive. The repetition of one item many times over can create a pleasing pattern, especially if attention is paid to color placement and to making sure the display is always full and neat. The customer looking at a massed display gets the impression that the store believes strongly in an item (otherwise why would there be so many of them?), and that the item is probably not very expensive. Many customers appreciate the fact that a massed display allows them to help themselves rather than looking for a sales associate for help.

Glass fixtures and wood furniture can, of course, also be used to put out large quantities of each item. Mass merchandising traditionally uses fixtures such as wall systems, wire grid cubes, rounders (circular clothing racks), bins, and the omnipresent *gondola*, a freestanding display with adjustable shelving along the two long sides and merchandise on the end caps as well.

Creative alternatives to traditional shelves and racks can give your store a unique look. Crate & Barrel started out using shipping containers to display their wares. We have also used terracotta pipes and clay flower pots to show merchandise, as well as heavy plastic buckets and tubs. We use lots and lots of baskets in our displays, most of which are also for sale.

Many stores use pedestals of various heights to display merchandise and find that these units are also useful in window displays. Small, round display tables can be found in inexpensive versions made of particleboard, or even cardboard and plastic, and covered in a wardrobe of tablecloths to match the season or the merchandise. Often a floor-length round tablecloth is used to drape, or skirt, the unit, and then a smaller contrasting square cloth "topper" is used under the merchandise. Basic platforms, raised a few inches off the floor, help highlight big stacks of packaged merchandise being massed on display, a sales technique colorfully referred to as *tonnage*.

In displaying clothing, the use of varied heights also effectively highlights fashionable merchandise. Instead of rounders, which display everything in a circle, all at the same level, consider waterfalls, t-stands, and wall units with hooks at various heights.

Wall Display Units

There are several systems for using walls, and the back panels of gondolas, to hold hooks and shelves. Pegboard was once considered a versatile and attractive way to hold merchandise, but it now looks dated. *Slatwall*, a grooved panel system available in many wood, laminate, mirror, or paintable finishes, is the current favorite for specialty shop retailers (see Figure 3-2). A wide variety of hooks, clothing merchandisers, acrylic shelves, and bins are available to hook into slatwall. Slatwall allows displays to be changed quickly and easily, although the surface color of the

Figure 3-2 The Connecticut Audubon Society uses slatwall to display a wide variety of products including cards, gift bags, boxed notes, books, T-shirts on hangers, and small apparel items in bins.

(Photo: Richard J. Boucher.)

slatwall itself may be more difficult to alter if it is made of one of the durable laminated materials. Slatwall can be put around a column to take advantage of space that might otherwise go to waste. There are also slatwall spinners that can be used with shallow shelves or short hooks to create compact but effective displayers for small items. The drawback to slatwall is that its horizontal pattern can be monotonous if overused. Areas of slatwall need to be broken up by occasional flat surfaces or other textures or patterns.

Wire grid systems can be used to hang merchandise on hooks or hangers, and can be used as a free-hanging display rather than up against a wall. A sporting goods store, for instance, could hang a wire grid panel with mittens and gloves clipped onto both sides, or hung on hooks made for grid systems. We have two grids hanging from the ceiling to show our line of stainless ladles, tongs, and spatulas. We keep a few extra grids on hand for customers who want to use the same idea to store the utensils in their own kitchen.

Remember that whatever fixtures you choose, the merchandise should remain the primary focus. Display fixtures should allow the goods to be displayed attractively and help keep them neat. Traditionally, shelving for massed merchandise is adjusted so there is a standard 2-inch space between the items and the shelf above. This is not practical when shelf is used for an assortment of merchandise of varying heights, but it can be used to create an efficient and attractive display of uniform items.

INTERIOR SIGNAGE

A thorough design plan should include interior graphics that reinforce the store's name and logo and point customers to the rest room and various merchandise departments. If you carry brand-name merchandise, the company's familiar logo may be a positive selling point that should be featured in your signage, and vendors sometimes help pay for this type of sign. Signs can be painted on hanging wood or acrylic panels, or directly on the walls. Fabric banners are an effective way to communicate information. They add color to the store design and can easily be changed.

Consider painting the store name or logo on the wall behind the cash register, and using your logo typestyle for signs throughout the store. Our hand-painted imported English pub-style sign couldn't survive outside in the harsh midwestern winters, so we display it over a fireplace mantle inside the store. It is surprising how many customers, even with a visual cue like this, still aren't sure what store they are in. Word-of-mouth advertising is the best kind, so it's important that customers know and remember your store name so they can mention it to their friends. Be sure the store name is clearly posted by the cash register for those writing checks.

Signs That Speak

Many shops show great care in selecting coordinated display fixtures but forget to pay attention to the need for a well-designed program of product information signs throughout the store. The colorful retailing term for these signs is *shelf talkers*, because they communicate prices, sizes, and the benefits of the products to shoppers. You can never have enough sales staff to explain every item to every customer. Signs that are beautifully made and thoughtfully worded can give the impression that you are speaking directly to the shoppers, telling them what you'd like them to know.

A visit to a dozen specialty shops in New York's SoHo district reveals that almost every shop has a distinctive look for its shelf talkers. Each store uses a recognizable background paper, type style, and frame for its signs. Careful thought has obviously been given to selecting a look consistent with that shop's decor. A garden accessories store uses natural kraft paper signs with its logo at the top, whereas a bed linen shop prints signs on a paper with a subtle floral pattern.

Signs located near a display in the store are sometimes referred to as POP (point-of-purchase) advertising. These signs can be strictly factual, giving the sizes and prices for each item, announcing new arrivals, or highlighting a sale. But some of the best POP signs are almost conversational in tone, pointing out the virtues of a product and telling the customer something about where the item was made or about the craftsperson or tradition behind the product. Think of what you would say about the item if you were enthusiastically describing it to a customer or writing about it in a catalog. Use your signs to "talk" to shoppers who are browsing and are willing to take the time to read them. Video stores and bookshops use shelf talkers to tell customers which selections are favorites of their staff members. Shoppers especially appreciate this service when it includes a few lines by the employees expanding on their recommendations.

We recently developed a standard sign with our logo on it that we keep on a computer disk. We add the text and print them on sheets of perforated 3- by 5-inch white cards made for the laser printer. It takes just a few seconds to add some color to each sign with orange and green highlighters and to insert them into inexpensive acrylic frames. After years of typed and handwritten signs, it is a big improvement to have all the signs in the store present the same look.

If your store doesn't have a computer, ask if anyone on your staff or in the neighborhood has calligraphy skills. Or you could purchase a P-Touch machine, which allows you to print out strips of words in neat black type on self-adhesive tape that is either clear or colored. We use our P-Touch machine to label shelves and even to put descriptions or prices on display samples of products.

THE CHECKOUT AREA

Every detail in the planning of the customer's side of the checkout area should contribute to making the experience of buying something from your store simple and pleasant. The sales associates will spend much of their time on the other side of the counter, so careful attention to planning the behind-the-counter area will pay off in a more efficient and contented staff.

The height of the check writing area of the counter is usually 42 inches, however this is too high for customers in wheelchairs. Providing one counter 29 to 36 inches high or a pull-out shelf at wheelchair level is a courtesy to disabled customers; in addition, it may be required by local building codes and is specified in the Americans with Disabilities Act. Find out about these regulations before finalizing your design.

For the comfort of employees, some stores have the customers' side of the counter at standard height and the sales associates' work area behind it somewhat lower so the employee can be seated on a stool or standing while ringing up purchases, bagging, and wrapping. You should also take into account whether the design of the counter and the area behind it would allow an employee in a wheelchair to wait on customers. The Americans with Disabilities Act, together with local and state building codes, mandate equal access to jobs for all potential employees.

The length of the counter is determined by how many cash registers will be on the counter, as well as any additional electronic equipment, such as scanners and data capture machines. Because there is no way to predict the future of retailing technology, it is wise to allow extra space and electrical outlets for changes. Also be sure to allow ample room on the counter for the customers' merchandise, especially if you intend to have small displays of impulse items by the register.

Behind the Counter

Comfort and safety are primary concerns for the employee side of the counter. Flooring should be easy on the feet, and stools should be provided for occasional rest breaks. To discourage money theft, the area directly adjacent to the cash register drawer should be accessible only to staff. A telephone or intercom for easy communication with other parts of the store should be within easy reach.

The back side of the checkout counter is often used to store sheets of tissue, a bin of shredded tissue for cushioning items being boxed, flat merchandise bags, and gift boxes. The more shelves you have, the better for separating gift box sizes, so that each size has its own compartment. Staff members can put their hands on the right size box or lid in a hurry, and restocking these supplies every day is easy. Shopping bags can also be stored under the counter or hung nearby.

If there are two registers at the same counter, the most commonly used supplies should be duplicated on each side so sales personnel don't have to reach across each other to get at them. It is also useful to keep pens, pins, additional register tape, scissors, tape, note paper, tissues, customer request forms, and business cards under the counter, along with a waste basket and recycling bin.

Additional supplies for boxing and wrapping are often located in an adjacent counter area or behind the checkout counter. Stores that sell many items that need to be wrapped in tissue paper may wish to have a slightly lower "well" in the wrap counter to fill to counter level with a stack of tissue sheets, ready to use. Spools of ribbons, bins of premade bows, and rolls of paper for gift wrapping can be hung on the wall behind the register, together with gift wrap samples for customers to choose from. Remember that any area that is visible to customers must be kept neat and attractive.

We put merchandise in boxes, with bows and ribbon, behind the checkout counter, but have our gift wrapping department located elsewhere in the store. We try to make the best use of limited space in our small building, and there just isn't room for rolls of wrap behind the counter. Customers don't seem to mind having to go to another part of the store to have packages wrapped, and this does cut down on the congestion around the checkout counter when we are really busy. Some stores that normally do gift wrap behind the counter set up a second wrapping area during the hectic holiday season.

A filing cabinet behind the checkout counter is useful for storing frequently consulted product information files, as well as wedding registries and forms for services such as shipping, layaway, gift certificates, and special orders. We also keep a folder for each employee in the cabinet behind the counter (mostly for paychecks, notes, and newsletters) and a file for concert tickets we have agreed to sell for local arts groups.

We keep a change box with rolls of coins in a cabinet behind the checkout counter. When a register needs change, a sales associate "buys" a roll from the change box with money from the till. As part of our reconciliation at the end of the day, we double-check to make sure there is still the correct amount in the change box.

During the slower months, our sales staff checks in merchandise behind the counter. This lightens the work load of the stock staff and also makes the time go by faster when the sales associates do not have many customers to wait on. We try to keep a work surface clear for this activity and have all the supplies for pricing nearby. A large shipment can make quite a mess behind the counter, so ideally only small orders are brought up to be worked on. It is a challenge to be ready to help customers at any moment while also unpacking merchandise, but we emphasize to the staff that no matter what else they are doing, customer service is *always* their top priority.

Signage near the checkout counter should promote gift certificates, gift wrapping, and any other special services. There should be a sign explaining the store's return policy and indicating which credit cards you accept. Have a supply of business cards on hand, lots of pens for customers to use when writing checks, and a small sign showing how to spell the store's name. You might also have a self-inking stamp made of the store name so customers don't have to write in the store name on checks. We keep a self-inking endorsement stamp by the register to stamp the back of each check as we receive it, saving us time at the end of the day and preventing anyone from being able to steal and cash our checks.

BACKGROUND MUSIC

Stores should not be silent. Customers feel self-conscious walking into a quiet space, intimidated by the fact that the sales staff can hear every word they say. Background music not only helps customers relax but can help create a memorable atmosphere that reinforces your store image. The music you choose should be pleasing to the majority of your customers and agreeable to your staff. Since staff members listen to the background music for hours and hours, it is important to have a large selection of management-approved music to help prevent audio boredom. Music choice and volume level should not be left up to chance or the staff's whim.

What type of music is best for your shop? Some specialty shops will be able to find music that carries out the store's theme, such as seasonal music for a Christmas shop or music with sounds of nature for an environmental store. Others will need to look at what type of music creates the best mood for their customers. Studies have shown that instrumental music is in general less distracting than vocals, although customers might be drawn into a shop selling retro clothing by the sound of Billie Holiday singing the blues.

The volume level is a crucial factor in creating a pleasing audio atmosphere. Music should not distract customers from their shopping or intrude on conversation. Nor should it be so quiet that it can barely be heard.

Many shops play a commercial radio station in the background, complete with ads, news, weather, and announcer chitchat. Not only can this be distracting, but the ads may include some for your store's competition—not exactly what you want customers to hear when they are shopping. Noncommercial radio is a good alternative during the times of day when the programming is all music. Be sure to make a contribution to your local public radio station if you use their service. Cable television companies sometimes offer a commercial-free music service, and the much-maligned Muzak may be available in your area. These services provide a variety of music all day long, with few if any repetitions, but, of course, you and your staff have no control over the individual selections.

A cassette player with a continuous-play feature, especially one that alternates between two different cassettes, can provide background music all day without anyone having to change the tapes. We used cassettes for many years before switching this year to a CD player that rotates six different CDs. This new system saves us from having to listen to the same song once every hour, which was often the case with cassettes. Our musical choices tend toward instrumental classical, folk, and light jazz—as long as there are no saxophones. I think I'm allergic to squeaky saxophones, so I assume some of my customers also may be.

Playing music in the store brings up the thorny issue of paying for the rights to use the recordings commercially. Technically a store playing the radio, cassettes, or CDs is required to pay an annual licensing fee to either ASCAP or BMI, or both. These fees, which go to the artists whose music you are playing, are based on the number of speakers used in the store. The only legal way to avoid paying for licensing is to play only recordings that you sell and to which your supplier has the rights.

CREATING AN AROMATIC ENVIRONMENT

The effect of fragrance on the mind is a relatively new field, and at the moment, few stores use fragrance to create atmosphere unless the scent is part of a product being sold. Customers can be turned off by too strong a fragrance, such as burning incense, either because they dislike the aroma or because they don't wish to have it clinging to their hair and clothes when they leave the store. A pleasant, light aroma is known to have a pleasing effect on most people. The scent of pine and cinnamon can help create the right atmosphere in a Christmas shop, even if the weather outside says summer. A shop promoting bathing suits in the winter could use shells and a sea-scented potpourri to help set the mood. Potpourri, room spray, and scented candles can be used to establish a subtle aroma in a store. We often bake bread on busy Saturdays in the bread machines we sell, because we know how pleasurable the scent of baking bread is for most people. (Those who are lucky enough to be around when it is finished get to enjoy eating it too.)

Anita Roddick of The Body Shop sprayed strawberry essence on the sidewalk leading up to her first shop in order to attract the public's attention.

STORAGE, OFFICES, LOUNGES, AND OTHER BACKSTAGE NEEDS

The high cost per square foot of many retail locations makes it tempting to devote almost every inch to the sales floor in order to maximize display space. Certainly the area devoted to merchandise display is the most important part of a shop, but few stores could survive without a rest room, unloading area, storage space, and an office.

Customers and staff alike appreciate access to a clean rest room. In most states, stores are required to provide a rest room easily accessible to customers and large enough for use by someone in a wheelchair. The rest room should have a safety bar and other features specified by the Americans with Disabilities Act.

A comfortable and efficient office, stock area, and employee break room make for a happy bookkeeping, buying, and stockperson staff. But few stores, including ours, have enough room to make these areas as spacious as they should be. Remodeling money tends to get put first into the parts of the store where customers can see it.

In designing behind-the-scenes spaces, remember that staff members need a place to eat lunch and to keep their coats and other personal items.

We keep a small refrigerator stocked with cans of soda for our staff and have a microwave on hand for them to heat up food. If you have room, it is a good idea to provide individual lockers (with locks) for employees' purses and other personal possessions.

Stock arriving by truck should not come in through the front of the store, and there should be a place for unpacking merchandise without making a mess on the sales floor. Ideally, the space for unpacking merchandise should be located near the freight entrance and should be roomy enough to accommodate new arrivals as well as merchandise not yet checked in. Supplies such as price guns, tags, pens, knives, and forms for checking in and routing merchandise should be close at hand. Bins for sorting trash and recyclables should be nearby. Our stockpeople work in a rather cramped area near the back door, processing as many as 160 incoming packages a day with surprisingly good humor.

A store can never have enough storage space. It is not a luxury; rather, storage space is often a key to good customer service. Customers find it frustrating when a store is out of an item they want. Adequate storage space allows the store to carry enough depth of stock in key items to prevent "outages" that result in lost sales. Of course, too much storage space can encourage costly stockpiling of merchandise, but few retailers feel that they have enough room for the stock they need, especially on-site. Many stores with multiple locations take advantage of less expensive storage in a nonretail area and supply each store's needs from a central warehouse. Individual stores also sometimes find space in another location, such as commercial rental storage units, to store merchandise, displays, and supplies. We rent a nearby garage to store boxes and bags, since these items do not require the security of a locked unit. Be sure to check your insurance coverage for any items stored off premises, even if the storage is in your own garage or basement. Keep storage areas clean and neat, with aisles clear for employees carrying boxes of merchandise. A messy stockroom can be a fire hazard, as well as an inefficient way of keeping merchandise close at hand and in perfect, salable condition.

A store also needs a place to keep supplies such as brooms, vacuum cleaners, and snow shovels. Cleaning supplies that may contain harmful chemicals should not be stored unlocked in a bathroom available for customer use. Trash and recycling awaiting removal needs to be stored. Shops often find that trash left outside is gone through by scavengers looking for discarded merchandise. We have installed locked bins behind our building for general trash and rent a dumpster for recyclable paper and cardboard.

Quiet Times

You will probably spend as much time at your store as you do at home, at least during the first few years, so include a few amenities to make your life more comfortable. A small kitchen area with a refrigerator, microwave, and sink will be appreciated by your staff as well. Make sure there is a place to relax, with comfortable seating and good reading light. During the day, the store belongs to the public, but in the early morning or late evening, it's all yours. Enjoy the calm and solitude, and the opportunity to get some work done without the distractions of customers and staff. There's no reason not to have a pair of bunny slippers tucked under your desk and a collection of favorite music to listen to when you're working late.

4

MERCHANDISE BUYING

A local discount appliance store used to boast in its radio ads, "How do we do it? We buy right!" The key to keeping retail prices down and profit margins up is to buy right. Good customer service also hinges on good buying, because you need to have what customers want, when they want it.

But how do you know what to order, especially when you begin planning your shop? Mel Ziegler, founder of Banana Republic and The Republic of Tea, states, "I would not think of starting a business unless I was its first customer." You should know and love the type of merchandise you plan to sell and be familiar with the strengths and weaknesses of the products available in the field. Start with what you know you want your store to offer, and through focus groups and other discussions try to learn what else your potential customers would be interested in buying. Visiting stores similar to yours in other areas will show you the types of products they feature. If a successful store stocks an item in depth, it's probably because it is selling well.

The main types of merchandise you decide to carry will dictate the related products that customers will expect you to stock. A camera store, for example, must have film, camera cases, and other accessories. These less expensive add-on items may attract more repeat visits from customers and produce more sales than the basic stock. A variety of merchandise can also make a store more visually appealing. A store selling dresses, for instance, can create interesting displays by also carrying jewelry, scarves, hats, and other accessories.

First orders should be *broad* and *shallow*, which means you will be buying a sampling of a wide variety of merchandise without stocking a large quantity of each item. You do need to order enough merchandise to do an inviting display of each line, but not so much that you will have a "deep" back stock if it doesn't sell well. You can always place a reorder once you see which items sell best. It is important that your merchandise assortment features a variety of price points. Once your store is open, sales will show you what price range your customers are most comfortable with.

You will also learn what items customers expect to find in your store by what they ask for. Have a notebook or file to keep track of these requests, watching for any trends that emerge. You cannot be all things to all people, but you should respond to customer requests that are within the focus of your shop. The ability to find out what customers want and get it for them quickly is one of the strengths that sets a good specialty shop apart from its mass market competitors.

TARGETING THE TYPICAL CUSTOMER

When doing your market research, you started to think about the customers you hope your store will appeal to. This profile of your typical customer will help focus some of your early buying decisions, because he or she will be your primary market. When you imagine a customer walking through your door, who do you see? What can you can tell about that person? Male or female? Age? Any idea about income or education level? Interests? A model train shop, for example, might assume its target customer will be a middle-aged male with disposable income who is interested in trains as a hobby. This shop's buying decisions will be different from those of the train buyer for a toy store whose typical customer is the mother of young children. Keeping your target customer in mind can help guide your early buying. It can also be helpful to get the input of any staff members you have already hired and the members of any focus groups you worked with during your early planning stages.

When thinking about your typical customer it is important to balance the picture by realizing that although the average shopper in your store may be a forty-three-year-old white female with a family income of $50,000, you will undoubtedly also attract many customers who do not fit this profile at all. Selling to a wide range of customers is one of the delights and challenges of retailing. At Orange Tree Imports, our shoppers range from five-year-olds spending their allowance money on stickers to Buddhist monks buying rice cookers, so we need to be prepared to serve this diverse customer base.

ESTABLISHING A BUYING BUDGET

The amount you spend on your initial inventory will be determined in part by how much money you have available. You need to keep funds free to pay overhead expenses and to buy additional merchandise once you see what sells well. There is a direct correlation between how much merchandise you have on hand and the sales you can expect to generate. Ideally, the amount of merchandise you have at retail should result in at least three or four times that amount in sales, a figure referred to as the number of times you are *turning your inventory*. The more inventory turns the better, up to a point (if your inventory is turning six or more times a year, you are probably often sold out of items customers might buy), but few shops actually achieve more than four turns a year. Most are probably closer to two, which means that maintaining an average inventory of $100,000 at retail will produce $200,000 in sales—*if* your merchandise selection and location attract sufficient customer traffic.

The total amount spent on inventory is a key figure, but it is also important to allocate these dollars wisely. Think of your inventory purchases as investments. By setting up merchandise categories in your store, you will be able to see which types of merchandise sell best and plan to put more money into those areas in the future. We code our merchandise with the letters of the alphabet to divide the inventory into twenty-six broad merchandise categories such as glassware, cards, toys, and jewelry. When purchases are rung up, each item is keyed into the appropriate category. The categories are designed to group similar items together, although some items, such as foods (but not candy) are in the same category because they are not subject to sales tax. Other categories isolate groups of items such as cookbooks or electric appliances that traditionally have a lower than 40 percent profit margin. This information is useful in converting each category's retail figures into wholesale costs when taking a physical inventory and also in tracking which areas are most profitable for the store. Categories with lower markup may still be very important because of their high volume.

Divide your inventory dollars carefully into the categories you establish for your store, and track these wholesale purchases by category as you pay the invoices. By comparing retail sales and wholesale inventory purchases by category, you can see whether your inventory dollars are correctly distributed based on the ratio of sales to stock. Merchandise categories that sell best should get a higher percentage of the buying budget.

You may also wish to use a similar system to check whether the amount of space in the store allotted to a category reflects the percentage of sales, and profits, generated by that category. Keep in mind, however, that a category that starts out with more shelf space and more merchandise is bound to outperform one with less of each.

Open-to-Buy Budgeting

Once you have established your merchandise categories and collected some sales data over the first few months your store has been open, you may choose to set up a formal system of budgeting merchandise dollars by category. Department stores often use this method, called *open-to-buy budgeting*. An open-to-buy allowance simply refers to the amount of money available for receiving orders of new merchandise for a particular merchandise category during a monthly or quarterly time period. This figure is determined by looking at the starting inventory and the seasonal sales history for that category. Cookware, for example, usually sells well in January. By determining the anticipated sales of cookware in January and knowing the amount likely to be left at the end of December, we can set a budget for how much cookware we want to have arrive in January. This system prevents a slow category from taking up too many inventory dollars and also ensures adequate stock on hand for busy sales months.

Do most specialty shops use open-to-buy budgets? Not in the strictest sense of the word. Many stores have a general idea of what categories are strongest for them, and order accordingly. Space on the sales floor is also allocated informally along these lines in many shops. But a real open-to-buy system requires sharp attention to sales and inventory figures and to delivery dates. Despite the fact that we realize budgeting would make our inventory dollars work more efficiently, most of us just aren't that disciplined. We also realize that the ability to spot a hot trend and order accordingly, no matter what sales history tells us, is one of the strengths that allows specialty shops to compete with big budget–encumbered department stores. If you enjoy working with data and taking a scientific approach to buying, you may enjoy using an open-to-buy system. There is one available specifically to small retailers that is designed by Mort Haaz, a former retailer who believes passionately in the virtues of inventory planning. For information about OTB Retail Systems, call him at 800-444-4682.

WHAT TO ORDER

An exciting, eclectic selection of merchandise is one of the key components to a successful specialty shop. Customers have the option of spending their dollars many different places, and to a great extent the same goods are available in most stores. The specialty store distinguishes itself by presenting shoppers with products carefully chosen and enticingly displayed. Stanley Marcus, chairman emeritus of Neiman-Marcus, points out that customers want the specialty shop buyer to edit the options for them and present those they think are the very best, or the best value at a good price.

Specialty shops constantly need to look for products unique in their market. As soon as an item turns up in a discount store, the time has come for the small retailer to drop it. Whenever possible, the specialty shop buyer should look for items not available to mass marketers. This helps eliminate price competition, which is a game that's hard to win when you don't have the buying clout of a big chain.

Are there still products that are not being sold to the big stores? One way to find out is to shop these stores regularly, paying attention to new merchandise. Ask your customers where else they shop, and look for weaknesses in the merchandise and services being offered by those stores. Make sure you offer something different—perhaps by doing some direct importing or by commissioning products from craftspeople or small manufacturers that will be unique to your store. You can also favor lines whose marketing is focused solely on the independent retailer.

Although specialty shop customers do not tend to focus solely on price, price is an important factor in most buying decisions. When I consider a product, I need to determine right away whether it is in a price range appropriate for my store. Since it is very difficult to run a store profitably at only *keystone*, markup of 100 percent on top of the wholesale price, another price consideration is whether the item would be likely to sell at a slightly higher markup.

One way to maintain a good margin while still offering attractive prices is to get the lowest possible wholesale price. We are constantly looking for good prices, special discounts, and extended terms from suppliers. Whenever possible, we buy in *case packs*, which often offer a lower price per piece than *broken*, or *partial*, *packs*. We try to buy directly from the source rather than through a distributor or middleman. Other stores band together to form buying groups, combining the orders of many independent small shops into single large orders to get better terms and lower prices. Buying groups, or co-ops, have already proved successful for bookstores, pharmacies, and hardware stores. Other types of specialty shops may find the idea will work for them as well.

Many buyers choose items only on the basis of whether they like them, but, of course, they are not going to be the retail customers buying the merchandise. One exasperated supplier said, "I'd like to banish the words 'I don't like it' from buyers' vocabulary! It doesn't matter if they like it or not—if it fits well in their shop, and if it is selling well, they should try it." Another salesperson reported that a buyer wouldn't carry cat items in her shop because she didn't like cats. If her customers like cats, and some of them undoubtedly do, she should consider carrying cat items—unless, of course, her shop is called The Dog House. This is not to say that you need to carry merchandise that you find to be in poor taste, or offensive. We draw the line at war toys, for example, and we won't carry Halloween decorations that make irritating electronic noises—no matter how well they might sell.

When considering new merchandise, try to imagine where a line will go in your store and how you will display it. What category will it fit into? Do you need more merchandise in that category? If you use an open-to-buy budget, are there dollars available in that department for the time period in which the order will arrive? Don't rush your buying decisions. You may wish to wait until after you have compared several lines before deciding which one to buy. Try to test new lines in your off-season so you can reorder heavily if they sell well.

DETERMINING QUANTITIES

It can be very difficult to determine how many of each item to buy. When my husband, Dean, came into business with me, I was shocked by the size of the orders he wrote, and twenty years later, he still sometimes orders by the gross while I order by the dozen. He is often right, so he will have enough of a good seller on hand to break sales records. But when testing a new item or line, I feel safer ordering conservatively. Still, you must order enough of a line to "make a statement," or present it fairly. If a line has several different items, styles, colors, or price points, consider ordering a variety of products in order to make a display. As a rule, order at least two of each item ("one to show and one to go" is an old retail expression). Otherwise you will never know if more than one customer is interested in the product.

It stands to reason that the more merchandise you order, the less frequently you will need to reorder, saving time and effort. Ordering in large quantities will usually also get you better prices and sometimes special invoice terms. Consolidating orders into a few big shipments instead of many small ones helps keep freight costs down. The flip side of ordering in depth, of course, is that you will have to store the additional merchandise until you can sell it and your money will be tied up in the stock. This is referred to as *opportunity cost*—the fact that the money used to purchase certain inventory is not available to use for some other purpose.

There is also the risk, especially early in your retailing career, that you will purchase a large quantity of an item that bombs. Reserve quantity purchases for items you have tested already, or merchandise that is basic to your stock. Avoid buying in quantity just to get a bargain. It's not a bargain unless you can sell the entire shipment, and in a reasonable amount of time.

BUYING ON CONSIGNMENT

One way to stretch your inventory dollar is to purchase on consignment, which means you don't pay unless the product sells. The risk of stocking the merchandise is thus placed on the seller, not the store. Problems may arise, however, if merchandise on consignment is damaged or stolen. And you need to take into account that your shelf space is valuable, so consignment merchandise still carries some overhead cost, despite the fact that these items don't tie up inventory dollars.

Goods sold on consignment also usually have a lower markup than merchandise purchased outright, so your profit margin will often be 40 percent or less. A consignment arrangement makes it less risky to try unusual merchandise you are not sure will sell but would like to try. It is a method best used for art, crafts, or expensive items such as antiques. Keep careful track of consignment goods so that at the end of the predetermined period you remember to return the remaining portion of the order and to pay for what you have sold. A price tag with a tear-off stub that can be removed at the time of purchase is one way to track consignment merchandise. Another way is to assign a code for each consignment vendor, and to write down purchase information in a journal by the cash register.

> Innovative Appalachian gift shop owner Ginger Hill uses the front area of her store for a changing display highlighting the work of one local artist or craftsperson. Although most of the store's merchandise is not consignment goods, the items brought in for these special exhibits are paid for only if sold.

Another way to produce sales without tying up inventory dollars is to take special orders for custom merchandise such as personalized gifts and imprinted stationery. For these special-order items, you may need only a sample or two for display or an album showing the choices available. Special-order merchandise can give a good return on very little inventory, but there is usually an investment of staff time in working with a customer placing an order.

DEVELOPING YOUR OWN PRODUCTS

One way to ensure a unique selection of merchandise in your shop is to arrange to have merchandise produced exclusively for you. Fillamento owner Iris Fuller particularly enjoys encouraging artisans to create items for her to sell in her award-winning San Francisco store. She commissions jewelers, for example, to use their talents to design articles for home decor. We carried a line of silkscreened cards by local artist (and scientist) Vaughn James, and one night I had a dream that Vaughn turned his card designs into T-shirts. We've been selling his shirts ever since. (They are the one item in the store I literally dreamed up.)

There are also manufacturers willing to put your store name and logo on their products, a process called *private labeling*. Private label merchandise reinforces your store name and image and gives the consumer the impression that your operation is large enough to include manufacturing. It is also hard for consumers to compare prices on private-label products, so extra markup can often be taken on these items. Chain stores often feature one or more private-label brands of clothing and other merchandise, and the profit on these products is considerably greater than on competitive name brands.

Private-label manufacturing usually requires placing large orders, if for no other reason than the expense of printing full-color labels. Look for products that can share the same label, perhaps with a separate sticker indicating the size, style, or fragrance. You might also be able to do your own packaging of items purchased in bulk , such as candies, seeds, beads, or soaps. Use a distinctive package, and add a fancy sticker or ribbon giving the store name. Figure 4-1 shows a sample gift basket featuring private-label products.

Customizing Merchandise for the Tourist Market

Someone once said that a good souvenir is an item that is a good buy and not readily available back home. As all products become more widely distributed, it gets harder to find something to offer tourists that is not available elsewhere. Locally produced items or regional specialties are often too expensive to be considered a good buy by most tourists.

One solution to this problem is to buy merchandise that has been *souvenired*, personalized with the name of the area or tourist attraction. The most common souvenir item is, of course, the T-shirt. Many T-shirt manufacturers will add the name of the city or state to any of their designs for a small additional charge. The minimum order for this service is usually just two or three dozen shirts. Magnets, ornaments, and mugs can also have the tourist destination added to stock designs.

In order to develop a coordinated program of custom souvenir items, Beth Engh, gift buyer for the Brookfield Zoo in Chicago, suggests designing a logo and one or more visual images and selecting a set color scheme. Use the same designs and colors on a wide range of impulse items—key rings, pencils, buttons, T-shirts, mugs, water bottles, and so forth—to create a coordinated look in your souvenir area. The same images can be used on slightly more expensive items, such as embroidered sweatshirts, wooden boxes, and tote bags. Numerous companies manufacture souvenir items, and many of these vendors can be found at wholesale shows aimed at the tourist trade.

Figure 4-1 A Southern Season, an innovative gourmet shop, catalog, and restaurant in Chapel Hill, North Carolina, customizes its gift baskets with private-label foods under the name "Carolina Cupboard."

(Courtesy of A Southern Season.)

Young customers are a prime market for souvenirs, especially at attractions visited by school groups. Be sure to carry a good selection of impulse items aimed at young buyers. Open acrylic bins, well labeled with price signs, are an effective way to display these small items, although shoplifting can be a problem. Plan to have at least one employee other than the one behind the cash register available to assist young shoppers when a large group comes in the store. This should help curtail shoplifting and can be a great help to the teachers or chaperones.

Not every tourist wants to buy an inexpensive souvenir. A selection of higher-quality, more expensive items will help make the shop look more sophisticated and can lead to larger sales. Look for merchandise representative of the area, preferably locally made. You may also want to stock guidebooks and other educational materials relating to the local attraction. Keep in mind that visitors may have to walk some distance to their car, so heavy or bulky items may need to be shipped or delivered to the customer's hotel.

Almost every tourist buys postcards, and these should be a staple of most souvenir shops. For the added convenience of your customers, consider stocking a supply of postcard stamps (for domestic and overseas postage) to sell at face value. Many visitors also like to buy candy or other snack foods. An enticing selection of small treats by the cash register is almost guaranteed to sell well.

INVENTORY CONTROL

It is easy to make the mistake of buying too much or buying without enough thought as to whether there are enough customers for certain items. In fact, it is much harder to say no to a line, especially when it is presented with a convincing sales pitch, than it is to say yes. New merchandise invariably looks fresher and more exciting than the stock on hand. Learn to stand your ground and turn down goods you don't need.

You should also plan to routinely clear out old goods that haven't been selling well so that you will have the money and space for fresh stock. Some experts even recommend budgeting a certain amount for markdowns each month. It is certainly helpful to track your markdowns, so you know whether the high sales in a line of table lamps comes from the fact that most of them are being sold at 50 percent off. You'll also want to know what you've marked down as clearance so you don't reorder these items.

There is a saying in retailing that the first markdown is the most important. One Dallas gourmet shop had a rule that anything that hadn't sold in a year went into a trunk in which every item was $10—no matter what its original price had been. You can bet that its clearance items moved out quickly, since the trunk was the first spot every customer checked on entering the store. Take a less Texas-sized discount than this retailer as soon as you realize that an item isn't selling, so that you can recoup your investment and not "sit on dead merchandise," as it is so colorfully described in the trade. Keeping slow movers on the move allows you to continue buying new goods with a clear conscience.

Consider what you will do if a line doesn't sell well *before* you place an order. Most items can be marked down and sold, but if you have invested in special fixtures, you may not be able to reuse them. Be especially cautious with programs that involve stocking items personalized with a range of names, initials, zodiac signs, or months or years of birth. It is notoriously difficult to sell down to the last pieces of these items or to display them when there are not many left (no one wants to see a zodiac display with only Aries, Taurus, and Libra!). Some companies offer a buy-out program for these products, giving you credit toward other merchandise if you return a certain percentage of your original order. This return allotment, however, may be considerably less than what you have on hand when you decide to discontinue carrying the line. There have also been cases of the supplier's no longer being in business (ask anyone who invested in personalized gift wrap in the 1980s) when it comes time to cash in on the guarantee. These programs are sometimes very profitable, but try to be certain that the product is good, the company is reliable, and your shop has enough traffic to sell it in quantity. It is also difficult to close out products that are seasonal, fashion oriented, artsy, or edible. Special caution is necessary when buying goods for these categories.

Few items continue to sell well forever. The fluctuations in an item's popularity is called its *product life cycle*. New merchandise that is well received by your customers may demonstrate a marked increase in sales every time you reorder, until suddenly sales drop off. Pay close attention to customer buying patterns, and listen to what sales reps are saying about an item's popularity. When you begin to sense that the sales of an item are slowing down, reorder cautiously or not at all. It is better to bring in new merchandise than to continue carrying an item just because it has been popular in the past.

Tracking Sales for Reorders

Every store has certain categories of steady sellers, called *bread-and-butter items*, that should never be out of stock. Most other items get reordered a few times, until sales slow down. Still others are ordered once, and then replaced with something new.

A point-of-sale (POS) cash register system will compile records of what merchandise has been sold, alerting you to dangerously low inventory levels. You can set a minimum inventory level for each item, based on how long it usually takes to receive a reorder and how many units you are likely to sell each day or week. The POS system can even generate a reorder; in fact many chain stores use a system called EDI (electronic data interface), which provides a direct link between the store's computer and that of major suppliers. Someday this technology may be practical for smaller stores heavily dependent on a few key vendors.

In a single store location, you can control inventory levels by watching what is selling and doing manual counts. For items we reorder regularly, we use a perpetual inventory sheet (a sample is shown in Figure 4-2), recording the quantity of each item received and the quantity left on hand a few weeks or months later. By tracking the number sold, we know how many to reorder. The quantity left from the first order, plus the quantity received on the reorder, become the new starting figure that we use to compare the amount left on hand the next time we are ready to order.

A perpetual inventory can be taken weekly, monthly, or just whenever stock seems low enough to warrant placing an order. Many vendors have a fairly high minimum reorder, so you can't order just one item that is out of stock. It also helps to reduce freight costs if you order a large number of items at a time. The trick is not to wait so long that a popular item is completely sold out before the new stock arrives. Keep track of which suppliers ship in a few days and which ones need to receive orders a month or more before they can ship.

Another way to track the inventory of certain items is to use a price tag with a detachable stub listing a product description or code number. When an item is sold, the stub is removed and put in a box, to be tallied later. We use this system to track collectible items such as Department 56's lighted houses. A record book kept by the cash register shows how many pieces of each house we have on hand or receive, and the employee in charge of this area counts the stubs every day or two and marks off those sold. This system gives us a fairly accurate picture at all times of how many pieces are in stock and is easier than asking each sales associate to find the book and mark off a piece when it is sold. (We also use detachable stub tickets on our store supplies, removing the stub when, for example, a new case of gift boxes is opened. This helps us reorder these supplies before we run out.)

Many stores do not reorder exactly the same item of merchandise more than a time or two in certain categories, so even a simple perpetual inventory system may be more record keeping than is necessary for some lines. There is nothing wrong with checking to see how many teddy bears have sold by just taking a look at how many bears are on the shelf and in the stockroom.

Figure 4-2 Sample perpetual inventory form.

PERPETUAL INVENTORY SHEET

Note: Be sure to mark "NR" next to any item ordered but not received.

PRODUCT DESCRIPTION	ITEM NUMBER	Retail Price	Wholesale Cost	Date Starting Inv.	Date On Order	Date On Hand	Date On Order	Date On Hand	Date On Order	Date On Hand	Date On Order	Date On Hand

Vendor: **Category:**   page___ of___

87

SEASONAL PLANNING

Long before the first snowfall signals the start of the Christmas season to most shoppers, buyers who order seasonal merchandise will be turning their attention to Easter bunnies and Valentines. And while most people are anticipating the arrival of spring, retailers who stock seasonal goods will be pondering ghoulish jack-o-lanterns and wintry Christmas cards. Seasonal buying is somewhat like working the night shift; you always feel a bit out of step with the rest of the world.

Anyone would find it difficult to remember which Easter candies sold best while ringing up Halloween treats. If you add to this the fact that the buying season for holiday merchandise has gotten so long that Christmas ordering takes place over almost a nine-month period, it becomes clear that it is an ongoing challenge to keep track of whether there are enough (or too many, which is often worse) gift bags, tree toppers, or jingle bell ornaments on order.

Many shop owners have discovered that some form of seasonal planning is a must. There are two real dangers in ignoring this need. The first, and more obvious, is that having too much merchandise on hand leads to excessive inventory at the end of a holiday that may have to be carried over in storage for a year. Some of these goods, of course, can be marked down and sold for cost within a few days of the holiday. Department stores have developed the after-Christmas sale into one of their biggest events of the year. But few small shops have the traffic to ensure that all of the postseasonal merchandise is sold within a few days of a holiday. A postseasonal sale should not be allowed to go on for very long; goods that haven't been sold while the holiday is still on everyone's mind are not likely to sell. I once visited a hospital gift shop in April and saw Christmas candy still on sale. The bad impression made by these stale boxes of chocolate cast a pall over all the other merchandise on display.

The second, less obvious, problem with not planning for seasonal sales is that you may have too little inventory on hand. You cannot sell twelve Santa figurines if you have only four in stock, unless you are lucky enough to find a supplier who can ship a reorder at the last minute. "You can't sell from an empty cart," the saying goes. Customers want what appears to be a full selection to choose from right up to the holiday itself. They usually will not buy the very last item on hand, even at closing time on Christmas Eve.

Creating a Seasonal Planning System

A seasonal planning program can make life easier for anyone who buys holiday merchandise and should lead to better inventory turns and a more profitable operation. It is especially helpful to new buyers, including the hospital shop's volunteer who is asked to order seasonal goods without having any experience of her own to rely on.

The basic premise behind a seasonal planning system is that the buying patterns of customers can be predicted based on their past patterns. If you sold thirty dozen Valentines in 1996, you are more likely to sell thirty-five dozen in 1997 than you are to sell three dozen—or three hundred dozen. And if hand-painted Easter eggs sold out early this season, you will probably want to make sure you have more on hand next year.

A new store will not have any history to go on, of course, but it is never too early to start keeping records to help plan for future years.

Watching for Changes

Although it is generally true that future sales can be predicted based on past sales, a number of factors can alter these predictions, and they should be taken into account when making buying decisions. First are the local factors. Are the store's sales increasing or declining? How is your community's economy and that of your particular mall or shop location? Do you know of any special factors, such as a feature story in the news about your shop, or bad weather, that influenced your sales figures last year? Do you know of anything that will have an impact on this year's sales? The opening of a competing store or roadwork in front of your shop may influence what you will need to buy.

Look closely at any changes in the holiday you are buying for. Easter, for example, can fall in March or in April, and an early Easter is generally an indication of a slightly weaker season because of the shorter sales period. Halloween and Valentine sales are influenced by whether they fall on a weekday or weekend. And finally, be alert to trends in consumer holiday celebration and buying. Fashions in holiday decoration, cards, and gifts all change to some extent from year to year.

Despite these variables—all of which contribute to making retailing a constant challenge—it is possible to significantly increase your chances of doing a good job of holiday buying through consistent seasonal record keeping.

Setting Up a Planning System

A large three-ring binder works well as a seasonal planning note-book, since it is portable and can expand to fill your needs. Pages can be added easily, and notes can be taken out and copied to take to trade shows. You might also consider keeping the records on a computer, print-ing out copies of whatever data you need to take with you.

Arrange your records by holiday, subdividing the larger holidays by merchandise category if necessary. We keep our records in chronological order, progressing from one season to the next. Even if we are working on Mother's Day in January, at least Father's Day still comes next. We also have a category for calendars, an increasingly important part of the sea-sonal mix for many retailers.

The seasonal record book could be used to organize photographs of the store's holiday displays and advertising, along with pictures of display ideas from trade magazines and vendor catalogs. Trade magazines often feature articles with useful ideas for seasonal promotions that can be clipped and saved. We keep a calendar in the front of our seasonal plan-ning notebook with the dates of all the major holidays over the next few years. These are sometimes available in trade magazines, or from the li-brary's reference department.

Counting Counter Cards

Many shops carrying greeting cards find that there are a number of holidays for which cards sold individually (*counter cards*) are a major sea-sonal product. If all of the store's cards come from one source, such as Hallmark, the vendor will undoubtedly take care of setting up an inven-tory system. But shops that carry a number of card lines will find it useful to track how many are on order from each vendor, how many are left from the previous year, and how many are left after the holiday (see Figure 4-3). This will show which lines sell best and give a total figure for the number of cards sold. By totaling the column of cards sold, you can get an overview of all the cards sold and compare the sales to previous years. Any card line that has sold particularly well should get a larger portion of the seasonal orders the next year.

The number left after the holiday becomes the starting inventory for the next year, although it is a good idea to first weed out any shopworn, one-of-a-kind, and out-of-date cards. Odds and ends of cards are welcome donations to nursing homes, where residents often can't get out to shop for cards. Some card companies allow seasonal cards to be returned for

Figure 4-3 Sample seasonal counter card tracking form.

Vendor	Left 1996	Received 1997	Left 1997	Sold 1997
Swan Cards	2 dz.	8 dz.	6 dz.	4 dz.
Baroquet	3½ dz.	6 dz.	3½ dz.	6 dz.

credit toward everyday merchandise or the next season—well worth doing if the volume is great enough to warrant paying the handling costs of the return.

To calculate the number of cards needed for the next year, multiply the total number of cards sold by 120 percent, plus any projected increase in sales. Twenty percent "overage" is an arbitrary figure, but it is generally considered a desirable amount to have carried over from one season to the next. If you have about that much left over, it means that you had enough stock on hand to maximize sales right up to the last minute. Subtract the salable stock left from the current year from your projection and you will know how many new cards to order. Consult the seasonal planning notebook for the performance of each line as you write orders for the coming year, and fill in the amount ordered as you place each order. This system also works well for tracking boxed holiday cards.

The Good, the Bad, and the Merely O.K.

The hundreds of other items carried seasonally by specialty shops can be followed in as much detail as is necessary for the size of the store. The most basic record is simply a listing of three columns: good, bad, and O.K.—with your impression of the items that sold most quickly, those that were slow sellers, and those in between.

A more detailed record would include everything ordered for a particular holiday, by company, with notes as to how well each item sold. You could even make copies of the purchase orders or invoices and insert them in the notebook for note taking. A simple yes or no next to each item will help you remember what to order more, and less, of the following year. Take a quick count a few days before a holiday to note any items that sold out early enough to warrant an increase for the next year. For example, there may be no Valentine candy hearts left after Valentine's Day, which means that all twenty-four boxes sold. But if there were no candy hearts left four days *before* Valentine's Day, it is a safe bet that more than twenty-four would have been sold had there been more on hand.

Counting leftover seasonal merchandise when you pack it away at the end of a holiday saves time on inventory day. Put a copy of this list in the seasonal planning notebook for easy reference when doing future ordering. If you are going to use the inventory for planning, however, list items by company or by category so that you can see at a glance what your carryover is on a certain item.

More detailed buying records may help avoid duplication not only of items still on hand from the previous year but also from vendors offering similar merchandise for a holiday. Rubber bats, for instance, are available in almost every company's Halloween line. If you order one line in January and another in July, you may end up with bats by the bin. To avoid this possibility, the seasonal planning notebook can be set up by product category (e.g., Halloween rubber toys and novelties; costumes and masks; Halloween candles) as shown in Figure 4-4. Enter items left

Figure 4-4 Seasonal planning records by category.

🎃 HALLOWEEN INVENTORY RECORD 🎃
Category: Party goods   Year: 96

DESCRIPTION	PRICE	VENDOR	start inv.	ordered	Oct. 25	end inv.	yes/no
Harvest Pumpkin			'95	'96			
beverage napkins	1.95	Amscan	2	24	12	7	yes
lunch napkins	2.50	"	8	o	o	o	yes
7" plate	2.50	"		12	8	3	no
10" plate	3.00	"	4	o	o	o	no
orange candles	3.50 pr	A. I. Root		12 pr.	6 pr.	1 pr.	yes
Small favor cups	50¢	Collector's Pr.	48	o	40	36	clear out

from the previous year; then make a note each time a seasonal item is ordered, noting the vendor and the price point.

Leave space for a postholiday inventory, possibly both before and after any half-price sale. The latter figures will become your starting numbers for next year's plans, minus any older or shopworn items that should be taken out to be sold at a clearance sale. Make a note by each item as to whether to reorder it for the following year.

PLANNING FOR DISPLAYS AND PROMOTION

Keep display and advertising in mind when you do your buying, always staying on the lookout for items that will be good draws when featured in ads or store windows. Advertising, promotion, and display should be coordinated, with any item featured in an ad prominently displayed in the store. Never have the last one of an item in the window; plan ahead so you will have an adequate quantity of every item being highlighted. You may also wish to order a few oversize items to use mostly as display props, but priced in case a customer wants to buy them.

When you order a new line of merchandise or even just a new item, have some idea where you will display it in the store. If special fixtures will be required, order these to arrive at the same times as the goods. In addition to working toward a full and interesting variety, think about how the various lines you order will complement each other, and look for colors and textures that go well together. The merchandise you order will become the basic material you will use to create in-store and window displays to excite customers and make them want to buy.

WHERE TO LOOK FOR MERCHANDISE

There are countless ways to find goods for your store, from reading trade magazines in bed at night to traveling like Anita Roddick of The Body Shop to meet with native suppliers on the floor of the rain forest. Companies often send catalogs to you by mail or have sales representatives (called *sales reps*) call on you to present their line. You can also travel to wholesale trade shows around the country, or around the world, looking for merchandise.

When you first start planning your shop, you may be puzzled as to how to find out about the trade shows and publications in your field. Start with a trip to the library. You'll be surprised how many trade publications are available at a city library, and the reference librarian can help you find the names and addresses of others. Trade publications have information about wholesale shows, and advertisements for vendors that will send you catalogs or put you in touch with their sales representatives. You should also visit stores similar to yours in other communities. Ask the owner or manager to take a few minutes to tell you about the trade shows and publications in your field. Once you have read a few periodicals and visited your first trade show, it will be easy to find out about additional sources of merchandise.

The wise buyer remains open to new ideas from all sources and will give thoughtful consideration to any new merchandise. I am always surprised that some buyers refuse to see reps or never go to shows to look for new lines. Certainly your time is valuable, but you should *always* be on the lookout for new items that fit with your merchandise mix. Shopkeepers without the time and energy to find new items for the store need to delegate some of their other duties.

WORKING WITH SALES REPS

We see sales reps by appointment only. If a new rep calls without any lines we already buy (this is tough for reps to do; it's called *making a cold call*, probably referring to the chilly reception they receive from most buyers), we ask a few questions before deciding whether to give an appointment. Obviously this is an easy decision to make if the rep is selling jewelry and your shop doesn't carry jewelry, but often you really can't say yes or no to new lines without seeing them. On the other hand, once a rep is in your store, it's hard to say no to them. Ever since we saw *Death of a Salesman*, we've had great sympathy for the trials of the sales rep, and we rarely turn anyone away without some sort of an order. If we think we may have to, we grant the appointment with the qualification that we may just be taking a look this time. That way the rep can decide if it's worth coming to see us. We both know that if we don't order anything, the rep won't get paid for the sales call.

I use a system of seeing reps at 11:00, 1:00, and 3:00 three days a week. This gives some structure to my workday, and lets the reps know that each appointment must take no longer than two hours. Other stores have a policy of seeing reps only one day a week, which can be a hardship on reps trying to plan their travel schedule.

A good sales rep can be a real asset to buyers, conveying information about best sellers, giving display ideas, arranging for help with promotions and advertising, and assisting with any problems that may arise. A rep may know where else the merchandise is being sold, a concern if the competitor is nearby or is planning to discount the line. Some reps even set up displays, restock them, and take inventory counts for reorders. These services are often provided to department stores and other large accounts; small retailers may have to ask for them.

It is useful for buyers to be aware of how the sales rep system works in order to form a mutually beneficial relationship with those individuals who call on the store. A company rep works for only one vendor, usually receiving a base salary plus a commission on products sold. Other sales reps are self-employed or work for a sales organization, and represent a number of different lines. Their income is usually based entirely on commissions from the variety of products they sell. Commissions vary greatly depending on the type of product, but generally fall into the 5 to 20 percent range. Travel expenses are usually paid out of pocket by the rep. Sales organizations negotiate with vendors for the lines to be carried, assign them to reps throughout a certain territory, and often maintain a permanent or temporary showroom at wholesale trade shows.

In most cases, it will be clear which rep covers the territory in which your shop is located, and this is the person you will work with. Unfortunately some companies have been known to assign more than one rep to a territory in the hopes of opening more accounts. In this situation, the buyer is in the awkward position of not knowing to whom to give the order, and this can be especially difficult if by unhappy coincidence the two reps are in the store at the same time. When this happened to us, I called the company for clarification, and was told that the real rep for my area was someone else—four states away!

Most sales reps are not paid their commission until the vendor's invoice is paid, and they may not receive any commission at all if your payment is very delinquent—another reason that it is important to stay current with your bills. Keep in mind also that sales reps' time is valuable. If it looks as if you won't be placing an order or will place only a very small one, try to take up as little of their time as possible. Reps are usually understanding of the fact that you may be interrupted to wait on customers or to attend to problems that come up.

A good sales rep will help you make wise buying decisions and will not encourage you to order too much, in the hopes that you will want to reorder. I knew one buyer who asserted his independence by refusing to buy anything a rep recommended—so he missed out on all the items that were selling well in other shops in his area. Sales reps call on many different businesses in their territory and can spot trends in customer buying patterns that may be very useful to you.

Unfortunately there are also unethical sales reps who will encourage a naive shopkeeper to buy too much or will even add to the order after it is written (this is called *padding the order*, and has happened only once to me). Be conservative when you order initially, and match up what you receive with what is specified on your purchase order.

BUYING TRIPS

One of the joys of retailing is being able to travel while scouting out new goods. Even visiting gift shops in some popular resort area can yield samples of items that would sell well in your shop (although the Internal Revenue Service would probably still not consider a day at the beach to be a business trip). We used to make a game of memorizing the name and address of a supplier before leaving a shop, since it seemed impolite to write it down in front of the shopkeeper. But it would be even better to pay full retail for a sample of the product—much as this hurts when you are used to getting items wholesale. Unfortunately, not every item is labeled with its source—in some very competitive locations, retailers actually go to the effort of obscuring any information that could give away the source of an item, and frequently manufacturers neglect to label their product. But you may find some friendly retailers who are willing to look up information and share it with you, as long as it is clear that your shop is outside their trading area.

Visiting arts and crafts shows is an excellent way to find small suppliers with handmade wares, which can be a wonderful addition to the merchandise selection of many specialty shops and are rarely carried by mass merchants. Artists who have never sold merchandise wholesale may need some help developing special products to sell to a store. We ask that artists selling to us not sell the same merchandise directly to the public— for example, at an art fair—at prices much lower than our retail price. This often means they need to decide which items they will sell wholesale to stores and which they will sell themselves.

There are several special trade fairs of crafts where artists already familiar with selling goods wholesale exhibit their wares for shop buyers. These artisans have already developed a line of crafts that they can produce at a low enough price to be viable when retail markup is added.

Most other product categories are also marketed through large wholesale trade shows. These shows are usually held once or twice a year, often with a combination of temporary exhibits by suppliers and sales reps and permanent showrooms of merchandise, set up like small shops. Trade shows are an excellent source of merchandise, display ideas, and contact with fellow shopkeepers. A retailer who does not feel any need to go to trade shows is one who is not interested in growing a thriving business.

Some specialty shop fields, such as the bookstore and museum shop trade, have one national show each year. But for broader categories such as gifts, there are trade shows held two to four times a year all over the country. Some of these shows are large and thus offer more potential suppliers, but a small show, especially one in another part of the country, can be the source of items that other stores in your area may not have discovered. In order to make your shop unique, you'll want to find some products your customers can't find elsewhere.

Sales reps may not get any credit for orders written out of their territory, so it is important to attend the show nearest you in addition to any you travel to in other parts of the country. If you have a good working relationship with a rep, you might also ask if they get full credit for the orders they write at the show in your area. Since this is not always the case, they may appreciate your taking notes on new items and writing the order with them in your shop later.

Tips for Trade Show Attendance

Perhaps the most valuable hint anyone can give a new trade show attendee is to wear comfortable shoes. If you are not used to standing on your feet all day, you will find that your buying decisions are being impaired by foot fatigue before the day ends. Come to a show well prepared to place orders, with a sheet of credit references (described later in this chapter) and a credit card or business checks if you plan to make any purchases that are cash and carry or need to be prepaid. In addition, you will need the proper business identification for getting into the show, or your show badge and identification if you have preregistered. Preregistering saves time when you arrive, and it will usually save you money on registration fees, if there are any. If you haven't preregistered, call show management before you leave home to find out what credentials are required to get an admission badge at the door. Be sure to ask about travel specials on air fare and hotels. Trade shows reserve large numbers of hotel rooms and make special deals with airlines in order to offer attractive prices to those attending the show.

One trick of the trade show trade that seems simple, yet is always appreciated, is bringing along a sheet of stickers with your store's name, address, and phone number on them to put on the "sold to" and "ship to" sections on purchase orders. You will need a good supply of these, since many orders are written in multiple copies (all of which, except your own copy, will need a sticker), but harried salespeople seem to appreciate this time saver—and you can be sure that your name and address will be legible. On a buying trip to England, we took along an almost worn-out rubber stamp with the store name to use on orders. We threw it away, as planned, when we were done, but a conscientious cleaning person found it in the wastebasket and insisted that the show office track us down at our London hotel to return it!

Many trade shows are a good source of catalogs, price lists, and even samples (although merchandise usually may not be purchased and taken home from a wholesale show), so be sure to bring a bag big enough to carry these papers and miscellaneous items, as well as your credit references, pens, business cards, and a notebook. Sticky notes, a calculator, and a highlighting pen are also useful, as is a folder for your copies of the purchase orders. If you are in a field such as jewelry or crafts that allows purchases to be made at wholesale shows, be sure to take along business checks or a credit card.

It is always good to bring some notes so you have a clear idea of what you need to order at a show. (Don't overdo it. Once I was surprised to see a buyer at the Atlanta Gift Show pulling a luggage cart behind her with all of her store's inventory records.) It is usually enough to have a general idea of what you have on hand and perhaps some specific inventories of lines you know you'll be reordering. Bring copies of customer special-request cards, and a list of new items you hope to find. If you work with an open-to-buy budget, bring a chart of your monthly figures, and make a note of purchase totals by category and delivery month as you place your orders.

You might want to bring along a granola bar or two; food at trade shows can be hard to come by when you are in the middle of a long aisle of exhibitor booths. And although the food in meeting halls may not be very good, take a break occasionally and eat something. If you are lucky enough to be attending a show where food and drink are provided by the showrooms, by all means take advantage of this hospitality. You may want to pass up offers of alcoholic beverages, however, until your buying day is over.

Be sure to keep receipts for meals, transportation, and lodging when you are on buying trips. Although the Internal Revenue Service doesn't allow meals (at either MacDonald's or The Four Seasons) to be fully deducted, 100 percent of all other legitimate travel costs are considered business expenses. If you drive to a trade show, you can even reimburse yourself for mileage.

We like to take our full-time staff members to trade shows. It gives them an opportunity to learn more about our merchandise, to see what other products are available to our shop, and to participate in buying decisions. The excitement of going on a buying trip to another city can be a good motivational tool, especially if you treat everyone to good food and stay at a nice hotel. Having additional staff at a show can sometimes be distracting, but it can also be beneficial to have more people looking for new merchandise ideas. You can split up and ask staff members to look for certain items you might not have time to research, and have them report back to you before the show is over so you can visit the booths they recommend. When you bring staff members to a trade show, have business cards made for them beforehand so they feel like professionals. If you don't want to go to the expense of ordering a large quantity of cards for each individual, print a single page of business cards on your store computer using special perforated sheets.

Allow enough time at a show to walk past every booth and showroom at least once. After all, you've come to the show to look for new merchandise, and unless you see everything, you may miss out on a potentially popular item. Try to attend shows on weekdays rather than the more crowded weekends, so that you will have the undivided attention of the sales representatives. If at all possible, stay long enough to be able to visit some stores in the area. No matter how long you've had your shop, you can always learn something new from other retailers.

Writing Orders at the Show

There are two schools of thought about writing orders at a trade show. Some buyers like to order merchandise as they see it, selecting from samples rather than pictures in a catalog. Others want to see everything first, so they pick up literature to study later and then make their decision. Exhibitors are often hesitant to give out expensive catalogs to those who don't write an order, because experience has shown them that most people who take a catalog don't order later. And if an order is sent in to the home office, the salesperson in the booth usually does not get credit for it, which makes it in their interest to encourage you to write the order at the show.

Request a catalog only if you are fairly serious about a line and unable to place an order on the spot. If you do request a catalog and the exhibitor promises to send one to you, make a note to follow up in case it doesn't arrive. (Many companies don't come through with catalogs they've promised at trade shows.) There are also many lines that don't produce catalogs, which makes it imperative that you order from samples at the show unless they have a sales rep who can call on you. It just isn't practical for a small company, or one that sells many one-of-a-kind items, to make a full-color catalog of its products.

Companies sometimes offer *show specials* in order to encourage customers to place orders—perhaps free freight, a discount, special delayed dating on the payment of the invoice, or free goods. As with any other sale, it is well worth taking advantage of the offer if you really need the merchandise. But don't feel pressured to order a line you aren't quite sure about, just because the show special is valid only for the few days of the show. If you show serious interest, you may be able to get the special terms extended until you have returned to your shop to count stock on hand or review other factors.

Companies that offer show specials don't always consider the fact that their sales reps may lose a sale on the road because of an attractive special offered only at a show. They are trying to cover the high cost of exhibiting by maximizing the orders written on the spot. If you know your rep will not get full credit for an order written at a show, you might ask if you can get the show special on an order placed with your rep within a few days of the show. This considerate attitude toward sales reps will be much appreciated by reps who have developed a mutually beneficial working relationship with a shop.

The exhibitors at trade shows are often weary by the end of the day as well, because standing is even more tiring than walking. Buyers who know how their customers like to be treated in their shop should extend this same courtesy to those who are selling merchandise at a trade show. If you are not interested in a line, say so politely. If you do want to place an order and you have brought a number of staff members with you, confine the actual decision making to one or two people. This is a courtesy to others who may wish to look at the same merchandise while you are ordering, and makes it easier on the order taker as well.

You may feel nervous about placing orders at the first trade show you attend, especially if your store is not yet open. Bill Haefling, principal owner of the rep group Haefling and Haefling, suggests that you be frank about your novice status and ask for help. Stores go out of business every year, so new stores are vital to the future success of every vendor. Let the experienced guidance of the exhibitor help you select the merchandise most likely to sell well in your new store.

DIRECT IMPORTING

Goods ordered to be shipped from the country of origin right to your shop or a port of entry nearby are said to be *direct imports*. Merchandise purchased this way is almost always less expensive than goods bought from an importer or dealer, but importing has its own headaches. You must, as a rule, purchase in quantity, especially if you are ordering factory-made goods. Unless you have an agent working on your behalf in the other country, you will be trusting the company you buy from to send you merchandise in perfect condition. You will need to pay for freight and often customs fees and the services of a broker. Freight claims for merchandise damaged in transit can be difficult to resolve.

Direct importing has two main advantages: paying a lower price gives you a better margin when you set your retail prices, and you sometimes can find merchandise that no other store in your area offers. Another advantage is that there are many trade shows abroad, offering the retailer who can afford it (it may be deductible, but it's not free) the opportunity to travel.

Finding lines to direct import can be a challenge for a small shop, especially since most goods with a well-developed market in the United States are already brought into the country by large wholesale importers. We once ordered some hand-painted Christmas ornaments at the Frankfurt Trade Show in Germany, only to find out that the exclusive U.S. importer of the line visited the booth a few minutes later and tore up our order. Nevertheless, there are small suppliers in other countries still willing to export to individual shops. We buy dressed felt bunnies every Easter from a woman who lives on an island off the coast of England. Our customers know spring can't be far behind when the English bunnies arrive at Orange Tree Imports. The bunnies come to us airmail, so there is no chance of their being lost at sea.

> Chicago's Brookfield Zoo worked with importers and native artisans to develop custom products imported directly from the coastal region of Peru for the "The Living Coast" exhibit's gift shop. Traditional pottery, jewelry, and textiles found in Peruvian markets were commissioned from local craftspeople featuring artwork of the coastal animals that are the focus in the zoo's exhibit.

Larger shipments of heavier or more expensive goods are usually shipped by boat and may require a letter of credit in payment and the services of a broker to process them through customs. You may have to pay to truck the merchandise to your shop from the port of arrival, where U.S. Customs may hold the goods for some time while levying the customs charges. All of these factors and costs need to be taken into account when deciding whether to import a line of merchandise directly from overseas.

If you are buying an item in large quantities through an importer, ask about getting better pricing by doing a direct import of the goods. Some suppliers, especially those dealing with department stores and large chains, are set up to assist you with overseas shipments if your order is large enough. A small shop might consider getting together with other retailers to place larger consolidated import orders in order to make this economically feasible. A word of caution, however: be clear about who will pay for what, and when. Goods not paid for on arrival at the port may incur storage costs or shifts in the currency market that can negate any savings.

A professional freight consolidator combines large orders from several stores and arranges to ship them in from overseas. The consolidator brings the goods through customs and then sends them on to the individual businesses. While not practical for small orders such as dressed felt bunnies, the services of a freight consolidator can be the key to doing direct imports of larger items for shops not large enough to do huge orders on their own.

Many countries maintain trade offices in their embassies or consulates in the United States to assist buyers in planning business trips abroad and arranging for direct imports. It is in the economic interest of other countries to encourage exports of their goods to the United States, so they are happy to provide information about trade shows, visas, buying offices, export regulations, and so forth. State and federal trade offices here can assist with customs and other import regulations.

CREDIT REFERENCES

The purpose of the *credit sheet*, or list of credit references, is to establish your credibility and reliability with a new supplier. You are asking the supplier to believe that your business is credit-worthy enough to receive valuable merchandise on account and that you will pay for it when the invoice is due. Think of the credit reference sheet as a resumé for your store. When you apply for open credit terms from a supplier, you want to make a good impression. The credit reference sheet should be neatly typed and present all the pertinent details about your business:

- Name
- Address
- Phone and fax numbers
- Date the store was established
- The store's legal entity (corporation, partnership or sole proprietorship)
- The name of the store's owner(s)
- Resale number
- Name and address of the store's bank
- Names of some of the store's major suppliers

Figure 4-5 shows an example of a credit reference sheet.

Be sure to give the address and phone and fax numbers for the suppliers you list as references and the account number assigned to your business by those companies. Some companies are not willing to serve as a credit reference and will not give out information if asked; check with potential references in order to avoid listing companies that will not be helpful in establishing credit terms. It is a good idea to give a mix of companies in different parts of the country and of different types if you can. New suppliers may prefer to contact a company they know, either because it is nearby or because it is in the same field.

Once you have been in business for some time, you will be approached by the credit reporting firm of Dun & Bradstreet. Dun & Bradstreet compiles credit rating information from you and from the suppliers you buy from, and it assigns your business a code number (your *D&B number*) and a rating. If you are punctual in paying all your bills and have a healthy balance sheet, your positive D&B rating should help you get open credit terms quickly with new accounts.

Figure 4-5 Sample credit reference sheet.

We also use the credit reference sheet as an opportunity to mention our policy of not accepting back orders of under $50 unless the supplier pays the freight. Other shops may give their preferences for certain freight companies or other details that will affect their orders. You could even make your credit references more impressive by including a photograph of the store and listing any awards you have received.

If you are new in business, you won't have much information to put on a credit sheet. Nevertheless, put it together with whatever data is available, even if your only references are local businesses, such as an office supply store, that have extended you credit. You may find that new vendors will still insist on payment terms such as COD (cash on delivery), prepayment, or payment by credit card, but at least you have established yourself as a professional business.

Even a well-established business will often be asked to take the first order from a new vendor COD or to prepay. Checking references can take time, delaying the order by several weeks, and can be a somewhat costly process for the vendor. By stating that no first orders will be on open account, companies avoid setting up accounts for one-time buyers and have some credit history of their own with the retailer when they check references for an open account on reorders.

Try to avoid prepaying orders in full at the time the order is placed, even if you have a short credit history. Vendors often can't ship every item you order and are reluctant to refund the difference. Offer to pay 50 percent down and the rest on *net 30* (due thirty days after being shipped) terms, or to pay in full when a *pro forma invoice* requesting prepayment is issued at the time the goods are ready to ship. We also accept COD orders, although it is sometimes inconvenient to drop everything and write a check when a delivery arrives.

THE PURCHASE ORDER FORM

For orders written in your shop, especially those faxed to reps or suppliers, you may want to produce your own purchase order form with the store's name, address, phone and fax numbers, and other pertinent data already listed. A sample form is shown in Figure 4-6. Leave room for the name of the supplier and its address and phone number. It is also useful to leave a space for the name of the sales rep, if there is one, and the account number assigned to your shop by the vendor. If the line is new to your store, you

Figure 4-6 Sample purchase order form.

STORE NAME
ADDRESS
PHONE
FAX

PURCHASE ORDER

To:_____

Fax number:_____	BILL AND SHIP TO:
Telephone:_____	STORE NAME
Address:_____	ADDRESS
_____	CITY, STATE, ZIP

Our account #:_____   Order date_____
Our sales rep.:_____   Ship date_____
Ship via:_____   Cancel date_____

Please note that we accept back orders of under $50 only when the vendor pays the freight.
❏ No back orders. ❏ No substitutions. ❏ Please cancel past back orders.

quantity ordered	item number	Description	wholesale cost	total amount	retail price
				ORDER TOTAL:	

p. 1 of ___   Order placed by_____

will need to send a copy of your credit references. You would then write "references enclosed" on the line for the account number.

The body of the purchase order form is the space for the quantity, item number, description, and wholesale price of the items being ordered. Since we use the purchase order to check in the merchandise, our form has a column to the left of the quantity ordered for checking off the number received. The column to the right of the wholesale price is used for our retail price and category code, usually written in after the order is placed. You may wish to ask that all orders be written on your customized purchase order form. If this is the case, you will need copies for the sales rep and the vendor. Print a supply on carbonless carbon paper with at least three copies, and remember to take a supply with you to trade shows.

If you send or fax an order to a sales rep, you will often receive a copy back in the mail as a *confirmation copy*. This copy is usually created when the rep copies the order onto his or her own form in order to get credit for the sale. After comparing the confirmation copy with your copy for accuracy, you may choose to discard it or to staple it behind the original purchase order.

We file purchase orders alphabetically by company name, which sometimes necessitates writing it in above the rep group's name on the top of a purchase order. Other stores file purchase orders by ship date, especially if they place orders with only a few suppliers.

PLACING PURCHASE ORDERS

In addition to specifying the items and the quantities being ordered, the buyer specifies when the order should be shipped and the method of shipping to be used. If the merchandise is needed by a certain date, state a ship date a week or two earlier. If the goods will not be of any use to the store if received after a specific time, specify a cancellation date for the order. If the supplier ships the goods after that date, you have the right to refuse the order.

You may also want to place a series of orders, called *program orders*, with staggered ship dates. In this way you plan your purchases for many months at a time and can cancel orders if the line does not sell as well as expected. Some vendors like having an idea of your needs far in advance; others find the cancellation of orders very problematic. Check with the vendor to find out whether program orders are welcome.

Suppliers often have a set minimum dollar amount for a wholesale order. This *minimum order* discourages individuals from buying wholesale for their own use and also assures the vendor that the orders are large enough to be handled efficiently. The minimum order is usually larger on the first order, since the vendor will have to go to the trouble of establishing a new customer number and account for the store. Companies also want retailers to order enough of their line to show a good representation in the store. Reorder minimums are often lower in order to encourage shops to reorder the best-selling items as soon as they have sold. For customer special orders, companies sometimes waive the reorder minimum or allow a small order if you pay an extra charge.

The Laurel Burch designer line once decided to raise its minimum reorder to $500 at wholesale, thinking that this would encourage stores to offer a complete assortment of Laurel's jewelry, mugs, shirts, and stationery. This strategy works well if the initial minimum is high—and some lines require as much as $5,000 for a first order—but it was a real problem when applied to reorders. Customers wanting a pair of earrings in a certain color or a shirt in a certain size had to wait until the store's entire stock had gotten low enough to warrant a $500 order. It was not long before the word came from Laurel Burch that there was no longer any minimum at all on reorders.

Vendors are often out of certain merchandise, especially imported items, and may choose to ship them when they arrive. Items that are out of stock when the first part of the order is shipped are referred to as being on *back order*. If you don't want to receive any items later, be sure to specify no back orders. You can also set a minimum for the size of the back orders you will accept. Small back orders often have high freight charges, so we tell vendors not to ship back orders of less than $50 unless they are paying for the freight. If you have established special terms for the original order, such as free freight or a 10 percent advertising allowance, these terms should apply to back orders as well. When reordering a line, specify whether you want any items still not shipped from your first order kept on back order or canceled.

Some suppliers prefer to substitute items that are in stock for those that are out of stock. We specify "no subs" if we want our selections or nothing at all, especially when it comes to greeting cards. Suppliers sometimes ask if a shop uses a purchase order number, and we find that using the date the order is written as the purchase order number helps track the order if there is ever any question about it.

If you have already established an account with a company, you may be asked to specify the *terms*—when you will pay the invoice. Usually this will be dictated by the company's policy, and will be net 30 or sooner. A discount may be offered for paying earlier than the due date—for example 2%/10 net 30, which means you can take 2 percent off the invoice if you pay within ten days of the invoice date. A discount of 2 percent may not seem like much, but when calculated over a long time period, these discounts add up. By paying a $1,000 invoice twenty days before it is due, you save $20. If you were to invest that $1,000 in a bank for twenty days instead, you would have to make over 35 percent interest to get a better return on your money.

After my first new-buyer orientation talk at the Chicago Gift Show, a man came up and shyly asked me, "What's dating?" It took me a moment to realize he was asking a legitimate business question. Vendors sometimes offer more than thirty days to pay, especially on seasonal merchandise that they want to ship as soon as they can. It is not uncommon to find *seasonal dating* on these lines, with the invoice due close to the holiday or season in question. *Delayed dating* means you have the merchandise to sell for a long period before you have to pay for it, always a plus.

Terms such as net 30 and beyond give the store a grace period in which to sell the merchandise before paying for it—a great help to the store's cash flow and a nice benefit provided by the supplier. Taking excessive advantage of this situation by paying bills late is called *leaning on the trade*, and is an unfair way to generate cash flow. Department stores are notorious for not paying bills on time, which gives the specialty shop that is a prompt payer an advantage over these pokey giants in the eyes of a supplier. Many suppliers belong to trade associations that share information about delinquent accounts—another reason to stay current on all bills.

SPECIFYING SHIPPING PREFERENCES

More often than not, your store will pay the freight on an order, so it is your right to determine how it is shipped to you. Freight costs can have a significant impact on the profit margin of your merchandise. Consider shipping options and distance when selecting merchandise. Shipments from companies in your part of the country will almost always have lower freight costs, but some vendors offer to pay part of the freight cost on large orders so that they can compete with companies in other regions. Freight cost will not vary so much on small orders or lightweight merchandise, so the location of the vendor is not as important with jewelry, for example, as it is with jams and jellies. Heavy, inexpensive merchandise such as bottles of lamp oil may incur freight costs almost equal to the wholesale price of the merchandise. Ordering a larger quantity at a time helps reduce the freight cost per item.

Many shops simply put "cheapest and best" under "ship via." This allows the supplier to choose whether to send the goods with a less-than-truckload (LTL) trucking company (also called a *common carrier*) or with a small-package service such as UPS or RPS. The size of the cartons and the total shipping weight usually determine which type of service is most economical, although UPS recently initiated a service, UPS Hundredweight, for larger, heavier shipments.

There may be some special considerations to take into account in selecting the most economical way to ship merchandise. Small shipments of books, for example, may be sent inexpensively by parcel post's special book rate. Bulky items such as piñatas must be shipped by common carrier, adding two or more dollars in freight costs to each burro or bull. Merchandise that is urgently needed by a customer may require shipment by Federal Express or some other overnight service, and customers may be willing to pay extra for this speedy delivery.

To minimize freight costs, try to avoid placing small, fill-in orders for heavy items. Remember to add more markup to the retail prices of items with high freight costs. Look for special shipping terms from suppliers, such as free freight or a partial freight allowance, terms often available when an order reaches a certain size or if it is prepaid. When calculating freight allowances, keep in mind that a 2 percent discount for freight means 2 percent off the invoice total for the merchandise, whereas *half freight* or *full freight* refers, respectively, to deducting half or all of the amount of the actual freight charges.

A purchase order sometimes states at what point the shipment becomes the responsibility of the store. The term *FOB* means that freight costs must be paid by the store after the merchandise has been delivered to the shipping company. FOB stands for "free on board," a throwback to the days when a supplier might actually deliver a bundle of goods shipside instead of just handing the package over to a friendly delivery person.

SETTING RETAIL PRICES

Merchandise must be purchased at a considerably lower price than it is sold for if you don't want to fall victim to that old retailing joke: "I'm taking a loss on every item, but I'm making up for it in volume!" Traditionally, most merchandise is purchased at a *wholesale*, or *net*, price that is half the retail price. This means there is a 100 percent markup (or 50 percent margin) on each item. The 100 percent markup has been standard for so many years that it is referred to as *keystone*. Most experts agree, however, that keystone markup is no longer enough to keep a store profitable. Some items must be sold at a higher retail, at least at keystone plus a portion of the freight cost. Merchandise that is prepriced, such as books and greeting cards, allows no fluctuation in retail pricing (and, unfortunately, none of our current card suppliers prices their cards at higher than keystone markup). Luckily other items can be priced however you wish, providing you don't break your state's minimum markup laws. In Wisconsin, for example, it is illegal to set retail prices below wholesale cost—hardly a practice we would ever consider, but when the law was passed, one of our kind customers asked me with great concern whether this new regulation would hurt our business.

We are always looking for closeouts and other items on sale from our vendors, or available with special terms such as free freight, that will allow us to take markup that is higher than keystone and still offer prices customers will find attractive. We also look for *blind* items—unique merchandise that customers don't have a preconceived idea of how much it should sell for, so we can price these items slightly higher without hurting sales. One way to create blind items is to bundle several items together, such as a soap dish, soap, and scented candle, and sell them as a set. Conversely, you can buy items in sets and then price them separately at a slightly higher total retail than the set price. Selling items individually that are normally sold prepackaged is a service to the customer, who may not want a large quantity of an item.

Keep markdowns and perishability in mind when setting retail prices. A nursery, for example, will price plants as high as 300 percent above wholesale cost. Plants require high maintenance until sold, and a certain percentage may not survive. Seasonal or trendy fashion apparel often needs to be cleared out at a reduced price after just a month or two in the store. Added markup is necessary to maintain some profitability when selling a significant amount of merchandise at clearance prices.

I write the retail prices on the purchase order soon after I've written an order, so the merchandise is still fresh in my mind and I can remember which items I feel can be sold for slightly higher than keystone. When I place orders at trade shows, I try to get all the orders retailed before the end of each day. I occasionally catch errors when reviewing orders to price them and will contact the rep to make a correction before it is too late.

In determining retail prices, I pay close attention to the even price points such as $5, $10, and $20. If an item wholesales for $2.50, I almost always keep it at the $5.00 price point. An item that wholesales for $6.00, however, will sell just as well at $12.50 as at $12.00. This type of discretionary pricing requires some consumer psychology. You need to look at each item and try to determine how much above keystone you can go without acquiring a reputation for high or, worse yet, unfair prices.

Customers love a bargain, so when we are able to offer a lower price because of a quantity purchase or manufacturer's special offer, we often draw attention to the price by using a white price tag to indicate the "regular" price and a red one preprinted with the word "special" to flag the lower price. We indicate this on the purchase order by noting the white and red tag retail prices side by side.

Competing with discounters will require you to occasionally settle for less than keystone on some items and to make up the difference on other merchandise. There are also categories, such as books and electronics, that traditionally are sold at a lower standard markup. In order to protect your profit margins when going up against a discounter or when featuring low markup merchandise, you need to buy very carefully, looking for volume discounts, dating programs, and other special offers. It is essential to have a diverse product mix so that some of your merchandise will provide you with a higher potential margin.

Pricing Shortcuts

Many items are sold wholesale by the dozen. When placing an order, I mentally calculate the approximate retail price per piece by dividing the dozen price by six. Price is very important to my customers, so I need to figure out the retail price before I can decide whether to order an item. Although I may eventually price the item at slightly higher than keystone, this quick calculation tells me what the minimum retail price will need to be.

It is more complicated to determine the retail price of items of graduated sizes wholesaled as a set. If three baskets, nested inside one another, wholesale for $17.00 and you want the set to retail for $36.00, the individual baskets will range from $8.00 to $16.00 in price. Here's a trick for calculating nested set prices:

1. Starting with the number 2, add one consecutive number for each item in the set. For three baskets, add 2 + 3 + 4 = 9.
2. Divide the retail price by that number. Since $36.00 ÷ 9 = 4, the factor in this example is $4.00.
3. Multiply the original numbers you started with (2, 3, and 4) by the factor: 2 × $4.00 = $8.00, 3 × $4.00 = $12.00, 4 × $4.00 = $16.00.

At this point you may want to adjust the figures to take into account facts such as the greater desirability of the largest size. Starting with the evenly spaced prices, add to one what you subtract from another. The price of the largest size could be adjusted up to $18.00, for example, and the smaller two down to $7.00 and $11.00.

Marking the Purchase Order

In addition to noting the retail prices on the purchase order, indicate the alphabet letter or numerical code for the merchandise category of each item. Some vendors carry merchandise in only a single category, such as soaps; others may sell a range of products requiring a variety of category codes. This category information will be useful for pricing the merchandise, if you use codes on your price tags, and also will assist the bookkeeper in tracking merchandise purchases by category. If you are using an open-to-buy budget, total each order by merchandise category, and subtract the amount spent from each category's budget for the month when the order is expected to arrive.

Any special terms, such as dating or return privileges, should be specified in writing on the purchase order. We also make a note on the purchase order of the names and phone numbers of any customers waiting for specific items from the shipment. Use a highlighter pen to emphasize special instructions or pricing so this information will catch the attention of those checking in the order when it arrives.

DEVELOPING VENDOR RELATIONS

The suppliers you buy from should be partners in your success. Your store cannot thrive without good-quality merchandise for customers to buy, and vendors cannot get their merchandise to the buying public without retailers as the link. Ideally, this partnership works well for both parties.

Retailers help vendors by:

- Ordering conscientiously.
- Not canceling orders capriciously.
- Displaying all merchandise well.
- Reporting damage and defective claims fairly.
- Paying invoices promptly.
- Giving the supplier feedback from customers about the merchandise.

Vendors help retailers by:

- Providing quality, fashionable merchandise.
- Communicating regularly with retailers about new merchandise and specials.
- Filling orders completely and on time.
- Settling damage and defective claims quickly.
- Not selling the same goods to discounters and neighboring stores.
- Offering special terms such as free freight or early payment discounts.

It stands to reason that a good retailer will favor suppliers who make a sincere effort to support specialty shop accounts. Some stores track vendor compliance to see how many orders are received close to the date specified and how many items are defective, incorrect, or on back order. It is also important to note which suppliers are selling to other stores in your area, especially mass merchandisers, by shopping your competition often. When goods become commonplace or are discounted, they are usually no longer as viable for a specialty shop.

The speed with which a vendor can ship reorders, called the *replenishment time*, is important in determining how much merchandise you need to keep on hand. If suppliers can furnish you with new goods quickly, you will have fewer dollars tied up in stored inventory. Some suppliers, especially those dealing with imported goods, have great difficulty shipping promptly and completely, but it stands to reason that you should favor those that make an effort to do so. Your life is certainly easier when goods arrive just when you want them.

Because specialty shop customers expect high quality, the condition of the merchandise when you receive it is also important. We inspect items carefully upon receipt and expect our vendors to take back merchandise that arrives broken or does not meet our reasonable quality standards. If a customer returns an item as defective, we often contact the supplier for credit. It is usually only by hearing from us about a problem that the vendor will know if the consumer is dissatisfied with a product.

It doesn't hurt to ask if special terms or pricing are available from a vendor, especially if you are placing sizable orders. Be sure to ask the supplier's advice about what items in the line are selling well, as well as what items are new. Order writing should reflect the partnership relationship you are working to establish with each vendor.

How many vendors should you buy from? Having too few vendors puts your store in jeopardy should one of them fail or begin selling to mass merchandisers. Too many can be difficult to keep track of and can lead to an unfocused look in the store's merchandising. Some buyers also point out that by concentrating on large orders to a number of key suppliers, stores can become important accounts to these vendors and will receive preferential treatment in return for their loyalty.

We are always looking for new, unique merchandise, so we open many new vendor accounts each year. This becomes somewhat of a headache for our bookkeepers, but it means we constantly have new goods to offer our customers. We favor certain exemplary vendors with larger reorders, but we rarely drop a line of really wonderful merchandise just because of poor performance in shipping or some other aspect of vendor compliance. We want our store to feature the very best selection of merchandise available, and working with many vendors is one way we are able to do so.

5

VISUAL MERCHANDISING

Buying for your store can be like shopping for a living, and sharing the exciting new merchandise you've found with your customers is enjoyable and rewarding. But in between these two stages come two tasks crucial to the success of your store. First, the goods need to be accurately and efficiently checked in, inspected, and priced. Mistakes or delays in the receiving area can be expensive. The merchandise then needs to be displayed in a way that will invite shoppers' attention and enhance the appearance of your store.

Books about retailing—and I've read more than my share this year—are full of mathematical tables and formulas to help fledgling shopkeepers figure out where all the money is going, but very few of them talk about the artistic side of retailing, technically called *visual merchandising*. The ability to display even commonplace goods in an attractive and effective manner is a skill every bit as important as being able to calculate return on investment, and I think it's a skill that's a lot more fun to develop. Many of us go into retailing because we love the merchandise we sell, and we want to show it to our customers in a way that will make them love it too.

CHECKING IN MERCHANDISE

Before a shipment of new merchandise can be put on display, it must be checked in and priced. Some stores hire employees especially for stock work; others add this to the duties of the sales staff. Accuracy in checking in merchandise can have an important financial impact on the store's operations. Not only is it essential that items be priced correctly, but shipping errors on the part of vendors are not unusual; they can be costly if not caught and reported. You must be certain that what you receive is what you ordered and that the vendor's invoice matches the purchase order.

In the front of our file of purchase orders is a lined sheet, the *arrivals chart*, with room to write down which shipments arrive each day, listing the vendor name, our purchase order number (we assign the date the order was placed as the purchase order number), whether the shipment arrived COD, and how it was shipped to us. This chart helps us track all packages that come into the store and can be useful if there is a disagreement later about what we received. For a sample arrivals chart, see Figure 5-1.

Figure 5-1 Sample arrivals chart.

ARRIVALS CHART

DATE	VENDOR	# BOXES	P.O. DATE	UPS/RPS	TRUCK	OTHER	COD?

When a shipment arrives, it is entered on the arrivals chart, the purchase order is pulled, and the date of arrival is written on the purchase order form. Most shipments include a list of contents, the *packing list*, which we staple to the back of the purchase order. If an actual invoice is enclosed, it is forwarded to the bookkeeper. Invoices and packing lists often look the same, but an invoice has the shipping costs added and is totaled. If an invoice is mistaken for a packing list and is stapled to the back of an order, it may not get paid, so it is important to be sure this does not happen.

Ideally, the wholesale price you wrote on the purchase order is the same price you will be charged for the goods. We calculate retail prices when we write an order and put them on the purchase order form so that the merchandise can be checked in and priced as soon as it arrives. Other stores wait until the invoice arrives in order to see what the shipping costs are and whether there have been price changes. But some vendors are rather slow in getting their invoices sent, which might mean that merchandise sits in the store for days without being priced and put out to sell. The sooner merchandise is displayed, the better.

Dealing with Back Orders

If you have elected to have back-ordered merchandise shipped to you when it arrives, you will receive shipments that do not have a purchase order on file. The reason is that the original order was pulled and processed when the first part of the order arrived; it is necessary to find this order and check to see whether the back order is correct.

We use a special form to check in back orders (a copy can be seen in Figure 5-2). When a back order arrives, we begin by looking up the original order date and then enter the date the back order arrives. The wholesale and retail information is taken from the original purchase order. This is a rather tedious process, which makes it even more inviting to specify "no back orders." Not accepting back orders, however, might mean that you are unable to get certain very popular items that are often out of stock. Most stores put up with some back orders in order to get the choicest merchandise, but it is smart not to allow a supplier to send numerous small back orders instead of consolidating them.

If you have merchandise on back order and are writing a new order with the supplier, be sure to note if you want to keep items on back order (which may mean that you'll be first in line to get them when they arrive) or if you will be reordering these items on the new order. The latter is

Figure 5-2 Sample back order check-in form.

BACK ORDER CHECK-IN

Vendor Name:_____

Original Order Date:_____   Date Received:_____

Original order specifies: ☐ Dating   ☐ Freight allowance
                            ☐ Price-off promotion   ☐ Ad allowance
                            ☐ Free goods (gift with purchase)

quantity	item number	description	wholesale cost	retail price

sometimes advantageous when you need to get your new order up to a certain minimum dollar amount or if you don't want to have to look up information on previous purchase orders when the merchandise arrives. Simply write "cancel back orders" on your new purchase order. You might want to call the supplier first and find out if the back order has already been shipped.

Dealing with Problems on Shipments

Ideally, when you open a shipment to check it in, every item looks exactly the way it did in the showroom or catalog, and the quantities match those on the purchase order. The prices on the invoice are the same as the prices you were quoted, and the terms are the same as the ones promised. Nothing is broken, and the order doesn't include pizza unless you ordered pizza. (The partially eaten piece of pizza, sent to us with a shipment of picture frames by a well-respected eastern manufacturer, is legendary in our receiving area.) Usually the incorrect items packed in with an order are pieces of merchandise from the line not on our purchase order. Often the person packing (or "picking") an order will transpose the item number, sending us #5462 instead of #5426, or perhaps the company was out of #5462, so they send #5461 without checking to see if the substitution is okay with us first. If we order 12 of an item, we may get 6, or 18, or 120. Items sometimes arrive broken, cracked, or crushed. All of these problems are common, and they are costly to deal with.

We have a two-part "problem" slip, provided for you in Figure 5-3, which we use when there is some complication with an order. One part of it is stapled to the order, and the second part can get put with any incorrect items while they await pickup by the vendor. We have a policy of ignoring problems on orders if the amount is less than $10, because they just aren't worth the time and effort.

When there is a problem with an order, we contact the vendor immediately, usually by fax or telephone, to ask for a carrier *call tag* to pick up items we did not order or which were defective. This means that the vendor will pay the return shipping. If the merchandise is heavy and the cost of shipping it to the store was significant, it is certainly reasonable to ask that some of the freight charges on the invoice be deducted as well.

Broken merchandise may lead to a freight claim being placed with the carrier. Depending on the type of carrier, the goods may be automatically insured for $100, as is the case with UPS, or not insured at all, as is the case with the U.S. Postal Service. Common carrier trucking companies base their liability for damage on the released value of the goods, which varies from one type of merchandise to the next. The more fragile the goods, the higher the freight cost due to the higher liability.

When making a freight claim, you are supposed to keep the broken goods and both the outer and inner cartons for inspection by the freight company. As one of our suppliers, Coyote Found Candles, points out, "UPS will not pay claims for freight damage unless they can visit the injured box personally." Keeping the cartons may be impractical if you have limited storage space or if, as once happened to us, the goods have been damaged by someone else's shipment of pickled pigs' feet leaking onto them. Freight claims are a headache for everyone and, luckily, are less

Figure 5-3 Sample "problem" slip.

---

new arrivals
PROBLEM

Vendor:_____Date:_____

Purchase order number or date:_____

Staff member unpacking order:_____

1. We received_____(quantity) of_____(item)

_____

which ☐ we did not order

☐ was apparently substituted for _____

_____

☐ was_____more than we ordered

☐ was defective/poor quality/damaged (explain):

_____

2. We did **not** receive_____

which the vendor claims to have shipped.

Any incorrect or unacceptable merchandise has been put:

_____

Recommended action:

_____

Print this on two-part carbonless carbon paper (two per
8½ × 11-inch sheet). Staple the top copy to the purchase
order, and attach the second to any incorrect or defective
merchandise.

common than they once were. Perhaps carriers are handling goods more carefully, or vendors are packing them better. We also find that some suppliers allow a small amount of breakage to be deducted from the invoice rather than deal with the hassle of having a claim filed against the carrier.

Some suppliers take out additional insurance on a shipment, adding this cost to the freight charges for which you are billed. The freight charges on the invoice should reflect the actual cost of shipping the goods to you, plus any insurance charge. It is not unheard of to have an unscrupulous supplier overcharge for shipping, although this is not a common problem.

If an order arrives COD, a charge will be added for this service. UPS and RPS collect a nominal COD charge, but common carriers may add a significant fee to the shipping cost for this service. Another hidden shipping cost might be for inside delivery if a common carrier is being used. Truckers are not even required to bring a shipment from the truck to your door, although many will.

Late and Lost Orders

Vendors sometimes ship later than the desired ship date, but unless you have stated a cancel date, you can expect the merchandise to eventually arrive on your doorstep. If an order without a cancel date is late and you decide you can no longer use the goods, be sure to notify the vendor in writing that you don't want it shipped. You are under no obligation to accept goods that arrive unreasonably late if you have specified a cancellation date.

Periodically reviewing all orders still open is a wise idea. Call vendors to find out why merchandise due in the store has not arrived, or fax them a "when will you ship" reminder (there's one in Figure 5-4). Sometimes a supplier will have no record of receiving an order, and sometimes the supplier will not have been able to ship the merchandise for one reason or another. Good vendors will notify you of delays, but many do not. Open-to-buy budgeting depends on shipments arriving during the month specified, and unfortunately many of our suppliers are rather hit and miss in their delivery times. Some ship the day after receiving an order, and others take a month or two. Some ship every order complete, and others let the goods dribble in on numerous back orders. Dealing with these variables is one of the challenges in acquiring an optimal selection of merchandise for your specialty store.

Figure 5-4 Sample "When will you ship?" form.

STORE NAME
ADDRESS
PHONE
FAX

When Will You Ship?

To: _____ Date: _____

Attention: _____ Fax: _____

Our Account Number: _____

We are in urgent need of the merchandise we ordered from

you on: _____.

Please let us know by phone or fax when we might expect these goods.

☐ If you cannot ship by _____, please cancel.

☐ Please ship as soon as possible. We do not wish to cancel this order.

Thank you for your assistance. We look forward to hearing from you soon.

PRICING THE MERCHANDISE

Once a shipment has been received and checked against the purchase order or invoice, the goods need to be labeled with prices. If you are using a bar code scanning system, this may not be necessary, but you will need to make sure the price on the shelf and in the system are correct. One of the most frustrating experiences for shoppers is getting stuck in line waiting to check out while someone up ahead is arguing that the scanned price is not the same as the one on the display or in the ad.

If you are a small shop, you might want to hand-write your price tags. Be sure to print neatly, so that there is no question about the correct price, and be sure to indicate whether the price is for one piece or a set. If you are selling expensive items such as antiques, you might consider having your logo printed on attractive hang tags, with a calligrapher writing in the prices and any additional information useful to the shopper. If printing your logo right on the tags is too expensive, it could be applied using a label, perhaps one printed in silver or gold on clear adhesive stock.

Using a price gun to print and apply self-adhesive price tags saves time and usually guarantees legibility. You can purchase tags that have your store name already printed on them, and the price gun can be used to add more data, such as date of arrival and a vendor or category code. We use a letter of the alphabet to indicate the category and a jumbled number code to indicate the date of arrival. An item marked 71505, for example, means that it was received on May 15, 1997. This system allows us to make sure stock doesn't "age," or linger beyond a certain number of months, but customers (we hope) are not aware whether the goods are new. Try to include some type of date on your price tags, and establish a markdown plan for merchandise when it reaches a certain age without selling. For clothing, markdowns may need to be taken at sixty or even thirty days, whereas for other categories, between six months and a year may be acceptable.

The alphabet codes we use correspond to the twenty-six categories on our cash registers and are intended to help the staff remember what category an item gets rung up under. We probably no longer need to code wine glasses "G" for glassware, but some items, such as plastic drinkware for picnics, are harder to place. Do they get rung up with glassware or with picnic baskets? The codes on the tags make sure that everyone rings items up in the same way and that the cash register category matches the inventory purchase category for that item on the invoice.

Price tags come in many different colors, so you can use color coding to indicate a category, season, or sale status. For everyday specials, we use a fluorescent orange tag preprinted with the word "special," and for clearance sales we use a bright yellow. Colored dots can be added to price tags to give additional data about the item's status. We use a tiny green dot on T-shirts, for instance, to indicate that all of the stock of a particular style is out on display. If a customer asks for another size, we know that we don't have it.

Be aware that some items won't hold a sticker for more than a few minutes, no matter what you try. The porous and oily surface of many wooden items, for example, refuses to take a price tag. If taping the tag on doesn't work, the only other option is a tag that ties on. If even that fails, put an attractive price sign with the merchandise, and keep a list on or beside the register of unmarked products and their prices.

We use "dog bone" tags to fasten onto the strings of Christmas ornaments and to label some jewelry. These tags are shaped like dog bones, or barbells, with adhesive under the large round ends so that they can be pressed together after the tag is wrapped around the item. The tags can be imprinted with the store logo and are available in a no-tear material for jewelry stores concerned about customers' removing the tags instead of paying.

Store supply companies sell two-part tear-off tags that allow the lower portion of the tag to be removed and kept when an item is sold. Although handwriting the data on the two sections of these fairly large tags is not practical for small items, it works well for gathering data on the sale of large items such as collectibles or craft items being sold on consignment.

In addition to tagging merchandise with prices, consider adding a small, attractive label with the store name to consumable items such as candles, potpourri, boxes of stationery, and personal care products. They will help remind customers or gift recipients where to go to replace the item when it is used up.

Personalizing Your Price Tags

It may seem redundant to put your store's name on all your price tags, but this serves two purposes. It is an inexpensive form of advertising, reminding customers over and over again of the store's name, and it helps with identifying returns (if the consumer has left the tag on). Many department stores and discounters seem to use tags that are very hard to remove, making it easy to see if an item being returned actually came from a big store competitor. No one could overlook the bright orange remainders of those very stubborn Toys 'Я' Us price tags!

If you are using price guns, order rolls of labels with your name printed on them. Allow several weeks for the labels to arrive. For handwritten price tags, the store computer can print your name and logo on sheets of stickers or on business card stock to use as hang tags.

Tips for Removing Price Tags

The flip side of putting price tags on is taking them off again, especially when gift wrapping a purchase. Some self-adhesive labels are divided into little sections in order to discourage customers from switching the price from a less expensive item to a more expensive one. Some tags have a very strong adhesive, for the same reason. No matter what type of tags you use, removing them from certain products may be difficult. Lighter fluid and rubbing alcohol work for this purpose; so does a new product, Goo Gone. We keep all three products on hand, because each works better on some surfaces than others.

Price tags on plastic wrap may tear the wrap when removed, so they should be applied to an inconspicuous spot. If it is important to take a tag off without tearing the surface it was applied to, try a quick pass under a hair dryer to dry out the adhesive and release the sticker.

DISPLAYING THE MERCHANDISE

Now that the merchandise you have purchased is priced and ready to sell, it is time to give some thought as to how to display the goods to best advantage. A good display makes the goods look appealing and makes it easy for customers to purchase them. The back stock of merchandise needs to be stored in an accessible, safe place. (We use the cardboard tote boxes with handles available at many grocery stores to carry priced merchandise away to be stored and to bring out items to be put out display.)

As a general rule, most items should be put in displays that allow customers to handle them. Customers always prefer to touch an item before deciding to buy it. You may choose to put a large quantity of each item on display or to highlight the uniqueness of a piece by displaying just one. During the holiday season, consider putting a few already wrapped boxes of your most popular items on the shelf for quick purchase.

Merchandise that is easily shoplifted or broken can be displayed in locked cases, but customers are often reluctant to ask to see an item that is under glass. Stores with locked cases of merchandise need alert sales staff to offer help as soon as they see someone interested in a closed display.

When arranging merchandise on your display fixtures, keep the principles of color harmony in mind. Highlighting many items of the same color, called *color blocking*, makes a strong statement. Products that come in a variety of colors sell best when arranged in a pleasing order, such as following the color spectrum or progressing from light to dark. Color harmony has a positive effect on the eye and enhances the sale of the products.

Yankee Candle Company of South Deerfield, Massachusetts, manufactures a popular line of wax-filled glass apothecary jars in a wide variety of rich scents and colors. Research in Yankee's own retail shop, the largest candle store in the world, has proven that displaying candle jars in color spectrum order, like the rainbow, significantly increases candle jar sales.

Often shops have so many items for customers to look at that the result is visual confusion. Help draw shoppers' attention to individual items on a shelf by using a mirror or a small piece of fabric under a display, or by placing pieces of merchandise on a small riser to display items at slightly different levels, as shown in Figure 5-5. Plexiglas risers are available from display fixture suppliers, as are cubes made of cork, mirror, Plexiglas, and wood. Make your own inexpensive risers to match a display by covering cube-shaped cardboard boxes with fabric or gift wrap. Rubber-covered wire plate stands or easels are versatile accessories for displaying many different items upright and can also be used to hold signs.

Focal Point Displays

Many stores are designed exclusively around fixtures that hold merchandise, with little thought to special areas that can feature changing displays highlighting new or seasonal merchandise. Often the only display that changes from month to month is the end panel, or end cap, of the traditional freestanding gondola units. When we expanded fifteen years ago, we neglected to allow enough space for seasonal displays and for *cross*

Figure 5-5 Display merchandise at different heights, and against complementary background fabrics, to highlight individual items, as demonstrated in this display of Portmerion porcelain at our shop.

merchandising, the technique of displaying merchandise from different departments together, such as placemats shown with holiday china, brass candlesticks, green glassware, and a Christmas cracker (a traditional English decorative and amusing table favor). Our store atrium, originally conceived of as a restful area with a bench and a hibiscus tree, was soon pressed into service as a display area. We now change the atrium displays as often as we change the main window, with seasonal merchandise dominating in the fall and spring and featured items from one or more departments being highlighted the rest of the year.

Clothing stores often have mannequins or body forms positioned throughout the store, on platforms or on the walls above the hanging rods, showing coordinated outfits and accessories. Other types of specialty shops can make use of small areas of floor or wall space to create displays that can be changed periodically. Your store's regular customers should be rewarded for their loyalty by seeing something new each time they come into the shop. A focused display, even one using merchandise that is not new, draws customers' attention to the featured items.

Displays can be used to give decorating, gift, and use suggestions that customers find very helpful. Showing scented candles with bath salts, for example, evokes the image of a sensuous bath and suggests that candles, which most customers think of as a dining table accessory, are also appropriate for the bathroom. Displaying a number of different apple-related gift items together, such as bags of potpourri, apple-shaped cookie cutters, an apple corer, and towels silkscreened with an apple design, gives customers the idea of putting together a gift basket of apple merchandise.

Cross merchandising can also be done on the basis of color, leading to some unusual and interesting display combinations—for instance, red casseroles displayed with red Christmas ornaments and teddy bears with big red bows. Some stores display all their merchandise in cross merchandising settings rather than having a separate area for soap, candles, linens, and other categories. This is perfect for leisurely impulse shopping in a tourist area, but not ideal for shoppers hoping to find a specific item quickly.

Props can be used in store displays to add color and interest. A display of rugged suitcases, for instance, might also feature maps of Africa, binoculars, a pith helmet, and a top-quality plush lion. Some of the prop items might be for sale, whereas others should be discreetly marked "for display only." If the prop is from another retailer, a tag might mention where it can be purchased.

The area near any checkout counter, even in the finest specialty shop, is a prime spot for impulse merchandise. (We all know what a strong draw the candy display can be along most grocery store checkout lanes.) Leave room near the register for a compact display of add-on accessories, treats, or any small new items to which you wish to draw attention. Because checkout counters can become cluttered with impulse merchandise, it is important to limit and frequently change the items that are featured there. These displays may be the final impression that customers have of your store, so be sure that the merchandise on the counter looks as enticing as the goods shown elsewhere in the shop.

MAINTAINING GOOD MERCHANDISING

It is more work, and less fun, to maintain existing displays than to create new ones. As merchandise sells, it must be replenished. Customers will unfold the folded shirts, move items around, tear packaging, or put merchandise they've changed their mind about in the wrong place. Straightening and dusting the merchandise and shelves is no one's favorite job, but it has to be done regularly if displays are to look fresh and inviting. Merchandise and display fixtures must be kept clean, and all displays should be kept full. A full display always sells more than one that is half empty.

We divide up the task of maintaining displays by having a staff member in charge of every department. This employee does the merchandise display and also dusts and straightens that area. Standing items are turned to face the same direction, and soiled or damaged merchandise is removed. Folded items get refolded and restacked in a standardized manner. Some stores have employees use a folding board to be sure that all shirts and sweaters are folded uniformly. At Pooh Corner, a children's bookstore in Madison, Wisconsin, employees in charge of an area are expected to touch every item in their area every day, straightening the shelves and putting back any books that have strayed from their proper place.

The employee in charge of an area in our store also restocks the displays. We encourage employees to restock from the basement, looking to see what is in back stock and then making sure everything is on display. If the fixture seems full, those who restock from the display may not notice that an item is missing or that a new item has arrived. Staff members in charge of a department also do inventories for the buyer of that area, and in many cases they eventually do routine reorders of merchandise and perhaps even new merchandise buying. Even part-time staff members are in charge of a small area, so that maintaining the attractive appearance of the store is truly a team effort. With many stores offering the same items, we all realize that the way we present our merchandise is an important factor in our store's success.

USING SHOP WINDOWS EFFECTIVELY

The concept of store window displays is not very old; until the invention of plate glass, windows were very small and intended just to allow light to enter the shop premises. Early plate glass window displays took advantage of the larger space to cram in a sample of almost everything in the store, and some merchants today still follow this "more is better" philosophy. Others err to the opposite extreme, with so little in the window that it seems dubious that there is much in the store. Good window displays take a certain amount of artistic talent, as well as organized planning.

Window displays should be changed at least once a month, and in high-traffic areas, every two to three weeks. Establish a calendar that identifies themes and responsibilities for creating the displays several months in advance, and share this information with the store's buyers in case they need to order any special merchandise for a display. One of the cardinal rules for putting merchandise in a window is that there be a reasonable amount of back stock for customers to buy. A customer who wants to buy something displayed in a window will be frustrated if told it is out of stock. The goal of a window, after all, is to bring customers into the store in order to buy your merchandise.

Laurie Karzen and Charlotte R. Morrill, merchandising experts from the design, marketing, and consulting firm CRM&ME, recommend keeping a notebook of display plans, with a page for each of the next twelve months of window and in-store displays. Each planning page contains a description of the proposed theme, sketches, notes about sources for the tools and props to be used, and information about the merchandise to be featured, including when it will need to arrive. These pages can be taken along when doing the buying for the season, to be sure that all the items needed are ordered. When a window has been completed, Karzen and Morrill suggest, attach a photograph of the finished display to the planning page, along with an evaluation of which elements worked well and which ones did not.

Sources of Display Ideas

A good window combines the elements of good visual display and creative advertising. There should always be a unifying theme, although the theme can be as simple as a single color or texture. Other themes might be a season or holiday, a product category, a color combination, an in-store event, or even an individual new item. Sometimes display themes are small vignettes, or realistic home settings such as a dining room table or a bedroom dresser complete with all the accessories. The theme, which is sometimes referred to as the *story* the window is trying to tell, determines the materials, merchandise, and signage to be used.

Where can you find ideas for window displays? A walk through your store should give you some ideas; look for products that are visually exciting or are hot sellers. We keep a photo album of all past window displays to inspire future designs. We also watch for good displays in the wholesale showrooms from which we buy merchandise. Some companies allow retailers to take pictures of trade show and showroom displays they wish to replicate and provide information about the sources of any props or background materials used. Trade magazines often feature photographs of successful store windows you can adapt for your own use. There is even a special magazine devoted to display ideas, *VS+SD*, which stands for *Visual Merchandising and Store Design* (800-421-1321). Every year *VS+SD* conducts an international visual merchandising competition and carries photographs of all the winners in the July issue. In May, the annual Visual Marketing and Store Design Show is held at the Jacob K. Javits Center in New York, concurrent with the National Stationery Fair.

We occasionally do a window display that helps a nonprofit group publicize a special event or cause. Often we are able to tie some of our merchandise into the display, for example, adding picnic baskets and non-breakable wine glasses to a window promoting American Players Theatre, a nearby outdoor classical theater.

Look for window display opportunities outside your store. Seaside Silks draws customers to its shop by doing wonderfully colorful displays of scarves in the leased display cases of a nearby luxury resort. Convention centers, meeting halls, and even airports sometimes have display cases available to rent, or you could offer to spruce up a vacant store front by temporarily filling its windows with goods from your store.

Do You Do Windows?

In larger cities, there are professional window dressers, or *visual merchandisers*, who can take your design concept and bring it to life. You may also be able to find an artist who can translate his or her talents into store displays. We have always done our own displays, encouraging staff members to pair up and take turns doing a window. Near our main window is a sign giving the window dressers credit for their work. Some of our employees have turned out to be gifted designers, and it is nice to share the opportunity, and the challenge, of creating a new window display with our entire staff.

Art students, and even floral designers, are taught how to use complementary colors and geometric shapes to create a pleasing design—skills that retailers often have to learn on their own in order to do good window displays. Merchandise alone does not make a display. Consider the aesthetics of the display, in addition to the lighting, backdrops, props, and possibly signage. Good window design should take into account five key elements: balance (symmetrical or asymmetrical), proportion, contrast, harmony, and focus. The Crabtree & Evelyn display in Figure 5-6 is an excellent illustration of these essential elements.

The Tools of the Trade

Good window displays often create an illusion, for example, an imaginary garden or jungle. A number of materials that fool the eye but are lightweight and inexpensive are ideal for creating this magic. The first of these is Foamcore, a stiff "board" made of Styrofoam that can be cut into any shape using a sharp blade. Foamcore can be painted and pinned into, and it will not warp like many other stiff materials. It can be used to create a smooth floor, an archway, or a palm tree. Create a starry night background by punching holes through foamcore painted dark blue and inserting small Christmas lights from the back. Foamcore is available in large rectangular sheets from most art supply stores and some lumberyards. It comes in different thicknesses, from 1/4-inch sheets to 2-inch insulation Foamcore that can be carved with a knife.

Fishing line is an essential tool for window dressers. This sturdy monofilament, available in sporting goods stores, allows items hung in a window to appear to be floating. Fish line is also useful for reinforcing standing items, so they don't tip over during the time the window is on display.

I am a strong believer in the use of small white Christmas lights to outline window displays, especially during the holiday season. We have, in fact, outlined both of our buildings in little white lights, which helps to brighten our streetscape during the long Wisconsin winter evenings. There are other colors of little lights available as well; we have used orange ones in the Halloween window and pastel lights at Easter. Strings of lights can be woven through a glassware display, intertwined in a floral garland, or even used on a Christmas tree.

Prop Master

"Display and visual presentation are the theater of retailing," writes designer Martin M. Pegler in *Store Windows That Sell*. As in the theater, backdrops and props can be used to make a display come alive. These materials need not be items you sell, as long as the focus remains on the merchandise you *do* stock. You should constantly be on the lookout for

Figure 5-6 An example of an attractive and effective window display from a Crabtree & Evelyn store.

(Courtesy of Crabtree & Evelyn Ltd.; Jonathan Kannair, photographer.)

inexpensive items that can be used in displays. Buy props at antique stores or rummage sales, or borrow them. Many organizations are willing to loan out items in exchange for a credit in the window. Over the years, we have borrowed costumes from the *Nutcracker* ballet, a cast-iron bathtub, an antique table, a bicycle, and a baker's sample of a wedding cake.

It is wonderful to have storage space so window props can be reused. This storage need not be in the store, since it does not need to be accessible on short notice. Over the years, you can build up a useful collection of fabric, window shades, silk flowers, greenery, pedestals, and display props such as fake rocks and mannequins.

Here are some prop items that can be purchased inexpensively or borrowed to make an original window display:

- Toys, such as beach balls and hoops
- Masks
- Musical instruments
- Theatrical costumes
- Trellises and garden fences
- Terra-cotta pots
- Hammocks
- Ropes, rope ladders
- Standing mirrors
- Shopping bags with the store name and logo
- Silk trees and plants
- Plush animals
- Gift-wrapped boxes
- Sporting goods
- Paper or silk kites
- Life-size cardboard cutout figures
- Plastic flamingos or other lawn ornaments
- Natural materials (e.g., hay, vines, wood chips)

The Backdrop

The background of the window is not important if the window opens up into the store (although even in this type of window, some kind of railing, net, or grid may be helpful to keep customers out of the window). Closed windows, however, allow a backdrop to be an integral part of the display. We often use window shades made of bamboo, rice paper, or pleated fabric as a background, lowering the last shade carefully as we back out of the completed window. Fabric panels and woven throws are also useful as focal points in the background of a window. We often base an entire display around a background that inspires us.

Many other items can be used to form an interesting background in a display window:

- Flags and banners
- Panels covered with wallpaper or gift wrap
- Posters
- Fish net
- Sheet music
- Product photographs mounted on Foamcore
- Blankets and woven throws
- Window frames, shutters, doorways
- Fireplace mantles
- Large paper fans
- Bull's-eye targets
- Enlarged clip art or photographs
- Sheets
- Scarves
- Parachutes
- Maps
- Wood folding screens

Photographs, clip art, and other graphics can be enlarged for use in a window display by a local photographic outlet or printing service. Be sure to have signed permission to reproduce any photographs or artwork that is not clip art, which is sold free of copyright restrictions. Dry-mounting the enlargement on Foamcore will keep it from warping, although it may still fade when exposed to direct sunlight. A new process, the 3M™ Scotchprint™ Electronic Graphics System, allows computer images to be manipulated, enlarged, and reproduced onto a variety of Scotchprint™ films, ultraviolet-resistant materials that can be mounted as a window background or used as a flexible banner. (For further information, call the 3M™ Commercial Graphics Division, 800-374-6772, ext. 205.)

Mannequins

Fashions in mannequins change along with changes in clothing fashion. Stores selling clothes may choose to display their products on hanging rods or forms, or to invest in a cast of characters that will model the clothing in a more realistic manner. A recent trend is toward modern, faceless mannequins, which circumvents the problem of dated hairstyles and makeup. The question remains, however, whether customers can really relate to these androgynous, anonymous figures.

The futuristic look is appropriate for stores selling cutting-edge, youthful fashions. More traditional stores should invest in mannequins that offer flexibility in hairstyle and poses and expect to have to replace these figures periodically to avoid a dated look. Never leave mannequins undressed even temporarily in a window or with an arm or leg off. You wouldn't want to give some small child nightmares.

Words in the Window

Signage can often pull a window together, announcing the theme or the customer benefits of the merchandise. Department stores with full-time visual merchandising staff often apply the words directly on the inside of the window, a sophisticated technique that makes the words an integral part of the display's foreground. According to Jeanne Anderson of Area Code 212 Displays in Minneapolis, most sign companies can produce individual vinyl letters to apply to the inside of the glass. Request letters that are reverse cut, or self-adhesive on the "second surface," or front side. Keep in mind that light-colored letters show up best against a dark or colorful background, and dark letters work fine against light colors. Once the letters have been applied to the window, you will need a razor blade to remove them.

Static cling also holds letters and signs onto most glass surfaces, and your local sign or art supply store may have static-cling alphabets available. These letters have the advantage of being reusable when removed and stored carefully.

Many of us use signs in the background to add words to our window displays. Letters cut out of Foamcore, painted to match the display and mounted on a sturdy background can be quite effective. Words printed on the store's computer can be blown up and mounted on Foamcore or framed.

Special events can be effectively announced using commercially made banners with vinyl letters mounted on nylon material. We use this technique twice a year for a bright window announcing our annual street festival and our clearance, or "Lemon" sale, combining the banner with a window of air-filled balloons tied to our shopping bags with colorful ribbon strings. The balloons are slightly underinflated, to allow for heat expansion. They appear to float but actually are hung from the window's ceiling using a piece of fish line taped to the top of each balloon. (See Figure 5-7.)

How Many Ways Can You Say "Sale"?

We use banners to announce our clearance sales, but there are many other creative ways to get the message across. Chain stores sometimes print special "sale" shopping bags and show mannequins carrying them. You can make use of this idea by creating "fake" sale shopping bags using color photocopies of the sale message attached to the front of five or six of your regular shopping bags. For a colorful finishing touch, tie a few balloons to the handles of the shopping bags, anchoring them to the ceiling

Figure 5-7 The lemon-yellow balloons in this window appear to float.

with fish line. Shopping bags can also be spray painted to match the color theme of other windows, with a highlighting color of tissue or fabric tucked into the top of the bag.

In Denmark, we saw a window full of mannequins each wearing a T-shirt featuring a single letter to spell out the word "udsalg" (sale) in giant type. One could also print the word *sale* on balloons, flags, kites, umbrellas or any other eye-catching prop.

Memorable Display Ideas

Whimsy and imagination are often effective elements in a window. I remember a shoe store in Chicago's Water Tower Place that was holding a preinventory clearance sale. Rather than just showing shoes with sale prices, the window dressers created a vignette with an imaginary manager's desk overflowing with inventory forms, adding machine tapes, and spilled cups of coffee. At Bennett's on Union Street in San Francisco, gardening supplies were highlighted by moss-covered men made out of flower pots. Crate & Barrel in Chicago stopped passersby with a display of glassware hot-glued onto shelves angled dangerously to look as if they were about to fall.

In our era of sophisticated computer animation, you wouldn't think that having a moving figure in the window would still captivate customers, but there still seems to be a fascination with any character that rotates, waves, or does somersaults. Perhaps it is the element of surprise, since windows are usually static. Live mannequins, who are models practiced at holding very still, always attract a crowd.

DISPLAY MISTAKES TO AVOID

A number of years ago a store near ours read that the latest trend in window displays was the use of real food. The owners put together an attractive food display promoting the napkins and glasses they sold for tailgate parties. It wasn't long before the window also featured an impressive collection of dead bees and flies. We have been guilty of putting candles in the window without thinking about what would happen to them on a hot day (they droop), and have used paper backgrounds that quickly faded in the bright sunlight. After a display has been completed, check it daily for items that may have fallen over, melted, or self-destructed. Windows should be washed regularly on the outside and cleaned on the inside whenever the display is changed.

Window designers sometimes try to communicate too much through one window display. Remember that you have only a few minutes of the viewer's attention in which to make your point. Don't make potential customers work too hard to figure out what you are trying to tell them—like the book on window design from 1970 that suggested promoting liquor-colored clothing by having "a mannequin dressed in an 'intoxicating' color pushing a baby carriage with a lovely setup of matching accessories and a few bottles of the 'genuine article,' peeping out from beneath the covers."

Avoid window displays that are too cluttered or contain too many props in comparison to the amount of merchandise featured. Conversely, windows should not be too sparse, although there has been a trend toward minimalist displays featuring very little in the way of product, props, or background. This requires a truly artistic eye to make it look intentional and not just unfinished.

Seasonal windows create a holiday spirit and are an important part of the marketing plan for many retailers. One of the greatest display challenges, especially during a busy holiday season, is making sure that no seasonal display remains up more than a day after the holiday is over. Don't let Easter chicks or Halloween ghosts outstay their welcome. Plan ahead so that a seasonal window can be dismantled immediately after a holiday and replaced right away. An empty window can quickly start rumors that your store has gone out of business.

VISUAL MERCHANDISING IN THE FUTURE

For years the press has speculated that television, catalog, and now computerized shopping would replace traditional retailing, but as long as retailers do a good job of presenting merchandise in an attractive and inviting setting, this is unlikely to happen. Customers like to see and touch most types of merchandise before buying. Good displays can also give customers ideas of how to use products in their home or how to combine and accessorize fashions. At its best, a display can be as interesting or aesthetically pleasing as a work of art. You can't say that about a bunch of products shown on a television or computer screen.

6

STAFFING YOUR STORE

Conversation at a cocktail party turned to the subject of retail stores. A guest asked Linda Alanen, our employee and neighbor, the secret of Orange Tree Imports' success. "The staff, of course," she replied. I must admit that had I been asked, I would have been tempted to take some of the credit myself, but her answer made me realize that in the eyes of our staff and many of our customers, the employees *are* the store. Your store is only as good as your staff. The selection, training, and positive reinforcement of good employees are key to creating a winning specialty shop. And since you will be spending countless hours in your store, it is important to surround yourself with people you like to be with.

DO YOU NEED EMPLOYEES?

Many new business owners try to postpone hiring employees, hoping to avoid the expense and the many government regulations and forms. But this approach is shortsighted. Not only is it impossible to grow a business without employees, but going it alone exacts a heavy toll on the business owner's personal life. The total cost of an employee, currently less than $10 an hour, is not too much to pay to provide better service for your customers and to buy yourself some free time. Without employees other than your spouse or children, you cannot afford to be sick, go on buying trips, or take vacations. This lack of time off can take a heavy toll on you, your family life, and your business. If your shop is very small, consider starting with a staff of perhaps just one or two part-time employees, provided they can work full days if you are absent.

When you decide to hire employees, you commit to meeting a weekly or biweekly payroll, no matter how slow sales are. There may be times when you must go without a paycheck yourself or borrow money in order to pay your staff. As an employer, you have a moral obligation to provide your employees with a dependable income and a safe work environment—not a responsibility to be taken lightly—but creating meaningful jobs can also be a source of great pleasure and satisfaction.

BEING THE BOSS

Few new retailers have any experience at being a boss. The role may be an uncomfortable one, especially if you did not like your last supervisor. Owning or managing a retail store is an opportunity to show just how effective a leader you can be: educating, motivating, and rewarding your employees. Keep in mind that a good boss:

- Treats employees as individuals, caring about their success.
- Routinely spends time on the sales floor.
- Is always available to employees when they need guidance, support, or just someone to talk to.
- Welcomes the input of all staff members.
- Praises the contributions, large and small, that each employee makes to the store's success.
- Is generous in rewarding employees for their efforts.

Even a good boss cannot always please everyone, but as a leader you need to make sure all employees can count on being treated fairly and with respect.

If you have never managed employees before, read some of the many books available on personnel policies and business management. Enlightened management techniques can have an enormous impact on your employees' level of job satisfaction, and you will find that a happy and enthusiastic workforce is essential for providing good customer service.

We use an unusual but effective approach to store management. The technique, *participative democracy*, is a form of business management with the basic concept that employees should have a voice in all aspects of running the business. Our staff members are privy to all our financial data and give their thoughts on major decisions, from hiring to merchandising and remodeling. The final decisions still rest with us, but in order to make this technique effective, we realize we must share some real power with our employees.

Delegating Effectively

"Giving away responsibility and authority is the ultimate expression of leadership," according to Jammie Baugh, author of *The Nordstrom Way* and an executive at Nordstrom, the department store chain often referred to as America's number 1 customer service company. It may be particularly difficult for you as a novice boss to learn to delegate responsibility, especially if you are used to doing everything yourself. An employee will rarely perform a task exactly the way you would have, but in order to be an effective leader, you must learn to give employees the authority to "own" the jobs they are doing. Changing a display or second-guessing a customer refund decision undermines staff members' confidence. There is a fine line between wanting the very best in window displays, customer service, restocking, and product selection—for the sake of the store and its customers—and wanting to let employees set their own standards for their job performance. We continue to struggle with this issue.

The day will come when you begin to delegate buying responsibility beyond just the placing of routine reorders. Buyers need to understand the focus of the shop, and the criteria you use to evaluate merchandise, so the store will retain your personal touch. It is helpful to review all orders initially, especially if you do not provide a buying budget. Don't expect every item on every order to sell well. All buyers, even you, make some mistakes.

Being able to delegate effectively is an enormous advantage. The skills and ideas that our thirty-six employees bring to Orange Tree Imports allow us to do much more than we could if Dean and I were trying to run the store alone. The variety of ages and interests of our staff members reflects the diversity of our customer base, and their varied opinions help us keep in touch with different perspectives. And because we encourage them to take on as much responsibility as possible, our employees' many talents are reflected in creative touches throughout the store.

HIRING FOR SPECIALIZED JOB FUNCTIONS

Chances are good that the first employees you hire will be salespeople. Some stores call them clerks or cashiers; we use the term *sales associates*, because it has a professional sound. A dignified title is an inexpensive perk that can make staff members feel more important. A title may seem insignificant, but consider the attitude reflected by a local department store chain's decision to refer to its sales staff as "hourly units."

As your store grows, you will need more staff to supplement your own efforts. As you develop specialized job functions, write job descriptions stating exactly what responsibilities you want these employees to take and what skills the employees will need to have. Specialty shops often employ people with the following job functions:

- Housekeeper
- Stockperson
- Bookkeeper
- Operations manager
- Manager
- Assistant manager
- Delivery person
- Personnel manager
- Buyer or purchasing agent
- Department manager
- Advertising manager
- Display coordinator/visual merchandiser

If you decide to branch out, you will need a store manager, and perhaps an assistant manager, for each location. If you have many branch stores, you may wish to have a division manager to oversee a group of stores in a specific geographic area.

When looking for employees for special job roles, experience and training become primary concerns. Almost anyone with a friendly personality; average reading, communication, and math skills; and a willingness to learn can be trained to be a sales associate, but it is preferable to hire managers with managerial experience and bookkeepers with book-keeping experience.

Skills testing may be useful for qualifying candidates for these specialized positions. Some businesses also find that personality testing is helpful in finding which candidates are best suited for a certain job. The more you can find out about each applicant, through testing or extensive interviews, the easier it will be to choose the best person for the job.

THE ROLE OF THE STORE MANAGER

Many store owners find themselves overwhelmed by the endless amount of work to be done: waiting on customers, buying merchandise, dealing with personnel issues, filling in government paperwork, and on and on. If you find there is never enough time in the day to get everything done, it is probably time to hire your first manager. Having someone to help run some aspects of the day-to-day operation will allow you to concentrate your time and energy on those tasks you do best and enjoy most, as well as freeing you up to work on the long-range, "big picture" issues facing your business.

Hiring a store manager is a special challenge because this person will represent you to your staff and customers. It is important to hire a person who shares your values and your vision of what you want your store to be. Look for someone with a level head, good listening skills, and a consistently upbeat attitude. As the owner, you need to share real responsibility and authority with the manager. Encourage the manager to be a role model, providing excellent customer service. A manager who supervises other employees should work to earn the respect of his or her coworkers by treating everyone as benevolently and fairly as you treat your staff members yourself.

It is essential to establish open communication and an easy rapport with the one or more managers you hire, creating a strong leadership team for the store. In order to keep a positive attitude, despite the challenges of the job, a manager needs your ongoing support and encouragement. Having a manager means being able to delegate many store responsibilities, but there is still a real need for you as the store owner to remain enthusiastically involved. Don't let yourself get out of touch with your customers and their needs or with your staff and their concerns.

APPEALING TO A SHRINKING WORKFORCE

The dwindling pool of candidates, especially for sales jobs, is of grave concern to all retailers. In some areas, stores compete fiercely for employees, luring staff members away from each other with the promise of higher pay and better benefits. And yet surveys of employees show that the opportunity to do meaningful work, the feeling of being appreciated, and a sense of job security are as important to workers as the hourly salary and benefits. Of course, you should check to see what other stores are paying and offer as much as you can afford in order to attract the best candidates. But look beyond money and benefits to create jobs that people will enjoy. As a specialty shop owner, you are in a position to offer:

- A pleasant work environment.
- A generous discount on merchandise.
- Flexible scheduling.
- Opportunities for employee input.
- Seasonal employment.
- Social interaction with customers and fellow staff members.
- Creative work, such as designing displays.

These perks will automatically make your job listing more appealing to most people than job openings at a fast food restaurant or large chain store. If you can also provide better wages and benefits, who would choose to flip burgers instead of working in your store? The main competition for quality employees, however, comes not from fast food restaurants, other retailers, and service businesses but from companies offering considerably higher salaries and opportunities for advancement. Retailing, especially at the sales associate level, simply can't support the same wages as what my staff sometimes jokingly refers to as "real jobs." This means that employees may not plan to stay very long as sales associates, or even in higher-level retailing positions, if there are opportunities for better-paying jobs elsewhere.

A specialty shop has to work hard to retain these employees by making their work more enjoyable than the alternatives. Although we do have turnover every year, I'm very pleased that we also have three employees who have been with us over fifteen years. We celebrate staff loyalty by presenting employees with a silver orange tree pin on their fifth work anniversary and a gold one on their tenth. For every five years beyond that, a semiprecious orange stone is added. We celebrate the annual anniversary of each employee's date of hire with a thank-you card and either flowers or a restaurant gift certificate.

One way to keep employees is to offer opportunities for advancement. A small shop may have limited jobs to fill, but if branches are in the store's future, there may be opportunities for sales staff to advance to store management positions. Even with just one location, we are able to help employees train to do product buying or to take on new roles such as cooking school director, display coordinator, or bookkeeper. Employees who stay on can be rewarded with salary raises, especially as they take on more responsibility, and added paid vacation and sick days.

WHERE TO FIND GOOD EMPLOYEES

Traditionally, most applicants find out about retail jobs by reading the daily or weekly newspaper job listings. There was a time when a small ad would draw dozens of candidates. To attract good applicants in today's tight labor market, ads must be larger (which can be quite expensive—help wanted listings are a gold mine for newspapers) and more enticing. Romance the job and the excitement of working in your store, and be sure to mention the salary and benefits if they are attractive. Don't forget to specify the type of experience and skills you are looking for. Not only will this help you attract qualified candidates, but lack of experience can often be used to soften the sting of rejection to those who don't get hired.

Colleges, technical schools, and local high schools may have placement offices that will post job listings for you or even provide work-study training programs that allow students to get credit for time on the job. Students placed with a store as part of a course in retailing or business may well be interested in staying on after graduation.

Your state unemployment office may advertise job openings for you. Your community may also have a program for retirees looking for part-time work; as McDonald's has discovered, senior citizens often make excellent employees. For management positions, you might consider using an employment agency, although these services are often quite costly.

Ask your current employees if they have friends looking for work. If you notice someone giving exceptional service in a restaurant or even another retail store, you might slip the person your card in case he or she is interested in making a job change. Of course, the employee you lure away from another employer may leave you suddenly if a better offer comes along.

Should you hire family members or friends? Some authorities say no, cautioning that the employer-employee relationship may damage the personal relationship or that any favoritism shown toward the friend or family member will be resented by other staff members. Be sure that the person you hire is qualified for the job you offer and understands that you both will need to be able to relate to each other in a business-like manner. You may find it difficult to criticize employees who are friends or relatives or to assign them tasks they don't like. Although we are guilty of ignoring this rule, most authorities advise, "Don't hire someone you can't fire."

One of the best ways to advertise a job opening is to post a notice on your store door or in the store. Current customers who have shown an interest in your store and its merchandise may enjoy working in a shop they know they like. Some businesses put up large "help wanted" signs that are visible from the street, but I prefer something more discreet. You don't want to broadcast the fact that you are short staffed or that someone just quit. Out of respect for your current staff, don't post their hourly salary on the job opening notice. This is a matter that can be discussed with applicants later or mentioned in a memo attached to the application form. We find it useful to also list the job description and hours on a memo, so applicants know what we are looking for in terms of experience and availability.

Using Temporary Agencies

Hiring a temporary employee through an agency has many advantages: you can get help quickly, you don't have to do the initial screening of candidates yourself, and the agency takes care of the payroll paperwork. Employees acquired through an agency cost more per hour because of the agency fee, and, unfortunately, most retail jobs require more training, and trust, than the routine tasks usually assigned to temps. Still, keep temporary agencies in mind if you need short-term help with data entry, special projects, or physical work such as moving stock to a new warehouse.

THE HIRING PROCESS

Careful hiring can result in lower turnover of employees and a happier, more compatible staff. A written job application is useful for providing background information, and one or two in-person interviews will allow you to get acquainted with the applicant. Of course even two face-to-face interviews cannot tell you everything there is to know about a potential employee, but this process should give you some idea of each applicant's strengths and weaknesses, and how interested he or she is in the job.

The Application Form

The government doesn't care much about what merchandise you buy, how you display it, and whether you empty the trash each night, but it cares a great deal about almost all matters relating to employees. The application form you use to screen potential employees may *not* ask questions about marital status, age (unless under eighteen), sex or sexual orientation, race, religion, national origin, and whether the applicant has children. It is illegal to discriminate against potential employees on most of these grounds, so of course these same issues may not be discussed when interviewing candidates.

So what can you ask? Name, address, and telephone number are basic. I used to eliminate candidates who forgot to include their zip code, because I thought it showed a lack of attention to detail. Today's retail shops cannot afford to be so picky. Past work history and education are also important questions. We don't require a certain amount of education or experience, but this information gives us an idea of the applicants' interests and whether they have successfully completed a degree or held a job for some length of time. You may also ask about limitations that specifically apply to performing the essential functions of the job. A stockperson, for example, needs to be able to lift packages weighing over thirty pounds, but a bookkeeper does not. Unless the job schedule is completely flexible, ask about available hours, so you will know if the applicant can work during the times you need to fill.

Applicants should also provide the name, address, and telephone number of three references other than family members and friends. Past work references are seldom a source of much information now that companies are afraid of being sued for libel if they give a negative reference. Nevertheless, these past employers will at least confirm the dates of past employment and the salary range; if nothing else, this information proves that the candidate has told the truth about past work experience.

A sample job application is shown in Figure 6-1 for you to personalize and copy for your store's use. It was adapted by our personnel manager, Connie Nadler, using other application forms as samples. There are

Figure 6-1 Sample employment application.

Application for Employment

Prospective employees will receive consideration without discrimination because of race, creed, sex, age, sexual orientation, national origin, handicap or veteran status.

Last Name	First	Middle	Date

Street Address	Home Telephone ( )

City, State, Zip	Business Telephone ( )

Position Desired	Number of Hours Desired Weekly: Minimum: Maximum:	Salary Desired

Please list all commitments such as classes, other employment, meetings, extended trips, etc.

Are you legally eligible for employment in the United States? ☐ Yes ☐ No

Do you have any physical limitations that preclude you from performing any work for which you are being considered? If so, please explain.

Education

School	Name and Location of School	Course of Study	No. of Years Completed	Did You Graduate?	Degree or Diploma
Graduate					
College					
Business/ Trade					
High School					

Retail and Other Relevant Experience

Please indicate retail and volunteer experience relevant to this position.

Figure 6-1 (*continued*)

Employment and Military Service

List below your last three employers, starting with your present or most recent employer. Please give accurate, complete full-time, part-time and military employment information.

Company Name and Phone Number		Employment Dates - State month and year From To
Address		Rate of Pay
Name of Supervisor or Other Work Reference	Position	Reason for Leaving
State Job Title and Describe Your Work Duties		

Company Name and Phone Number		Employment Dates - State month and year From To
Address		Rate of Pay
Name of Supervisor or Other Work Reference	Position	Reason for Leaving
State Job Title and Describe Your Work Duties		

Company Name and Phone Number		Employment Dates - State month and year From To
Address		Rate of Pay
Name of Supervisor or Other Work Reference	Position	Reason for Leaving
State Job Title and Describe Your Work Duties		

We may contact the employers listed above unless you indicate those you do not want us to contact.	**DO NOT CONTACT:** Name: Reason:

Signature

The information provided in this Application of Employment is true, correct, and complete. If employed, any misstatement or omission of fact on this application may result in my dismissal.

I understand that acceptance of an offer of employment does not create a contractual obligation upon the employer to continue to employ me in the future.

Date   Signature

also generic application forms available by mail order or in office supply stores. These forms have the advantage of being revised constantly for compliance with federal and state regulations and are worth reviewing periodically to be sure your form is current.

Reviewing the Applications

A competitive job market requires you to act quickly on applications that look particularly promising. A delay of a few weeks may mean that the applicant has already been hired by another business. Look over the application for neatness and completeness as well as content. Any retail experience is of course a plus, as is any work or volunteer experience requiring interaction with the public. Very few applicants have academic qualifications that specifically apply to retailing, but a high level of education does reflect a capacity to learn and to commit to a program. Long-term commitment is something we value in an employee, especially since it is much more expensive to hire and train someone new than to retain a good employee.

Look for consistency in the education and job history. We once had an applicant with an unexplained ten-year gap in his work record. When we asked what he'd been doing those ten years, he replied that he didn't remember. Needless to say, he didn't get the job. Another applicant said she had been working on a cruise ship for two years, but we later found out she'd been in jail during that time period.

The application doesn't reflect the most important qualities of an employee—enthusiasm and a willingness to learn the job, to work hard, to serve customers, and to be a member of a team. For this reason, all applicants who meet the basic qualifications should be interviewed in person.

Preliminary Interviews

Our interviewing process reflects our participative democracy management style. One of the most important elements in the success of this approach is the entire staff's involvement in the interviewing process, hiring, and employee training. We have used this technique for many years, so all of our current employees have been hired by their colleagues.

The preliminary interview is usually done by the personnel manager, myself, and either another manager or a full-time employee. The candidates are invited to come for about a twenty-minute meeting in our office. The questions we ask are similar to those that are on the application form, plus some open-ended queries such as, "Tell us about an achievement you are particularly proud of" and "Give us an example of how you handled a difficult situation in one of your previous jobs." The applicant is given a chance to talk informally and to ask us questions about the job. The key to good interviewing is to put the candidate at ease and allow him or her to talk as much as possible.

The Staff Interview

The three or four candidates selected for second interviews after the first screening are asked to come before the store opens for a staff interview. As many as fifteen of our current employees usually attend these informal interviews, and all of those present have been hired in this way. We sit in a circle and meet with one candidate at a time, asking the applicant to tell us a bit about himself or herself. The staff is free to ask anything they want, except of course about topics prohibited by law. Questions range from, "What book would you take to a desert island?" to "Do you like to cook?" In the interest of fairness, we plant certain standardized questions so that every candidate is asked some of the same questions.

One employee usually tells the candidate a bit about what it's like to work at Orange Tree Imports and describes what the job entails. After the last candidate has left, the staff discusses the notes they have taken and then votes, by secret ballot (if it looks like it will be a close vote) or a show of hands.

Some candidates find it very intimidating to face a large group, and we take their nervousness into account when evaluating their interview performance. Positive details from the first interview will be brought up if the applicant appeared poised in front of two or three interviewers but not the entire staff. We look for indications that the candidate really wants to work at Orange Tree Imports, as evidenced by a positive attitude and by good grooming for the interview. The stress of the staff interview is not unlike facing a number of customers all wanting immediate attention, so the process helps us see if the candidate is comfortable talking with strangers.

The staff has a vested interest in the success of the new coworkers they have selected. The new employees come on the job having already met a number of the staff members and with the knowledge that their coworkers want them to be there. Of course, as with any other democratic voting process, candidates are sometimes selected by a narrow margin, but most staff members are comfortable with the concept of the majority vote ruling. I can think of one instance, however, when some members of the staff were so vehemently opposed to the final candidate for personnel manager that we started the application process over again.

Yes, even the personnel manager is hired by staff interview. The only exceptions to this process have been technical positions, such as bookkeeper, and employees who work when the store is closed, such as the housekeeper. Occasionally seasonal help is hired by a smaller staff committee, but we are committed to the idea of having employees hire employees.

We usually do not check references until after the selection process is completed. That same day, we make the references calls and offer the job to the candidates the staff has chosen as soon as we are able to get in touch with their references. Those not selected are given the courtesy of a telephone call and their applications are kept on file for future consideration.

GOVERNMENT FORMS FOR NEW EMPLOYEES

The first day on the job for a new employee involves a certain amount of paperwork. Your business will need to have obtained a federal EIN (Employer Identification Number) and W-4 forms for employees to fill in specifying their tax status, number of dependents, and federal tax withholding allowances. If your state has its own income tax, and most do, you will need to withhold state taxes. The W-4 form provides a space for the number of deductions being claimed for state as well as federal taxes.

A relatively recent requirement is that the employer have proof that the employee is legally entitled to work in the United States, as required on INS (Immigration and Naturalization Service) form I-9. Ask the new employee to bring one of the following:

- U.S. passport.
- Certificate of U.S. Citizenship or Naturalization.
- INS Forms 688 or 688a.
- A social security card or government-issued birth certificate, and proof of identity (e.g., driver's license, school photo ID, voter registration card).

"I'm sorry, but a Mickey Mouse Club card is just not acceptable proof of U.S. employment eligibility."

A number of other documents, such as a Native American tribal document, may also be used. If you have questions, call the U.S. Department of Justice or the INS information line (800-755-0777). The fine for hiring someone not eligible for employment in the United States can be stiff. The Immigration Reform and Control Act, which requires employers to establish their employees' right to work in the United States, also prohibits discrimination on the basis of national origin or citizenship.

THE EMPLOYMENT AGREEMENT

There is no government requirement that you have an employment agreement, or contract, but it does make good business sense. Spelling out the compensation you are offering an employee can avoid future misunderstandings. Stating your expectations lets an employee know exactly what the job entails. There is a sample employment agreement shown in Figure 6-2 for you to copy.

Figure 6-2 Sample employee agreement.

EMPLOYMENT AGREEMENT
(Complete form in duplicate: one copy for the employer; one copy for the employee.)

EMPLOYEE'S NAME _____

Starting date _____ Full time/Part time _____

JOB TITLE _____
See attached list for details of duties and responsibilities

PRACTICE WORK SCHEDULE (Your hours will be scheduled within these times.)

Usual days per week: S _____ M _____ Tu _____ W _____ Thur _____ F _____ S _____

Usual working hours: _____ to _____ Lunch _____ Breaks _____

Work schedules are posted _____

COMPENSATION

Starting rate: _____ Pay days are: _____

Basis for increases: _____

Vacation days: _____ Sick days: _____ Personal time: _____

Additional benefits _____

PERIODIC PERFORMANCE EVALUATION

Provisional employees will be evaluated _____

All other employees will be evaluated _____

TERMINATION

For each new employee, the first _____ weeks are a provisional period of employment.
During this time, the new employee may leave or be dismissed without notice.

After this period, the employee is expected to give _____ weeks notice.
If dismissed, the employee will receive _____ weeks notice or the equivalent in severance pay.

In the event of fraud, theft, illegal drug use, or unprofessional conduct, the employee will be
dismissed without notice or severance pay.

_____   _____
          Employee's signature   Employer's signature

156

Many employee contracts include a *noncompete clause* in the contract, asking that employees promise not to open a competing store within a certain distance of the employer's store within a year or two of leaving. Although these clauses often prove difficult to enforce legally, there is no reason not to request that at least those in managerial positions make this promise. Unfortunately it does sometimes happen that an employee privy to inside information uses that knowledge to open a new business or to benefit a future employer.

The employment agreement also usually states how often employee evaluations will be held and spells out the conditions for termination. It is standard to request that employees give two weeks notice when leaving and to promise an equivalent amount of notice, or severance pay, if the employee is dismissed for reasons other than fraud, theft, illegal drug use, or unprofessional conduct.

In addition to the employment agreement and the W-4 and I-9 forms, we ask new employees to fill in an emergency contact form. These forms, kept in the employees' personnel files, give us telephone numbers of close relatives or friends to contact in case of emergency. A sample of this form is shown in Figure 6-3.

Two Weeks on Trial

Two interviews are better than one, but even after two interviews, you will know very little about how well a new applicant will work out. Keep in mind that the process of dismissing an employee is difficult and often costly. Put your best effort into the hiring process, and if you don't find a candidate you and your staff are comfortable with, continue the search until you do. You can also insist on a two-week trial period for the new employee. This offers both the employer and the employee an easy out if the fit is not right. If a serious problem, such as tardiness, a negative attitude, or poor work habits, turns up during the first two weeks, the conditional period allows both parties to sever the relationship without having to give the usual two weeks notice or written warnings.

It is essential to let the employee know at the time of hiring if the first two weeks will be considered a trial period. The new employee may have quit another job in order to take the one at your shop, so dismissal even during the short trial period can be very problematic. Be sure that the employee has agreed to the idea of a trial period and that you and the staff do everything possible to make the person a successful member of the team.

Figure 6-3 Sample employee emergency contact form.

EMPLOYEE EMERGENCY CONTACT FORM

EMPLOYEE_____

ADDRESS_____

CITY AND STATE_____

PHONE:_____HOME_____WORK

SOCIAL SECURITY NUMBER_____

BIRTH DATE:_____

....

IN CASE OF EMERGENCY:

CALL:_____

PHONE:_____HOME_____WORK

OR:_____

PHONE:_____HOME_____WORK

ALLERGIES, MEDICAL PROBLEMS OR OTHER

IMPORTANT INFORMATION:_____

_____

TRAINING THE NEW EMPLOYEE

After filling in the necessary forms on the first day of work, our new employees are taken on a tour of the store, introduced to some of the staff, and given their own copy of the store's employee handbook. The actual job training is spread out over a week or two, because there is too much for anyone to learn in a few days. Our personnel manager conducts the procedures and product knowledge training, working from one of the training checklists to make sure nothing is missed.

The training checklist varies from job to job, but for sales associates, it includes cash register training and information about a myriad of small procedures, from selling gift certificates to calculating out-of-state shipping charges. We even include details such as what we want employees to say when answering the telephone and what my real name is. (This may seem silly, but since most people call me by my nickname, Orange, we have had several instances of new employees turning sales reps away when they ask for Carol Schroeder.) We cover important topics relating to customer service and help employees begin to be familiar with the benefits of all our products and how to find various types of merchandise in the store and stockroom.

At Office Depot, product location is taught during the initial training period using a treasure hunt approach and then reinforced through a quarterly, noncompetitive game. Sales staff members are given an opportunity to win movie passes by completing a quiz asking the location of sixty different items. Every employee who gets all the answers right wins.

Procedures are explained and demonstrated, and then the new employees practice them. Some of this training takes place when the store is closed, so the cash registers are available for practice. Role playing is used as a training method, with the personnel manager and new employee taking turns pretending to sell each other items, handle refunds, and correct mistakes. It is essential that these skills are practiced, not just explained. As the Chinese proverb says, "I hear and I forget. I see and I remember. I do and I understand."

After the initial training period, a sales associate is assigned to shadow an experienced staff member for several shifts. This buddy system allows the other staff members to get involved in training new employees and gives the new person a specific coworker to turn to with questions. We encourage new employees to ask questions. There is a lot to learn, and no one gets it all the first time.

After two weeks on the job, each new employee is given an evaluation. This is an opportunity for the personnel manager to sit down with the person and ask if there are any areas of the training process that need more work and to review the employee's first weeks of job performance. This is also a good opportunity to build the employee's self-confidence, pointing out how much he or she has already learned. Sometimes new staff members are a bit worried at this point, because they realize they don't know everything and can't remember some of the procedures they've been taught. We try to reassure them that it can take as long as a whole year to feel comfortable with all aspects of the store's operations.

THE EMPLOYEE HANDBOOK

My informal poll of small shop owners revealed that a surprisingly low percentage have employee handbooks or manuals. I wonder how the employees of these stores know what standards of behavior and appearance they are expected to live up to and what the store's policies are regarding issues that concern the staff, such as sick leave, paid holidays, and salary increases. For the sake of consistency and clarity, many personnel issues should be addressed in a handbook that can be given to each new employee.

In keeping with our participative democracy mode of management, we developed our first employee handbook many years ago with the input of a staff committee. Everyone who wanted to serve on the committee was welcome, and a group of five or six of us spent several months hammering out the store's first policy statements on such issues as dress code, tardiness, employee evaluations, and maternity leave. The process could have been abbreviated by not seeking staff input, but then the policies might not have been as willingly followed by our employees. Employees will support policies they help to create.

Our employee handbook starts out with a brief history of the store and a *mission statement*, which establishes goals for the staff to work toward as a team. A mission statement also reflects the philosophy of the business, and in some cases it may be worth posting for customers to see. Felissimo, a New York shop that refers to itself as a "specialty department store," includes a copy of its mission statement in the catalog it sends out to customers across the country; see Figure 6-4.

The remainder of the employee handbook is devoted to brief, clear statements about personnel policies and employee benefits, including, but not limited to:

- Payroll procedures
- Paid vacation and sick days
- Parental and adoption leaves
- Overtime policy
- Employee discounts
- Health, life, and other insurance
- Sales bonuses
- Opportunities for advancement and raises

Figure 6-4 Sample mission statement.

The Felissimo Philosophy

In the heart of one of the world's great metropolises, FELISSIMO has transformed a turn-of-the-century townhouse into an elegant, harmonious oasis that's almost timeless in feeling. We're dedicated to providing a new kind of shopping experience, one where beauty, art, function, and sophistication combine. We're committed to offering unique merchandise that's compatible with the natural environment. We showcase innovative designs that minimize waste and emphasize renewable, recyclable materials. We support and encourage designers whose work embodies these principles. We guarantee attentive, unobtrusive service. We look to employees who embrace our standards. We strive to help maintain the earth's delicate balance, not disrupt it. We seek out customers who share our concerns and our aesthetic. And we welcome their suggestions on how FELISSIMO can be a force for good in the world.

- Breaks
- Personal telephone calls
- Continuing education
- Business trip reimbursement
- Termination, exit interviews
- Drug and alcohol use policies
- Dress code
- Scheduling
- Changes in part-time or full-time status

The information contained in the employee handbook is intended as a guideline for all staff members. We try not to be too restrictive in the wording; it is not intended to sound like the Ten Commandments. Staff members can bring any policy up for review at any time, and in fact the entire handbook is revised periodically.

Dress Code and Name Tags

Customers appreciate being able to identify a store's personnel by the way they are dressed or by the name tags they wear. Some stores carry out the shop's theme in the employees' dress—for example, having all the staff wear referee shirts, lab coats, denim shirts and khaki slacks, or gardening aprons. I must admit that I've never been able to convince my staff that smocks and name tags are a good idea, much as I admire the effect in other shops. It is difficult to find a uniform that everyone thinks looks good on them, and some employees don't want customers to call them by their first names.

At Olson's Flower Shop in Mount Horeb, Wisconsin, employees are given a choice of floral pseudonyms for their name tags: Pansy, Rose, Daisy, and Fern.

A store that chooses not to provide an apron, T-shirt, smock, lab coat, or other uniform for its employees still needs to have a dress code for staff members. We keep ours very simple: no blue jeans or torn pants, no shorts, no T-shirts or sweatshirts with writing on them, no worn running shoes, and no low-cut or revealing clothing.

The employee handbook states that everyone is expected to practice good hygiene, and male staff members are required to shave, unless they have a beard. Employees are not allowed to chew gum while waiting on customers. By spelling out these details in the handbook, we hope to avoid having to criticize an employee's appearance. It isn't so bad to tell someone that they've priced an item incorrectly, but to ask an employee to go home and change clothes is an embarrassment for us both.

FLEXIBLE SCHEDULING

When your store first opens, it may be difficult to predict how many sales associates will be needed at any one time or to know how many hours a week specialized jobs such as bookkeeping will take. Many businesses, especially restaurants, hire more people than they actually need, on the assumption that a percentage will leave within the first month or two. If they don't, everyone's hours get cut back. It is better to hire a reasonable number of employees, favoring those who can be flexible in the hours they work. Employees willing to work fifteen to thirty hours can start out at fifteen and work more as the store gets busy.

With time, customer patterns will develop that make it easier to know how many staff members will be needed on certain days of the week or even at certain times of day. We know that Saturdays are always our busiest day of the week, for example, and that we need extra help the day before Valentine's Day. These are all factors for the person doing the hiring and scheduling to take into account. Payroll is usually a store's highest operating expense, so it makes sense to schedule efficiently. Use cash register records to determine which times of day and days of the week are busiest and which months require extra sales staff.

To make more efficient use of sales associates during slower hours, such as 2:00 to 4:00, we purchased a vibrating beeper that is set up with a speed dial number. When the employee at the cash register needs the assistance of the sales associate who is off working on a display or unpacking merchandise, he or she merely presses a few numbers in our phone system and hangs up. The message is relayed via satellite to the beeper on the second employee, who immediately returns to the counter.

Our staff is made up of both full-time and part-time employees. The full-time employees work thirty to forty hours a week, providing a wonderful sense of continuity by their being at the store so much. All of the full-time employees have duties beyond customer service, and as a result, these staff members are paid at a somewhat higher hourly rate. We also have a number of employees who work twenty to thirty hours a week, a position we call "special part-time." These employees have a real commitment to the store, despite the fact that they don't want to work full time. Some of our "special part-time" employees have been with us for many years, and all of them manage at least one department. Our very part-time staff is key to being able to offer flexible scheduling, because they fill in as needed and work more hours during vacations and the busy season. We also hire seasonal help for late November and December, ideally getting started with their hiring and training in late October.

We realize that flexible scheduling is one of the strong appeals of working at our store, but setting up a schedule that makes everyone happy is a major challenge for the personnel manager. We change the schedule four times a year, following the academic year for those in school or with children, plus a special holiday schedule to fill the extra hours we are open in December. Employees are invited to submit schedule requests, and we make every effort to accommodate them all. Weekdays are divided into two shifts, 10:00–2:00 and 2:00–6:00, plus the evenings when we're open late. These four-hour units allow us to schedule those who want to work partial days, as well as those who want a full eight-hour day. Anyone working eight hours needs a lunch or dinner break, which is usually covered by having a half-day worker come in early or stay late.

Employees who have paid vacation time as part of their compensation package are encouraged to schedule their vacations early and to avoid taking them during our busiest months, November and December. We do have a problem with too many employees wanting time off in August, so we ask that staff members try to schedule summer vacations in June and July. Some stores allow those with the most seniority to have first choice of vacation dates.

Weekends are the busiest time for most retail stores, and Saturdays and Sundays can be very difficult to staff. We make working weekends more appealing by splitting Saturday into two shifts, and by setting up an "A" and "B" weekend schedule, so employees have the option of working every other weekend. Dean and I work most Saturdays ourselves. Without the distraction of sales reps and telephone calls, Saturdays provide an excellent opportunity for us to have direct customer contact. We take Sunday and Monday off as our weekend together.

Job Sharing

Almost all of our specialized job functions are job shared—we have two bookkeepers, three stockpersons, and a management team—both the store and the employees benefit from this flexible arrangement. The essential work of an area does not come to a halt if someone is sick or on vacation, and staff members have someone to share their work load with. Parents enjoy being able to be home when children return from school or to stay home with a sick child. Usually those sharing a job develop a close rapport, working out on their own how to divide the tasks at hand and even sometimes setting up their own schedule.

A number of years ago we had a problem with a bookkeeper who fell desperately behind in her work, hiding the mounting bills and other problems from us. When we hired someone to job-share her position, it became impossible for her to conceal her inability to handle her part of the job. We made the painful decision to terminate her but have continued since that time to have two people in the bookkeeping department.

COMPENSATING EMPLOYEES

There are two basic methods of compensating employees: salary and commission. Most stores pay an hourly salary, plus some benefits at least for full-time employees, such as life and health insurance, sick days, and paid vacations. Others pay sales associates commissions based on sales, and some use a combination of the two methods. The commission method is generally practical only for stores providing one-on-one customer service to sell high-priced items such as electronics, expensive clothing, and furniture.

The advantage of paying commissions is that employees' income is directly tied to their job performance. Commissioned compensation encourages staff members to develop a customer base and to serve those customers well. But it does not always encourage team spirit, and commissioned salespeople can sometimes be too aggressive in their sales techniques. Stores such as Nordstrom pay an hourly salary plus commission, requiring employees to achieve a minimum average amount of sales per hour to justify their base hourly pay. Those unable to live up to this standard are either terminated or moved to nonsales positions.

An alternative to the commission system is to offer special rewards or bonuses as incentives for exemplary sales and service. Many retailers treat employees to lunch or give staff members a day off with pay when they reach specific sales goals. We add a dollar to the hourly base pay of employees performing certain "extra credit" tasks, such as doing a main window display or assisting with a cooking school class. In order to encourage sales assistants to substitute for each other, we give employees a "sub shift voucher" for every shift they take; ten vouchers entitles the employee to a $25 bonus.

Managers are often salaried, that is, paid a flat amount no matter how many hours they work. Sometimes a monetary bonus is added to the manager's salary, based on annual sales or on achieving certain sales goals or increases. This is especially appropriate if the manager is in charge of a branch store's operations and can be a prime motivation in attracting and keeping good managerial staff.

Overtime Regulations

We learned the hard way about the federal requirement that any employee, salaried or hourly, be paid overtime, or one and a half times the normal hourly rate, for all time beyond forty hours in a seven-day period. This law also applies to salaried employees who do not qualify as exempt under the labor standards laws. Unfortunately, in the United States a single-location specialty shop with the owner present, no matter how large, cannot exempt a salaried manager from overtime compensation. We were recently audited by the Department of Wages and Hours and had to go back through all our payroll records from the past few years. Even companies with branch stores must prove that the duties of the branch managers are at least 80 percent managerial, as opposed to such work as customer service and merchandising.

Needless to say, paying time (the hourly salary) and a half increases payroll costs significantly. We have always tried to avoid overtime by requiring employees to notify us in writing in advance of going over the forty-hour limit, so that we can try to replace them on the work schedule. The government takes a firm line on making sure no more than forty hours fall within a seven-day period. Your employees may not work thirty-nine hours one week and forty-one the next, even if you use a two-week pay period. Extra time worked during a busy week may not be saved up and used as time off during a slower week, unless it is repaid at time and a half (three hours of paid time off to compensate for two hours of overtime).

There are also special restrictions involved in hiring minors, and these regulations may be different at the state and federal level. Be sure to check how many hours high school students are allowed to work on school days and other restrictions. The fines for disobeying these regulations, even inadvertently, can run into thousands of dollars.

Payroll Procedures

Computer software and outside payroll service bureaus can take much of the headache out of producing payroll checks with the correct amounts deducted and then paying the government all the taxes and contributions due in a timely manner. Payroll checks may need to have state, federal, and possibly even local taxes withheld, and as an employer you will need to match your employees' contributions to FICA (social security) and Medicare. You are also responsible for paying state and federal unemployment taxes. There are strict deadlines for reporting and paying all of these taxes, and it will save a lot of grief if you set up a tight system of payroll accounting from the start. Falling behind in tax reporting or, worse yet, in making the required deposits or payments on taxes can result in heavy penalties. The government can put a lien on your business and will add significant interest to the amount you owe for every day you are late.

You may choose to pay your employees once a week, biweekly, or even monthly. Ask them to keep track of their hours on special time cards, conveniently located near their coats or lockers. The information gathered on these forms is essential for preparing the payroll, and it is useful for planning future staffing. We ask employees to give us a breakdown of how their time is spent, so we know what percentage of our payroll goes toward sales, restocking, meetings, bookkeeping, our cooking school, and other activities. Vacation and sick days are also noted on the time card, and entered on the employee's file when the payroll is compiled. An example of our time card is provided in Figure 6-5.

This honor system has always worked well for us, but some businesses feel more secure using a time clock to track employee hours. Staff members are given a form or code number to punch into the clock when they arrive and when they leave, so work hours are recorded with minute precision. A time clock, however, does not provide any information about how the employee's time is spent.

Be sure to keep all payroll records, including time cards, for the unhappy eventuality of a government audit. Some authorities recommend keeping these items for as long as seven or eight years.

Figure 6-5 Sample time card.

Time card for:_____

Period from _____to _____19____

number of hours worked

MONDAY ☐ 10-2 shift (4.25 hrs) ☐ 2-6 shift (4 hours) _____
other counter hours: from _____ to _____ _____
additional:task code ____ from _____ to _____ _____
task code ____ from _____ to _____ _____
☐ SICK PAY ☐ HOLIDAY ☐ VACATION _____

TUESDAY ☐ 10-2 shift (4.25 hrs) ☐ 2-6 shift (4) _____
other counter hours: from _____ to _____ _____
additional:task code ____ from _____ to _____ _____
task code ____ from _____ to _____ _____
☐ SICK PAY ☐ HOLIDAY ☐ VACATION _____

WEDNESDAY ☐ 10-2 shift (4.25 hrs) ☐ 2-6 shift (4) _____
other counter hours: from _____ to _____ _____
additional:task code ____ from _____ to _____ _____
task code ____ from _____ to _____ _____
☐ SICK PAY ☐ HOLIDAY ☐ VACATION _____

THURSDAY ☐ 10-2 shift (4.25 hrs) ☐ 2-6 shift (4) _____
other counter hours: from _____ to _____ _____
additional:task code ____ from _____ to _____ _____
task code ____ from _____ to _____ _____
☐ SICK PAY ☐ HOLIDAY ☐ VACATION _____

FRIDAY ☐ 10-2 shift (4.25 hrs) ☐ 2-6 shift (4 hours) _____
other counter hours: from _____ to _____ _____
additional:task code ____ from _____ to _____ _____
task code ____ from _____ to _____ _____
☐ SICK PAY ☐ HOLIDAY ☐ VACATION _____

SATURDAY ☐ 10-2 shift (4.25 hrs) ☐ 2-6 shift (4) _____
other counter hours: from _____ to _____ _____
additional:task code ____ from _____ to _____ _____
task code ____ from _____ to _____ _____
☐ SICK PAY ☐ HOLIDAY ☐ VACATION _____

SUNDAY counter hours: from _____ to _____ _____
additional:task code ____ from _____ to _____ _____
task code ____ from _____ to _____ _____
☐ SICK PAY ☐ HOLIDAY ☐ VACATION _____

GRAND TOTAL_____

Task Codes: (non sales counter hours only) H=Housekeeping,
B=Bookkeeping, D=Departments (restocking, ordering), W=Window Display,
G=Group Meetings/Seminars, S=Stock/Shipping, M=Management

BENEFITS AND PERKS

The hourly or annual salary is usually only one component of employee compensation. Some of the other benefits, such as paid time off for illness or vacation, and health, disability, and life insurance, are commonly granted to employees in big businesses. A small specialty shop may be hesitant to take on the cost of these perks, but without offering benefits, it becomes more and more difficult to compete for quality employees.

One solution is to offer a two-tiered system, with part-time employees receiving a lower level of benefits than those working at the store full time. Many of our part-time employees have full-time jobs elsewhere that provide them with insurance and other key benefits, or perhaps their spouse has a family insurance policy. Our full-time and even half-time staff do not have many other options if we do not come through with a decent benefits package.

Insuring Your Employees—and Yourself

It is ultimately in the best interest of employers to have a workforce that is protected by insurance against life's catastrophes. Some types of insurance to protect your employees, such as workers' compensation, are mandated by state law. *Workers' compensation insurance* provides disability coverage and life insurance benefits to employees injured on the job. Fortunately retailing is not inherently dangerous, so the premiums are not as high as they would be for, say, construction work. The amount of workers' compensation is based on the total payroll, and coverage does not include the store owner in the case of sole proprietorships. In some states workers' compensation is sold through a government program; in others it may be obtained through your insurance agent.

Most state governments collect *unemployment insurance* to fund payments to workers who are laid off. The cost is based on your total payroll and the long-term record of how many of your past employees have collected from the business's unemployment fund. We learned—again, the hard way—that the rules governing this program are complex. We lost over $5,000 from our fund by not having our lawyer help us read a form summoning us to a hearing about an employee who had collected unemployment from her former full-time employer, while she worked only the legally permitted four to five hours a week for us. (Next time I will seek legal assistance even if I think I understand the situation.)

Health Insurance Options

Having seen our health insurance costs rise astronomically in the past seven years, it is easy to understand the reluctance of many retailers to offer this coverage. But by the same token, it is the lack of benefits like health insurance that makes retailing an unattractive field for some top-quality candidates. It is also a dilemma for a caring business owner to see an employee suffer through a serious illness without adequate health care coverage.

There are many choices of health care programs available today, and most shops should be able to offer to provide at least partial coverage to its full-time employees. If your store is too small for a group policy, consider purchasing insurance through a local or national association, or getting together with other businesses to create your own group. The chamber of commerce in your area might also be able to help.

We belong to a health maintenance organization, which encourages our staff to get regular checkups and routine care, since there is no extra charge for these services. Our company policy is to pay 100 percent of the health insurance for those who work thirty or more hours a week and 25 percent of the cost for those who work twenty to thirty hours. This year we added co-pay prescription coverage, which requires the individual to pay only a small portion of each prescription. We do not, however, offer dental insurance because the cost is beyond our reach.

Disability and Life Insurance

Disability insurance for staff members is sometimes overlooked by new entrepreneurs, but statistics show that a disabling illness or injury is more likely to occur than an untimely death. Policies with a relatively long waiting period before benefits are paid are less expensive than those that begin at thirty or sixty days, but it is important to look for a policy that will continue to pay benefits until retirement age or death.

Life insurance may not be a very attractive benefit in the eyes of young employees, but it is not expensive to provide a small amount of coverage, such as the equivalent of a year's salary. We provide disability and life insurance for all our full-time employees. Term life insurance can be purchased as part of a package of employee insurance benefits or as a separate policy.

When selecting disability and life insurance for your staff, don't forget to check about extra coverage for yourself. If you are unable to work or if you die, the effect on the business and your family can be cata-strophic. Providing an adequate amount of insurance can cushion the blow. You might also consider *key-person* or *key-executive* insurance, which specifically protects the business, as the beneficiary, against loss in the event of your disability or death. The premiums for this insurance are not deductible as a business expense; however, if benefits are ever paid, they are tax free. Business loans often require a certain amount of this type of insurance in order to protect the interests of the lender. This type of in-surance is also available on important employees in your organization, such as branch managers. Businesses with one or more partners may wish to take out partner life insurance, which would provide the funds to buy out a deceased partner's share of the store without having to close or sell the business.

Retirement Plans

As the owner of a store, you need to save for your own retirement. At the same time, you have the opportunity to contribute toward retirement funds for your employees or to offer them a retirement plan into which they can put money from their salaries. Government regulations regarding retirement savings allow certain tax exemptions for plans that do not favor the employer at the expense of the employees. A number of different types of plans are available, including Keogh, or corporate, plans; the 401(k); and a version of the individual retirement account (IRA) called the simplified employee pension plan (SEP). You may wish to set up a profit-sharing plan in which a percentage of the store's profits, in good years, goes into a Keogh plan.

Employees often must wait a number of years to be fully qualified to receive their part of a retirement account. This policy, *vesting*, is used to en-courage job loyalty. Funds not fully vested when an employee leaves revert back into the accounts of those still part of the plan. A short vesting sched-ule is more generous than a long one, and there are federal regulations regarding how long it may take for an employee to become fully vested.

The 401(k) plan allows employees to contribute their own funds to-ward retirement by means of salary deferral. This money is not subject to income taxes, but social security tax must still be paid on it. Employees who are not covered by any pension plan at work may make tax-deductible con-tributions into individual IRA accounts. If you do not provide a pension plan, you should also be making contributions into an IRA each year.

Be sure to check with your tax adviser or CPA for the latest information about retirement plan regulations. Whenever the rules for these plans change, or you change your mind about your plan, administrative fees may be required in order to keep the business in compliance. Look for a plan you are sure you can afford and one that will appeal to your staff.

Discounts and Courtesy Cards

We offer our employees all merchandise at 10 percent above wholesale. This is our most popular "perk," and, of course, it really doesn't cost us anything. We do many special orders for our staff members. Occasionally one of our farsighted cookware or gadget suppliers will even offer a special discount to store employees, realizing that a salesperson who owns and uses an item can sell it more effectively. During the holidays, staff members are allowed to order any books they want through the large distributor that supplies many of our cookbooks.

We used to extend the staff discount to employee spouses, but not everyone on our staff is married, so we came up with a popular and fair alternative: the courtesy card. Each staff member is allowed to assign two annual 20 percent off courtesy cards to a spouse or the friends or relatives of their choice. There are certain exceptions to the discount, and these are listed on the back of the card. A copy of our card is shown in Figure 6-6. We print the cards on the store computer, using card stock with a design on it to prevent duplication, and assign each card an authorization number. If an employee leaves the store before the end of the calendar year, the card is invalidated.

Goal Setting and Bonuses

One way to get the staff more interested in the sales and even profit figures is to involve them in setting goals for the business. When there are real rewards associated with reaching these goals, the staff has a natural motivation to work toward them. Bonus program goals should be announced with fanfare, followed in weekly or monthly progress meetings, and celebrated when met.

We pay our entire staff, including employees such as the housekeepers and bookkeepers, a quarterly sales bonus representing 10 percent of any increase in sales for that quarter over the same quarter the previous year. This bonus is divided among staff members (Dean and I do not par-

Figure 6-6 Sample employee courtesy card.

STORE NAME
EMPLOYEE COURTESY
20% OFF DISCOUNT CARD

issued to_____

from_____
Valid until December 31, 1997, or the
employee's last day of employ, if earlier.
Please present card before checking out.
See reverse side for details, Code_____

---

front

PLEASE NOTE: THIS CARD
IS NON-TRANSFERABLE.

Exclusions: The 20% discount is not valid on
clearance items. It may not be used in
combination with other coupons or
discounts. Please note that there is an extra
charge for gift boxes and wrapping.

---

back

ticipate) based on their percentage of the total payroll during the quarter. Other stores share a percentage of profits with their employees at the end of each year or reward their employees with stock. These methods all help give employees a vested interest in the success of the store.

It is important that the time period being measured is short enough to keep staff interested, which is why we do a bonus quarterly instead of annually. We have a calendar showing the " figures to beat" for each day: the sales figures from the same day a year ago. We adjust for the day of the week before setting up these charts each year, so that the sales on *Sunday*, April 1, are not being compared to last year's sales on *Monday*, April 1, just because the date is the same.

In addition to measuring sales, you can set other goals, such as targeting two and a half inventory turns per year in certain departments, a certain percentage of gross profit margin on all sales, or an increase in customer traffic or the average transaction. Always target something that can be measured, and set goals that have a good chance of being met.

Employee Equity

"The best, most efficient, most profitable way to operate a business is to give everybody in the company a voice in saying how the company is run *and* a stake in the financial outcome, good or bad," states businessman Jack Stack in *The Great Game of Business*. Stack advocates using an employee stock ownership plan (ESOP) to allow employees to become partial owners of a business. Employee stock can be designated as nonvoting, so that the control of the business remains in the hands of the original owners. The employees still benefit from the growth and success of the business as their stock increases in value. Most ESOPs specify that employees must be with the business for a year before buying in or being given stock as a bonus. A vesting period of up to seven years may be set up, which means that employees must stay longer than seven years to receive the full value of their shares.

Employees who think like owners are much more likely to make a long-term commitment to a business. Absenteeism, employee theft, and wasteful expenditures are less likely to occur. The ESOP concept has proven successful in many different types of businesses, and although it is relatively untried in the field of specialty shop retailing, there is no reason to think that sharing equity would not work well for store operations large enough to warrant the legal work necessary to set up such a stock plan.

OPEN-BOOK MANAGEMENT

We have been using *open-book management* for years without knowing the name for it. With the exception of confidential personnel information, all the store's financial data is available to staff members. In *The Great Game of Business,* Jack Stack maintains that "the more people know about a company, the better that company will perform. This is an iron-clad rule. You will *always* be more successful in business by sharing information with the people you work with than by keeping them in the dark." In a retail store, it is a good idea to teach all staff members how the income generated by sales is spent and how the cost of goods sold affects the net profit. Most employees aren't aware of the overhead costs in running a store and don't realize that most of the store's profits go to taxes and to fuel growth. They also need to know how their work fits into the big picture and how important their efforts are to the store's success.

We find it especially useful to share sales figures, broken down by merchandise category, with our staff. Those in charge of a department are eager to see how their area is performing, even though their compensation is not tied to these sales figures. We periodically review the additional data on the income statement and balance sheet with the store's management team, which is made up of our personnel, advertising, and operations managers. We pay special attention to the payroll and advertising budgets, as well as sales figures and inventory turns. In a small shop, these are the main variables that we can try to adjust, since expenses such as rent and utilities do not fluctuate much. Although we do not focus a lot of attention on statistics, we do know a healthy bottom line is important to the future of our business.

EMPLOYEE EVALUATIONS

Employees and managers should be in continuous communication about issues of common concern, but a private annual or semiannual evaluation makes sure that every employee gets an equal opportunity to be heard. An annual private conference provides each employee a chance to bring up job-related concerns and to discuss future plans. There is real value in having this special opportunity to listen to an employee, and by holding these conferences in a safe and quiet setting, we show each staff member how much we value his or her input. We try to use the occasion to praise the employee for past accomplishments. If there is room for improvement, we list specific items under "future goals." At the next annual evaluation, or sometimes a follow-up meeting a few weeks after the first one, we check to see if progress is being made toward these goals.

We encourage employees to bring up their own issues to work on, such as needing to broaden their knowledge of the electric appliances we carry. This is the method our elementary schools use to get students excited about working toward goals they are interested in. (Our son, Erik, for example, told his fourth grade teacher that one of his goals was to conduct experiments involving explosives.)

When salary increases are tied to the annual evaluation, the money issue becomes the primary focus of the conference. An employee not receiving a raise may wonder why and may doubt the sincerity of any praise of his or her work. Ideally, salary increases should be given at other times of the year, such as when additional responsibilities are taken on.

We use a simple evaluation form that is filled in during the conference, signed by the employee, and kept in the employee's file. We also give staff members a questionnaire to fill in prior to their conference. Copies of both of these forms are shown in Figures 6-7 and 6-8.

Confidentiality

All employee evaluations, and most conferences, should take place in a private setting free of interruptions. Arrange the chairs so that everyone is face to face, without a big desk in between creating a physical and psychological barrier. If several people are participating in the discussion, arrange the chairs in a circle or oval, perhaps around a table. Everyone, management and staff, should be on equal footing. Encourage open discussion by promising that all matters discussed privately will be kept confidential, if that is the wish of those involved.

One of the most difficult challenges facing an employer using a democratic style of management is keeping confidences. When openness is the norm, it is painful not to be able to explain to other staff members that one of their colleagues is feeling particularly emotional because of a personal problem or to know that someone is leaving soon without being able to mention it. But part of employer-employee trust is promising that when something is said in confidence, it will not be repeated. Thankfully, no one has ever asked that my husband, Dean, and I not talk to each other about staff concerns, so we always have someone to discuss an issue with without violating confidentiality.

Figure 6-7 Sample employee evaluation questionnaire.

EMPLOYEE EVALUATION QUESTIONNAIRE

EMPLOYEE'S NAME_____

YOUR EVALUATION IS SCHEDULED FOR _____ AT_____

PLEASE ANSWER THE FOLLOWING QUESTIONS AND GIVE THIS FORM TO THE PERSONNEL MANAGER
AT LEAST ONE DAY BEFORE YOUR CONFERENCE.

1) WHAT QUESTIONS DO YOU HAVE ABOUT WHAT IS EXPECTED OF YOU IN YOUR JOB?

2) WHAT DO YOU BELIEVE ARE YOUR MOST SIGNIFICANT ACHIEVEMENTS FOR THIS PAST YEAR? WHAT GOALS DID YOU MEET?

3) LIST ANY WAYS YOU FEEL YOU COULD IMPROVE YOUR EFFECTIVENESS.

4) ARE THERE ANY GOALS YOU WOULD LIKE TO WORK TOWARD? HOW CAN WE HELP YOU ACHIEVE THESE GOALS?

5) IS THERE ANYTHING WE CAN DO TO HELP YOU IN YOUR JOB?

Figure 6-8 Sample employee evaluation form.

EMPLOYEE EVALUATION FORM

EMPLOYEE'S NAME_____

EVALUATED BY_____ DATE_____

NOTABLE ACHIEVEMENTS:

PERFORMANCE OBJECTIVES FOR THE FUTURE:

EMPLOYEE'S COMMENTS:

I HAVE PARTICIPATED IN THIS PERFORMANCE REVIEW AND HAVE READ
THIS EVALUATION.

EMPLOYEE'S SIGNATURE_____DATE_____

Employee records should be kept in a locked cabinet that can be accessed only by those entrusted with a key. Of course, an employee has the right to see everything in his or her own file at any time, but there is no reason for employees to see each other's records. We ask that employees keep their rate of pay confidential; nevertheless, everyone seems to know what everyone else makes.

Although we ask employees to keep the store's financial information confidential, we are realistic enough to realize that everyone talks about their work at home. We have never had anything that we were trying to hide from the outside world, so fortunately it has not been detrimental to have our store's operations be somewhat publicly known.

Correcting Performance Problems

Stores should have clear performance standards, spelled out in the employee handbook, and should hold all employees to these standards equally. When an employee doesn't live up to the store's standards, a discussion of the problem and any consequences that follow a poor performance should take place right away. I usually make it a policy to overlook any performance problem if it occurs only once, but if the error is repeated, a conference is called for.

It is never pleasant to criticize an employee's behavior. Discussions of problems should be held in private—*never* in front of customers or other employees. Cushion your criticism with encouragement and praise of the employee's strengths (this is sometimes called the "Oreo approach"—beginning and ending with positive points, with the problem sandwiched in the middle). Criticize the act, not the person. Make it clear that you are interested in helping the employee correct the problem, not in being punitive. Set goals for better performance, and arrange for a follow-up meeting to see if these goals are being met. If an employee does not seem able to correct a problem, perhaps a different job function would allow the person greater success. A staff member who is not good at waiting on customers, for instance, might excel at stock work.

Document any discussion with an employee about a performance problem, and list the goals and dates for follow-up. Written documentation not only shows the employee that the situation is being taken seriously but may also be necessary proof that you warned the employee of a problem before dismissing him or her. Progressive discipline is intended to ward off the necessity of firing an employee, but sometimes this action is inevitable.

THE LEGALITIES OF FIRING

Eventually you will probably face the unpleasant act of firing a staff member. We have learned the hard way that the laws offering employees protection against wrongful discharge are complex and can easily be used to bring a lawsuit against the former employer. No business can afford to fire someone without knowing the legalities involved, preferably far in advance of ever having to terminate someone. Check with your lawyer and other advisers for recommended sources of information, such as the local Small Business Development Center.

Problems should ideally be brought to an employee's attention, in verbal and written form, long before firing is considered. If an employee is chronically late, for example, have a private conference with the person and have him or her sign a dated document spelling out the consequences for continued tardiness. Keep a copy of the warning in their personnel file, and follow up on the deadlines set for improved behavior. Firing should be considered only after two or more written warnings. This progressive discipline can help prevent accusations of wrongful dismissal.

Some offenses nevertheless warrant immediate firing, and these should be spelled out in your employee handbook. Verbal or physical abuse, theft, drug abuse, insubordination, and embezzlement are automatic causes for firing in most businesses.

Firing should always be done in private, with a witness present if you suspect that the employee may pursue legal action. Have all the necessary papers prepared ahead of time, including the final paycheck, and details about severance pay, unused employee benefits, unemployment compensation information, and any optional continuation of insurance coverage. Ask where the employee would like W-2 payroll tax information sent and what information should be provided to future employers asking for a reference. Collect the employee's keys to the store, and make sure the person has all his or her personal possessions. Escort the employee out of the store without going past customers and other employees if at all possible. If you have an alarm system code, it is wise to have a policy that the code is changed whenever anyone is fired, no matter what the circumstances. You might also plan to have the locks changed.

Expect tears, rage, or defensiveness when you dismiss someone. Even when the firing is humanely handled, the employee will feel rejected and unhappy. The lawsuit a former employee files after being fired may be motivated in part by anger at the wrong they feel they have suffered. A lawsuit may also be the result of greed; it is often less expensive for you as an employer to settle out of court than to defend yourself against a disgruntled former employee, even if you know you would eventually win the case.

Despite the unpleasantness of firing, do not put it off once you realize dismissal is necessary. The unsatisfactory employee may be a drain on the staff's morale, and the situation will undoubtedly weigh on your mind until you take action. If you have to fire someone for the good of the store and the rest of your staff, do it as soon as possible.

You should realize, however, that a sudden dismissal may be very upsetting to the rest of the staff. Staff members may be in touch with the former employee, hearing his or her side of the story. For reasons of confidentiality, you may not discuss the reasons for the dismissal, which frustrates employees who are used to open communication. It is important to reassure the rest of the staff that their jobs are not in danger. Spending extra time on the sales floor may help to reestablish a feeling of trust and teamwork. In time, things will return to an even keel. Helping to hire and train a replacement employee can focus the staff's attention on the future instead of the past.

Employee Layoffs

Occasionally a retail store will need to lay off employees because of a decline in sales or profits. These layoffs may be temporary, or they may actually be permanent terminations. Make it clear to the individuals involved that the action has nothing to do with their job performance. Be realistic about whether you might be able to hire them back again if the store's situation improves.

State unemployment compensation is often available to employees who are laid off. Before taking action, find out what benefits your employees might be eligible for. This information may help soften the blow when you inform them that you need to lay them off.

THE EXIT INTERVIEW

Employees who leave for reasons other than termination should meet with the personnel manager or owner one last time for an exit interview. The employee can turn in keys or other store possessions and fill in a form giving information such as where the last paycheck should be sent. This is also an opportunity to ask the employee for suggestions regarding the store's staff training and management. Although it may be painful to ask an employee why he or she is leaving, the answers can lead to improvements that will increase the job satisfaction of the remaining staff members.

CREATING TEAM SPIRIT

Establishing a sense of community is key to creating a workplace that is enjoyable to employees and welcoming to customers. Sometimes a group of people develop this camaraderie naturally, especially if united by similar interests and backgrounds. But many stores, including ours, have a very diverse workforce: our employees represent a forty-five-year age span and very different lifestyles. We present opportunities for staff members to get to know each other at parties, on our annual picnic and play outing to a local outdoor classical theater, and during the social part of staff meetings. We set up smaller teams to work on special projects, such as spring cleaning. We encourage employees to do favors for each other, such as watching over a department while someone is gone or filling a "sub shift" on the schedule.

Part of establishing a team spirit is avoiding a gap between management and "hourly" staff. All managers should spend some of their time on the sales floor, waiting on customers and working with the sales staff. Managers' offices should not have closed doors. Dean and I don't have an office or even a desk. We meet with sales reps and do paperwork at the customer service table in the upstairs sales area or at any free spot in the bookkeeping office, which doubles as the store's gift wrap area. We try to be accessible to customers and to staff, and ask that the members of our management team do the same.

Employees want to feel a sense of pride in their workplace. Involving the staff in celebrating the store's successes is important. Be sure staff members know about charity donations the store is making and encourage employees to participate in fund-raising projects for nonprofit organizations. Instill a sense of belonging by providing the staff with T-shirts, jackets, or caps with the store name and logo. And most important, work with the staff team to create a successful business of which you can all be proud.

Staff Communications

We issue an in-store newsletter with the biweekly paychecks, covering important topics such as new arrivals, recently hired employees, and any proposed changes in scheduling or policy. Day-to-day communication is done in person whenever possible, but otherwise is handled by notes left on two bulletin boards: one for general announcements, such as ads we are running, and one for individual messages. We also post a daily "who's where" schedule listing the stations we want each sales associate to cover during the day, rotating the staff through the upstairs and the two downstairs sales counters to give everyone a little variety in their day. This schedule also allows us to pair an experienced employee with a less experienced one, and even on occasion to keep two employees apart who are not getting along.

At periodic staff meetings, important for staff morale, we always have refreshments and often give out door prizes or staff recognitions. At some meetings we brainstorm ideas for in-store and window displays, at others we discuss the season just past and how we can improve it next year. The agenda is kept informal so that the staff can bring up issues of concern to them. We arrange the seating in a circle if possible, and make sure that the sales staff and management team members do not divide into separate groups. All ideas are given careful consideration, and we try to act on as many staff suggestions as possible. Employees need to feel that they have a voice in their workplace and that their work is more than just a job.

Keeping It Light

According to Paul Hawken, founder of the Smith and Hawken garden stores and author of *Growing a Business*, "If you aren't having some fun, you might wonder just what you are doing in your business life. Laughter and good humor are the canaries in the mine of commerce. If employees, customers, and vendors don't laugh and have a good time at your company, something is wrong." Retailing should be fun, exciting, and interesting—at least some of the time. If things are getting too serious, set up a product trivia contest with real prizes, suggest a betting pool on some silly topic such as the next day's weather, or surprise your staff with a treat. Be sure your staff newsletter occasionally has some humor and personal interest stories in addition to the usual announcements.

Lillian Vernon, founder of the mail order catalog by that name, once said that if one of her female employees was having a bad day, she'd tell her to take a couple of hours off and get her hair done. Today that would not be a politically correct suggestion, but the sentiment is still valid. Employees are first and foremost people, and they need to feel the business cares about their joys and sorrows. Celebrate birthdays and other special events in the lives of your employees, and when things go wrong, send flowers or a note to let them know you are thinking of them.

For many employees, their fellow staff members form the community with whom they spend the majority of their time. Stories and photographs from past years are the group's family history and are important to preserve and share. We reminisce about former staff members, memorable customers, and other anecdotes that show we have a common history. We keep photo albums of all our past parties and window displays, and a box full of clippings and other memorabilia. We want employees to feel that they belong to a corporate community with both a past and a future.

On the wall of our bookkeeping office is a family tree, shaped (naturally) like an orange tree. All staff members, from the earliest day of Orange Tree Imports to the present, are listed on the tree. For our fifteenth and twentieth anniversaries, we hosted staff reunions, with our "family" photo albums and letters from former employees around the world displayed for everyone to enjoy. We've had about 125 employees over the years, and I'm pleased to say we've kept in touch with almost all of them. I guess Linda was right when she said that the staff is the main reason for the store's success. We certainly couldn't have gotten where we are today without all 125 of our past and present employees.

7

CUSTOMER-FRIENDLY POLICIES AND SERVICES

Exceptional customer service is one of the areas in which a specialty shop should be able to outperform all of its competitors. Customer service begins with the basics: greeting each customer, being available to offer assistance, ringing up a purchase promptly and correctly, and saying "thank you" when the transaction is completed. Yet how many times have we all experienced a lack of even these basics? We have been ignored by salespeople who talk on the telephone to their friends, waited in endless lines in stores with twelve checkout lanes but only two in use, and tried to get assistance in shops where staff members are vacuuming though closing time is still half an hour away. A store owner or manager who really cares about customer service would never permit these behaviors.

This emphasis on good customer service comes at a time when it is harder than ever to attract employees eager to serve. Putting someone else's needs before your own doesn't seem to come naturally to many employees; perhaps it is no longer part of our culture. It must be demonstrated by example, taught in training programs, and reinforced by recognition and rewards.

Fortunately, a shop with a reputation for fine customer service has a better chance of getting applicants interested in providing service, especially if it is willing to pay more than the going rate for its staff. Disney has shown how successfully customer service can become a part of a company's corporate culture. Cheerfulness and helpfulness are the norms at Disneyland and Disney World, which means that Disney undoubtedly attracts more than the average number of applicants comfortable with that expectation.

In *It's Not My Department*, Peter Glen's diatribe against poor service, he points out that "when customers have an adequate experience, they're satisfied, and they usually forget it. But people remember bad service forever. They form their opinion of entire companies or careers based on their worst customer experience. They remember every name and detail and they love to tell you how they suffered. . . . The simplest secret of selling and serving customers is: Find out what they want, and how they want it, and give it to 'em, just that way. Talk to customers about the thing they are most interested in: themselves. And that means it will be *different* with each customer. There is no one right way to approach the customer: there are as many different ways as the number of people who ever stand before you." Listening to what the customer really wants is essential.

Part of the training of any staff who will come in contact with customers—and this may not be limited to sales personnel—is the importance of placing customers' needs first. All employees should know that they are to put aside whatever they are doing when a customer approaches. Shoppers should never have to wait while employees chat or unpack merchandise. Employees should greet customers as they enter the store and offer assistance when appropriate. They should always try to find an answer to a customer's question, even if it requires calling a competing store. And a customer asking for a certain product should be shown where it is located, not just pointed in the right direction.

You need to decide if you want your employees to be salespeople who wait on customers or clerks who mostly just ring up sales. Since self-service is the norm in most stores today, be clear about your expectations. Salespeople need to be trained to give customer service that is attentive but not overbearing. There is a fine line between being available to help and ruining a customer's shopping experience by hovering excessively.

When approaching a shopper to offer sales assistance, employees need to remember that the question "May I help you?" almost always receives the reply "No, just looking." Encourage staff members to begin a conversation with a customer by making a positive comment on some general topic or about the merchandise he or she is examining. Once a conversation has been initiated, it is easier to find out what the customer is shopping for and to point out the positive points of any products the customer is considering buying. Sometimes customers need assistance in making a purchasing decision. Employees should be taught that reinforcing the fact that the customer is making a good choice or offering to go get the item in a box can help close the sale.

When ringing up a sale, the sales assistant might ask the customer, "Did you find everything you were looking for today?" or suggest an add-on item, such as film to go with a new camera. Some stores have contests to see which employees can sell the most add-on items at the time of purchase—which is fine *if* the additional items are products the customers really need and want.

MOTIVATING EMPLOYEES TO PROVIDE GOOD CUSTOMER SERVICE

Merchants everywhere try to motivate employees to give the kind of customer service that will win repeat business. Even in little Banffshire, Scotland, the government sponsors classes in "customer care," in the hope that more tourist income will result from sales clerks' smiling and speaking more slowly for foreign visitors.

There are four basic components to having employees who provide exceptional service: hiring people with a positive attitude; training them thoroughly so that they know all about the store, its merchandise, and its policies; giving them the authority to do what is necessary to make the customer happy; and rewarding them when they do well. Training and rewarding need to be ongoing processes, because people don't usually stay motivated on their own. As Carl Sewell says in *Customers for Life*, "Even when people know what they are supposed to do, sometimes they forget. That's why they hold church every Sunday."

Continuing Staff Training and Communication

New employees are usually given training in procedures and merchandise. They should also receive training in customer service standards. Do you want your employees to offer assistance after greeting the customer? To answer the telephone by the fourth ring? Clearly communicating your expectations can help employees live up to them.

It is unrealistic, however, to expect anyone to memorize every aspect of product knowledge, store procedures, and customer service in the first few weeks of employment, and of course a good specialty shop is constantly changing. Staff education must be an ongoing process if employees are always going to be ready to give exceptional service.

Many shops find it useful to have weekly or biweekly meetings an hour before the store opens in order to introduce new products, review upcoming advertising promotions, and discuss any problems with store procedures. If bagels and fruit are served and the tone of the meeting is informal, these meetings can also serve an important social function of helping to encourage a team spirit. Meetings should always have a topic or agenda, however, so that staff members feel their time is being well spent.

Because we carry many kitchen items that require some technical knowledge in order to sell, we often ask sales representatives to give hour-long staff seminars before the store opens. The reps are usually quite willing to come demonstrate their products, because they stand to benefit as much as we do from an increase in sales. They even donate door prizes for us to give away to those who attend, which has the added benefit of putting products into the hands of staff members who later will be selling them. Customers love to hear that a sales associate uses a particular item at home and really likes it.

A weekly or biweekly newsletter can also help keep staff up to date on new products, upcoming ads, and other store news. Instead of writing it all yourself, ask those in charge of different parts of the store to submit a short report. Birthdays, recipes, and other personal news can also be shared in the newsletter. When we hire a new employee, we include a short biography in the newsletter so that the entire staff knows a little about the latest addition to our crew. And when an employee deals with a difficult customer or accomplishes a goal, we share that news too. Use clip art (on computer disc or from any inexpensive clip art book) to make your in-store newsletter visually interesting, and distribute it with your staff's paychecks to be sure they notice it.

Everyone concerned with the survival of specialty shops in the era of discounters and megastores stresses that staff needs product knowledge, but they rarely mention that staff also needs to know about the other aspects of the store: what is on display in the windows, what is being advertised, the plans for new shipments, the store's procedures for handling difficult transactions, and so forth. Sizable sales can be lost if an employee doesn't know how to change the tape on the cash register or can't find the sofa featured in Sunday's ad.

If you want staff members who act like professionals, you may need to invest in some professional courses for them. Training in sales techniques, display, business procedures, and even specialized lines of products, such as gemstones, may be available in your community. Consider paying for tuition for some of these classes for your staff—and yourself. Although you might not be able to fund an M.B.A., as some big businesses do, staff members will appreciate any investment you make in them. Be sure to pay them their hourly salary for the time spent in class.

Trade shows and conventions often offer seminars for free or at a low cost. Time at a show is always at a premium for those doing buying, so you might consider taking along a staff member or two to attend some of the programs. Have them report any exciting new ideas to you and the rest of your staff.

Subscribe to the trade magazines in your field, and share copies with interested staff members, or put them in the break room for everyone to read. Clip out pertinent articles from popular magazines, and place copies of product catalogs where staff can read them during slower times. The better informed your staff members are, the better your customer service will be.

A Warm Welcome

When Wal-Mart started to institutionalize friendliness by stationing a greeter by their entrance doors, it meant that small shops had to go one step further in making the customer feel welcome. Creative retailers started offering valet parking, complimentary coffee and cookies, play areas for children, and free lectures on everything from canoeing to crafts. In the process, they learned that customers have so few positive shopping experiences (can you remember the last time *you* received really exemplary service?) that they are appreciative of even the smallest welcoming touches.

Telephone Manners Matter

To the customer calling by telephone, the person answering *is* the store. When someone calls Gloria Jean's Coffee Bean in LaCrosse, Wisconsin, the first thing the caller hears is, "It's a glorious day at Gloria Jean's! How may I help you?" This cheerful greeting makes a memorable impression. If your staff can't manage quite that much enthusiasm each time, they should at least answer promptly, give the name of the store, and ask if they can be of assistance. Perhaps you'd like them to give their first name, so that the customer knows to whom they are speaking. If they must put the customer on hold, it should be done briefly and with sincere apologies. Be sure your telephone system has a reminder tone so that no one is left on hold indefinitely. If you decide to use on-hold music, consider music that is appropriate to your shop, such as pleasant, instrumental Christmas music for a holiday store.

No customer likes to wait while a salesperson talks on the telephone to someone else. When you have a customer on the telephone and one standing in front of you, greet whoever came second and explain to them that you will be with them in just a moment. If it looks as if the call will take a long time, perhaps you can get someone else to help out or offer to call the customer on the telephone back in a few minutes.

SETTING STORE POLICIES

There are some services that most stores offer, such as the opportunity for the customer to pay by check or credit card, and a refund or exchange policy. Be sure your staff understands your payment and return policies so they can be applied fairly. All sales and return transactions should be pleasant for both the customer and the sales staff member. Clear policies help avoid unnecessary misunderstandings, and employees empowered to make exceptions to the rules can often turn a difficult encounter into a positive experience.

Your Store Hours

Surveys show that shoppers no longer prefer the traditional Monday through Friday daytime hours for shopping. Evenings and especially weekends are now prime shopping times, and of course your store may be in competition with a superstore open twenty-four hours a day. Small retailers can't possibly keep those kinds of hours, and they don't need to. But ignoring the importance of being open Sundays and some evenings is usually a mistake. Ask your customers what hours they prefer to shop, and talk to owners of other stores in your area to try to standardize open times for the convenience of everyone's customers. Add extra hours during your shop's busy season.

We list store hours in the white pages in the telephone book, saving many unnecessary calls. We also mention "added holiday hours." One

Christmas Eve a person called at 3:00 and was unhappy to learn that we had already closed. "It says in the phone book you have added holiday hours," she sputtered. I tried to explain patiently that we had indeed been open until 9:00 every weekday evening the whole month, but that on Christmas Eve we closed at 2:00 so we could enjoy the holiday with our families. She hung up angrily, only to call back a few minutes later to get the last word: "I just want you to know that it's people like *you* who turned Mary and Joseph away from the inn!"

Shopping centers usually require standardized hours, and customers like knowing all the stores in the mall will open and close at the same time. Nonetheless, some mall store employees anxious to get home begin closing procedures as long as half an hour before closing time. Open promptly at the hour promised, and alert your staff to the fact that shoppers arriving close to closing time deserve the same courtesy and attention as those coming in earlier in the day.

Kazoos Are for Keeps: Returns and Exchanges

A return policy may not seem like a positive customer service, but as trend spotter Faith Popcorn points out in *The Popcorn Report*, the shopper of the future wants "return policies that will no longer punish us for changing our minds." Employees also want a return policy that will reduce the stress of what is known as retailing's most unpleasant regular transaction: accepting a return.

Lands' End offers a return policy that is "Guaranteed. Period." Nordstrom, the department store chain renowned for its customer service, is said to have given a refund on tires, even though it doesn't sell tires. And yet some small shops still post unfriendly "No refunds. No returns" signs. The fact is that no one really wants to give a customer their money back. This is especially true of new businesses that need every dollar they receive to stay afloat. But Lands' End and Nordstrom have figured out that the increase in sales that comes from a generous return policy outweighs the cost of occasionally being taken advantage of by an unscrupulous customer. The vast majority of people are honest, and they have a valid reason for returning a purchase or a gift.

Some items, however, can't be returned for hygienic reasons. The Magic Flute Music Mall lets customers know at the time of purchase that kazoos, harmonicas, and mouthpieces may not be returned. Stores selling swimwear, jewelry, and lingerie may also need a policy regarding returns, and some states have special regulations about this issue.

Writing a Return Policy

In fairness to your customers and your staff, post your return policy, and be sure it is usually followed. Some states have mandated that stores have a policy and follow it, although the actual terms are left up to the individual business. Department and discount stores have led customers to expect a liberal return policy, so specialty shops need to be at least as accommodating as their competition. Here are a few guidelines to keep in mind in setting a return policy that is equitable to consumers and the store.

The merchandise should be from your shop. A recent test of return policies by a consumer vigilante group asked stores to take back a private-label shirt from another chain. Why should they? What would they then do with the shirt? Even Nordstrom, famous for taking back tires when they don't sell tires, sets limits. (The returned tires had actually been purchased from an Alaskan store, the Northern Commercial Company, which Nordstrom had recently bought.) You may choose, however, to take back an item you do carry, even if it was purchased elsewhere.

The purchase should be recent. Many stores set a thirty-day limit on refunds and offer exchanges after that time. It is difficult to sell items that are not from current stock.

The refund should be for the amount paid. This may be difficult if the customer has no receipt and the item may have been purchased on sale. For some clearance sales and second-quality merchandise, you may want to have a no-return policy. If you do, clearly explain it to each customer at the time of purchase.

Credit card purchases should receive credit card credits or merchandise exchange. Since you have paid a service charge to the credit card company, giving the customer a credit card credit or store merchandise credit is the only way to recoup that charge.

Large cash refunds should be paid by check. There may not be enough money in the till to give out a large amount of cash, especially early in the day. And occasionally a thief will take an expensive item from the back of the store, remove the tags and present it at the cash register demanding a cash refund. By asking for the customer's name, address, telephone number, and signature in order to mail the refund check, you will discourage this practice. It is also useful to take this information from anyone getting a cash refund from the till if you are troubled by frequent returns. A sample cash refund form is shown in Figure 7-1.

Decide if you want to wait for the check to clear. If you have a lot of trouble with bounced checks or if the refund is for a large amount, you

"I bet Nordstrom would have taken them back!"

might want to wait until the check clears the bank before issuing a cash or check refund. This policy should not be applied to people you recognize as good customers, however, because it implies that you don't trust them.

Decide about the need for a receipt. It is always more convenient for the store if the customer has a receipt with a return so that you know the date of purchase, the amount paid, and the method of payment. But it is awkward for someone giving a gift to give the recipient the receipt, so many returns are without a receipt. Some stores try to avoid this problem by putting a carefully coded sticker inside the lid of the gift box, referring to the date and amount of the purchase, but customers often reuse boxes, much to the embarrassment of anyone who tries to return a gift to the wrong shop. Other shops avoid this problem by filling in a coded return slip to be put in the box with the gift.

The fairest way to handle returns without a receipt is to offer a store credit, applicable on an immediate exchange or future purchase. But there will always be those who are unhappy with this policy, and it is probably

Figure 7-1 Sample cash refund form.

```
                    STORE NAME
                     ADDRESS
                   PHONE & FAX

              CASH REFUND FORM

     CUSTOMER NAME_____

     ADDRESS_____

     CITY AND STATE_____

     PHONE(HOME)_____(WORK)_____

     SIGNATURE_____

     DATE_____SALESPERSON_____

     ITEM/S_____

     REASON FOR RETURN_____

     MERCHANDISE AMOUNT_____SALES TAX_____

                         REFUND TOTAL _____

     FOR LARGE CASH REFUNDS, A CHECK WILL BE SENT
     TO YOU  BY OUR BOOKKEEPER WITHIN A FEW DAYS.

        ❑ CASH OR CREDIT CARD REFUND GIVEN.

        ❑ CHECK TO BE SENT.

        DONE BY_____DATE_____
```

Print the form (two per 8½ × 11-inch sheet) on two-part carbonless carbon paper, with one part for the customer.

worth avoiding their anger by authorizing staff to make exceptions and give a refund.

Keep on hand a supply of store credit forms, possibly on two-part carbonless carbon paper, with one copy for the customer and one for the store. Ready-made forms can be purchased at an office supply store, but a custom-made form (like the one shown in Figure 7-2) is more likely to fit your store's image.

Always take back defective merchandise. If something you sold is clearly defective, the first thing you should do is apologize. After all, the customer was disappointed in what you sold and has had the inconvenience of coming back to the store. Then ask what would make the person happy: a refund, a replacement, or a different item. Make it right, and then apologize again. You want the customer to come back.

Remove defective merchandise from the checkout area immediately and attach a form identifying it as defective (see Figure 7-3).

Post your policy. Signs clearly stating your return policy should be put where customers can see them. We also keep pads of 3- by 5-inch slips with our policy on them by the registers so that we can give one to anyone who asks. Some customers choose to put it in with the gift they are giving. An example of a return policy is shown in Figure 7-4.

Figure 7-2 Sample credit slip.

STORE NAME and LOGO
ADDRESS
PHONE & FAX

CREDIT SLIP

CUSTOMER NAME_____DATE_____

ADDRESS_____HOME PHONE_____

_____WORK PHONE_____

MERCHANDISE AMOUNT:_____(CATEGORY___)SALES TAX:_____

STAFF MEMBER_____TOTAL CREDIT:_____

PLEASE NOTE THAT STORE CREDITS ARE VALID FOR TWO YEARS.

Print the form (up to four per 8½ × 11-inch sheet) on two-part carbonless carbon paper.

Figure 7-3 Sample "defective" form.

DEFECTIVE

Please place this item on the defectives' shelf right away, with the top copy
of this form attached. The second copy goes to the merchandise buyer.

Item:_____Date:_____

Vendor:_____

Category:_____Price:_____

Nature of problem:_____

_____

❏ This item was accidentally broken, or discovered to be
 defective, while in the store.
or
❏ This item was returned by a customer, who received:

 ❏ a replacement

 ❏ a cash or credit card refund

 ❏ a store credit

Staff member _____

Recommended action:

 ❏ request replacement or credit from vendor:

 done by_____on _____

 ❏ discard, put in staff "free box," or donate to charity

 ❏ mark down for clearance sale, marked "as is"

Print this form (two per 8½ × 11-inch sheet) on two-part carbonless carbon paper.

Figure 7-4 Sample return policy.

STORE NAME
RETURN POLICY

•Cash refunds and credit card credits will be given within 30 days of purchase, when item is accompanied by a cash register receipt. Refunds of over $50 will be made by mail, with a waiting period of seven working days if the purchase was paid for by check.

•Items that are returned after the 30 day period, or gifts returned without a cash register receipt, may be exchanged for a store credit that is valid for up to 2 years.

•All items being returned must be in good condition, and unused. (This does not apply to items that are being returned because of a manufacturer's defect.)

•Clearance sale purchases are final. Please inspect these bargains carefully before buying.

CUSTOMER CONVENIENCE AND COMFORT

Many little touches can make the shopper's visit to your store more pleasant. I am always pleased when customers comment that coming into Orange Tree Imports cheers them up, because it means we are providing a pleasurable shopping experience. We try to think of customers as our guests and to make their time in the store as relaxing and enjoyable as possible.

Creature Comforts

At Sewell Village Cadillac in Texas they take pride in the fact that the floors in their customer rest rooms are washed every hour on the hour. When was the last time you were in a small store that even allowed customers to use the bathroom? A clean, well-lit, and well-stocked bathroom is a delight and a relief to the shopper who needs one. If you tell a customer to use the rest room across the street in the gas station or around the corner in a restaurant, chances are the person won't return after leaving.

There are dozens of excuses for not providing bathrooms for customers. Some are legitimate: an older shop without plumbing or a store in a mall where the rest rooms are in a central location. But many shops have a bathroom for their employees and choose not to allow customers to use it because it is in an inconvenient location, or management is afraid thieves will shoplift items by concealing them while there, or no one wants to bother cleaning it regularly.

Anyone who has shopped with a small child knows that a convenient bathroom can be the ultimate and most appreciated customer service. If you can, make one available to your customers, and make sure it is clean and attractive, not a storeroom for cleaning supplies. If you sell soap or potpourri, put some in the rest room, perhaps with a small sign indicating that it is available for purchase. Decorate it with posters or prints that relate to your store theme. And make sure it is always cleaned (at least once a day) and well stocked with toilet paper and towels. By using commercial-size rolls of toilet paper and paper towels or a dispenser that piggybacks smaller rolls, you will hardly ever run out of these supplies.

In many areas, stores are required by law to provide a customer rest room that meets access codes for disabled people. A wide doorway and grip bar make the rest room easier for all customers to negotiate. And in designing your rest rooms, don't forget mothers—and fathers—who may need to change a diaper while in your store. If you have room, provide a safe diaper changing area. Fold-down changing tables are a practical solution used in many small rest rooms.

When we remodeled our store, code regulations required us to install an e.w.c., which we learned is an electric water cooler. We balked at the expense at the time, but both our customers and staff have enjoyed having it. You might consider a bottled water system that allows customers to serve themselves a cup of water. After all, Wall Drug in South Dakota has attracted customers for years with their famous signs across the West offering "Free Ice Water."

Spouses and tired shoppers always appreciate a place to sit down. It is especially important that stores offering services that customers must wait for, such as prescriptions, repairs, or gift wrapping, provide a comfortable seating area. A few current magazines or a television quietly running an educational or entertaining video can make the waiting time seem shorter. If customers are likely to have a long wait, be sure to advise them of this at the start. Some stores use electronic pagers, or beepers, so that those who are waiting are free to browse around the store while they wait.

If you have the space, offer coffee or hot cider in cooler weather. Shops selling specialty foods may wish to have regular samplings available of the foods they sell. And stores that have customers who sit down to be waited on, such as a florist conferring about wedding flowers, might plan to offer iced soft drinks or hot tea in china cups to make customers feel really special.

Keeping Children Content

Shoppers with small children often feel particularly stressed by trying to get their errands done. They will be grateful if you offer an interesting play area or have some toys or coloring books that you bring out when a child needs entertainment. Star Market's newest store in Boston has a play space for its customers' children managed by a firm that runs day care centers. Shoppers pay as little as $2 an hour for childcare service if they spend $100 or more in the store. At Mitchells of Westport, a Connecticut shop selling fine men's and women's apparel, the children's area is staffed by a babysitter on busy days. In addition to supervising customers' children, the sitter helps keep refreshments for adults and children replenished.

My own children suggest that store employees make an effort to greet the child as well as the adult. I often start a conversation with an adult customer by saying something nice to the child or baby. This opener puts the adult at ease and is a welcome change from talking about the weather.

Special Customers, Special Needs

Traditional retailing wisdom suggests putting the most commonly purchased items, such as milk in a supermarket, in the back of the store in order to encourage shoppers to go past the maximum number of displays on their way to find it. This advice ignores the fact that the growing market of elderly and physically challenged customers need stores to make shopping as easy as possible.

Feather Hills Nursery, a new gardening shop and landscaping service in Durham, North Carolina, offers special classes in container gardening for customers in wheelchairs and any others who find it difficult to bend over to tend their plants.

Look at your store from the perspective of someone who has trouble getting around:

- Are the aisles wide enough for a wheelchair?
- Is signage large enough to be read by someone with less than perfect vision?
- Are there any unnecessary steps up or down?
- Is there a place for someone who needs a rest to sit down?
- Are there baskets or carts for customers to use to carry their purchases?

We are happy to open early for anyone who has difficulty shopping when the store is crowded. (We've also extended this offer to celebrities who are performing in our area, but so far none of them has taken us up on it.) We offer telephone shopping service to those who can't come to the store in person, and one of our housebound customers tells us that she displays the annual catalog pictures of our family in her living room. Some stores develop a relationship with nearby nursing homes, taking sample merchandise and catalogs in once a month and encouraging residents to place orders by telephone.

SERVICES BEYOND THE ORDINARY

Services you offer customers can be every bit as creative as your displays and promotions. Specialty stores that offer services beyond the usual and expected show an eagerness to please customers that sets them apart from the crowd. A unique service will also be something customers will talk about, and that positive word of mouth is worth more than any paid advertising.

There is no limit to the types of services your shop can offer if you use your imagination. Here are a few suggestions:

- Repotting house plants.
- Book signings by visiting authors.
- Hands-on crafts demonstrations.
- Antique appraisals.
- Cleaning and repairs.
- Loaners for customers while an item is being serviced.
- Party planning.
- Cooking classes or food sampling.
- Additional gift with a purchase, such as batteries with a clock.
- Valet parking or validated parking in a nearby facility.
- In-store appearances by artists.
- Free recipe cards.
- Crafts instruction sheets.
- In-home interior design consultation.
- Elegant wrapping of gifts from other stores.
- Complimentary installation or assembly of purchases.
- Telephone hot line for technical problem solving.
- Extended warranties or low-cost service contracts.
- A lending library of instructional books and videos.
- Trade-ins on used items.
- Twenty-four-hour a day telephone order service.
- Personalization or other custom work.
- Birthday and anniversary reminders.
- Same-day alterations.
- Storage of out-of-season items.
- Craft parties for children's birthdays.
- Office or home sales calls.
- Senior citizen discount day.
- Price matching with competitive stores.
- Rentals of tools or items for entertaining.
- Coffee or juice bar, possibly run by an outside firm.
- Guided tours led by a specialist from your shop.
- Tourist information.

Be sure to advertise your special services on signs in the store, as well as in your Yellow Pages ad. Make your special services part of your image advertising in all media, especially if these services help distinguish your store from competitors.

For Your Customers' Convenience

As an added service, some stores serve as a UPS pickup point for packages brought in ready to send. This convenience brings customers into the store, including some who may not have been in before. Other services you might consider include having a small official U.S. postal station in the shop or selling tickets for your state lottery.

Is there anywhere in your area to get copies made? Drop off film to be developed? Send a fax? Use a pay phone? Buy bus tickets or tokens? Get money from a cash machine? These conveniences won't pay the rent, but if they are in keeping with the nature of your store, they can generate goodwill and bring in extra customers.

Personal Shoppers

Stores with many repeat customers who enjoy personal attention should consider offering a personal shopping service. Department stores such as Nieman Marcus do this with great success. Print business cards for your salespeople, and encourage them to develop a list of customers who will work with them each time they come in or call. The salespeople should maintain records of their customers' purchases so that they can assist them in wardrobe planning, for instance, or offer reminders of special occasions requiring gifts. When new merchandise comes in that they feel will be of interest to their customers, staff members can call or send a note.

Not everyone appreciates this type of assistance, and not every store can offer it. Those that do may find a rivalry developing among sales staff members, especially if staff compensation is based on a commission. To avoid competitiveness, some stores have employees take turns *being up*, or taking care of the next new customer.

Many shoppers are grateful for service with a personal touch and appreciate being recognized when they shop in a specialty store. Whether the personal shopper you provide to customers is one special individual or all the members of your staff, personal shopping assistance will set your store apart from the masses. Encourage everyone to address customers by name, starting with whatever level of formality seems best, and make an effort to remember something about their interests, occupation, likes and dislikes. David Grimes, owner of the decorative accessories line Potpourri Designs, comments, "People like to be recognized, and it is really so very easy to do with just a tiny bit of effort. I have always told our folks that there is no excuse for not calling someone by name after they have written a check or given a credit card. It is right there in front of you. And after you do it several times with the same person, you will begin to recognize people and call them by name without having to refer to a check or credit card."

Employees should also be encouraged to send thank-you notes to important customers, telling them how much the store appreciates their business and inviting them to come in again soon. A coupon for a discount on the next purchase or a small gift could be enclosed. Provide your staff with attractive note cards with the store name on them, and keep a supply of cards and stamps near the checkout counter so that employees can fill them in during the quiet times between customers.

The Corporate Market

According to specialist JoAnne Stone-Geier, the corporate gift business is a $5 billion market. "Gift giving is one of the most advantageous communication skills of the business world. It creates an image, and sends a message of spirit and goodwill. It is a sensitive art. The '90s corporate-gift client is concerned with greater perceived value, creativity, showing a personal touch, environmentally correct wrapping, and probably supports a social cause. Significantly, the corporate-gift buyer is searching for new store resources and services."

There is a ready niche in servicing the needs of businesses buying gifts, imprinted holiday cards, awards, office products, flowers, or specialty advertising products. A shop that decides to pursue this market aggressively will need to develop a plan, supported by samples, materials, and sales work in the field or on the telephone. Once a relationship is established with a large business, the repeat orders may come easily. A bank, for instance, will probably call the same gift basket business or florist every time it needs a baby gift.

There is ample opportunity for the specialty shop that decides to offer its services to business clients, although the competition is strong. Start by researching the types of purchases local businesses are making and the sources they are using. Membership in a business or service club would be a good source for leads on corporate accounts. Even if you choose not to pursue corporate sales actively, you may want to give businesses a quantity discount if they come to you for a large number of items.

We sell many products that are used in restaurants and attract some of this professional business by offering a 10 percent discount card to be used on items for the restaurant. We may someday expand this market by doing regular mailings, or in-person visits, to the major local restaurants.

Consider using the names of distinguished business customers to strengthen the store's image. Corporate and professional clients may be willing to garner some free publicity by being mentioned on a sign listing the shop's exclusive customers. In America, shops can't claim to be the "Purveyor to the Queen" as shops in England can, but an upscale produce store could note that it sells to the finest French restaurant in town.

It's a Wrap

One advantage to customers in most specialty shops is that the merchandise they purchase will be packaged nicely and possibly even shipped or delivered. When the items the customer is purchasing are handled respectfully, the customer feels well treated.

Many shops package items by putting them in a bag, possibly wrapped in tissue. For this type of packaging, the bag and the tissue should be color coordinated and should have the store's name on them. But in most cases, especially if the item is being purchased as a gift, boxing and wrapping are services customers expect from a specialty shop. To paraphrase one gift box company's ad, if it's a gift, you'd better have a box for it.

Having boxes of many sizes and a variety of papers and ribbons requires a great deal of space and expense, but wrapping and boxing are services that are a good investment, providing an excellent means of advertising your store image to both the customer and the gift recipient. Your store packaging should be in keeping with the image you are creating for the shop. Remember to order these supplies, especially those that will be custom imprinted, at least six weeks before the store will open.

If you incorporate your name or logo into the packaging in a subtle manner, no one will object. Tiffany, for example, has such a prestigious reputation that customers actually *want* the store's name on the outside of the package, but most of us need to be more subtle. We use tissue paper printed with our store name and logo in heavy white ink on thin white tissue. Other stores use an overall repeat of their logo in colors to match the gift box, or they seal solid color tissue with a sticker with the store name.

The store logo can be hot stamped on the outside of a gift box, especially attractive when done in a foil ink that matches the ribbon and bow. However, some customers will not consider a package wrapped if the store name is on the outside and may even request gift wrap over an attractive gift box with an elegant metallic or textured finish and no store logo.

We have 3M™ Sasheen ribbon hot stamped with a repeat of our logo, and use this ribbon together with a matching solid ribbon to make bows on a special bow machine. These bows can be stored flat and fluffed up for use, allowing us to keep quite a supply on hand. Our staff isn't wild about making bows, so our children do them to earn pocket money. Other types of premade bows include the ingenious "pull bows" that store flat and pop up into full-size bows when two pieces of ribbon are pulled.

Inexpensive, narrow all-cotton ribbon can be imprinted with the store name and logo in a wide variety of colors. This ribbon can be curled and is wonderful to use on gift baskets and small packages. You can make hanks of this ribbon, mixing imprinted with a matching solid or stripe in loops, to store as ready-to-use bows, fluffing them up and curling the ends when you use them.

At Leonardo, a gift and decorative accessory shop in Copenhagen, small purchases are treated to a simple but elegant wrap: the item is wrapped in a bit of tissue and placed in a pretty floral gift bag, which is folded over at the top and sealed with a store sticker and a swirl of curled gold ribbon. We keep a supply of little bags in a colorful children's design to give to children for their stickers or other small treasures.

Some shops use a gift bag tote for wrap, filling it with tissue and tying ribbons to the handles. For a particularly memorable presentation, helium-filled balloons can be added. A special device allows you to insert small objects, including dollar bills and lottery tickets, in the balloons before they are inflated.

Many shops offer to put together a gift basket for customers or have premade baskets for sale. Baskets (or other containers) can be enclosed in bright cellophane or wrapped in special film that will shrink when heated with a hair dryer or special heat gun. The companies that sell these supplies can often give valuable suggestions for making eye-catching baskets. If you offer to customize baskets for your customers, The Gift Basket of Grand Rapids, Michigan, suggests allowing a day's lead time so you can make the gift look just right, even if the shop is busy with customers. The cost of wrapping materials and staff time should be built into the price of the gift basket.

How do you select gift boxes for your store? There are inexpensive, lightweight white boxes available, although they may not be strong enough to hold heavy items securely. If you offer gift wrapping, customers almost always want these plain white boxes wrapped in paper. A more elegant colored or earth-toned gift box, on the other hand, looks wonderful with a fancy ribbon and bow, saving time, money, and natural resources.

The cost of boxing and wrapping can be charged to the customer or included in the store's markup. Consider taking a little extra margin on items likely to be wrapped and offering gift wrapping as a complimentary service. As an alternative, you might offer free wrapping on purchases above a certain minimum, such as $5.00. A box, bow, and wrap can easily cost over $1.00, so it can be prohibitive to wrap every small item at no charge.

If you offer wrapping, make it as attractive as possible within your budget, and offer a choice of papers for different occasions. If you want to offer extra touches, such as a little ornament tied into the bow of a Christmas package, you might make this deluxe wrap available at a slight extra charge. Wrapping can be a wonderful creative outlet, as Nieman Marcus has found. It employs a number of full-time gift package designers, and customers look forward to the gift wrap as much as the gift.

Getting the Goods Out

Some specialty shops, such as florists, are expected to make local deliveries, often the same day the purchase is made. If you are one of these, having your own vehicles and delivery staff is essential for prompt service. A delivery vehicle presents another opportunity to advertise your shop, so be sure that your truck or van is attractive, clean, and well marked with the store name, tag line, logo, and address. Staff members making deliveries will be representing your store and should be as polite and neatly dressed as anyone in the shop. For special occasions such as Valentine's Day, you might want to hire actors or singers to make deliveries in costume or accompanied by a special song. Your regular staff members might not mind dressing up as an Easter bunny to do a delivery, but don't count on it!

When delivering gifts, don't miss out on the opportunity to let the recipient of the delivery know about your business. Be sure there is a card or sticker on the item with your store name, address, and telephone number.

You might even follow up with a call, asking if the gift was received in good condition and saying you hope the recipient enjoys it.

When you promise a delivery at a certain time, it is good service to call the customer if you will be late. No one likes to sit at home waiting for an overdue delivery. Equipping delivery vans with mobile phones allows delivery people to keep in touch with the store and the customer. For the added convenience of your customers, consider offering evening or weekend delivery.

Delivery service is essential if you are selling corporate gifts or bulky items such as furniture. If you do not have your own delivery vehicle, a local courier or taxi service may be able to help you on a per-delivery basis. You might also consider cooperating with a noncompeting store that has its own vehicles and would like to make fuller use of them.

Many shops offer to ship a customer's purchases via a parcel service. For a small charge, UPS will make daily stops at your store to see if there are any packages to go out. The customer usually pays the UPS charge and perhaps a small packing fee. The store needs to have an area set up with packaging materials, such as bubble pack or Styrofoam "peanuts" to wrap the purchases. You will also need a system for tracking these shipments in case of problems.

When a customer orders an item to be sent to someone else, a thoughtful touch is to send a thank-you note to the person making the purchase stating the date the package was shipped. If the order was placed by telephone rather than in person, enclose the credit card receipt as well. Figures 7-5 and 7-6 provide samples of a shipping form and a customer thank-you note you can adapt for your shop.

Wedding and Gift Registries

The tradition of bridal registry began with the bride and her mother selecting a china and silver pattern, but today both the bride and groom put together their wish list for wedding gifts—and that list is by no means limited to dinnerware. We've had couples register for fancy soaps and Christmas ornaments as well. People even register for occasions other than marriage, although showers and weddings are still the main reasons for using a gift registry. Many stores, even the big box discounters, now offer the service. In order to stand out, a specialty shop must offer something special.

Whether you use a computer (particularly practical for shops with multiple locations) or a manual system, the key to gift registry is to make

Figure 7-5 Sample shipping form.

```
                    STORE NAME
                     ADDRESS
                   PHONE & FAX

                  SHIPPING FORM

DATE:_____     SHIP ☐ ASAP OR ☐ ON _____

ITEMS_____PRICE_____

      _____PRICE_____

      _____PRICE_____

      SHIP TO:_____

              _____

              _____

      PHONE:_____

FROM:  _____

       _____

       _____

      PHONE:_____

      ☐ GIFT WRAP -- CHOICE OF WRAP:_____

      ☐ ENCLOSURE (CIRCLE: RECEIPT, CARD, OTHER)

METHOD OF PAYMENT_____

SALESPERSON_____

SHIPPING CHARGES:

WEIGHT_____UPS ZONE_____PACKING CHARGE_____TOTAL_____


FOR OFFICE USE ONLY:

SHIPPED ON_____BY_____SHIPPED WEIGHT_____
```

Figure 7-6 Sample shipped order acknowledgment on thank-you note.

```
                STORE NAME and LOGO
                     ADDRESS
                   PHONE & FAX

  THANK YOU FOR YOUR ORDER

  THE MERCHANDISE YOU ORDERED WAS SHIPPED TO:

  _____

  ON:_____

  WE APPRECIATE THE OPPORTUNITY TO SERVE YOU!
```

This form should be signed by the person packing the order. For mail and telephone orders, enclose the customer's receipt. Print up to four per 8½ × 11-inch sheet.

it as easy as possible for the person registering and for the person selecting a gift. We have a preprinted form listing lots of suggestions by category, following the layout of the store (more or less). After an introductory chat, the couple is given a clipboard and pen and encouraged to select as many items as they want. The more the merrier, in fact, because guests want a variety of merchandise and prices to choose from.

Other stores have a wedding consultant walk through the shop with the couple and make note of their selections. Traditionally, the consultant would offer advice to the bride and create a table setting showing how the bride's choice of china, crystal, and silver would look together. The table setting would then be displayed in the store together with the engagement picture of the happy couple. In lieu of this, some other listing is needed to show who is registered and the wedding date. We use a fabric wall sign holding an elegantly printed card for each registry.

After a couple has registered, we give them a small thank-you gift (usually a cake knife or guest book) and follow up with a note that includes a few preprinted cards indicating that the couple is registered at our shop. These cards may be sent directly to the engaged couple or to the bride's mother.

When a guest comes in to select a gift, we pull out the registry and go through the list of items the couple has selected, offering to show some of the items in the person's price range. At Crate & Barrel, guests can go to a self-service computer terminal and read through a wedding registry, printing out any information they need. In the future, a shop's wedding registry may be available on the Internet, allowing the guest to select an item without ever speaking to a live person.

We offer to gift wrap the wedding gift purchase and then mark it off as sold on the registry. We also indicate the date of purchase and the initials of the person who bought it in case the gift enclosure is lost.

> Shop of the Gulls, a resort gift and apparel store in Charlevoix-the-Beautiful, Michigan, will do anything it can for its wedding registry couples. When one of its registered brides ran short of housing for her guests, owner Jeannine Wallace put up their out-of-town priest in her guest room.

Registries are no longer limited to wedding couples, of course. Many children's stores offer baby shower registries, and others encourage children to register their birthday gift wishes. We tried a general gift registry at Christmas one year, providing customers with a handmade Christmas tree magnet that said, "Santa, I've been very good. To find out what I'd like for Christmas, stop at Orange Tree Imports." But most of our customers seemed reluctant to write down what they hoped to receive. A gift registry certainly would help us be of service to the harried husbands who come in and ask us if we have any idea what their wives might like for Christmas.

According to an article by Louise Lee in the *Wall Street Journal* (August 2, 1995, p. B1), Crate & Barrel used its gift registry to throw a shower for Aids-Care, a nonprofit organization that runs a home for people with advanced AIDS near the store's Chicago headquarters. Aids-Care registered for items ranging from kitchen gadgets to furniture and, as a result, hundreds of needed items were donated to the home.

Gift Certificates

Even with a gift registry, some people can't quite decide what to give, or want to let the recipient have the pleasure of visiting the store and selecting something. Every shop should have gift certificates available for these occasions, and they should look as festive as any gift you sell.

There are preprinted gift certificates available from store supply houses, but it is more exciting to create your own. Use your computer or a local artist to come up with a certificate that reflects the nature of your shop. When opening a new store, be sure to order gift certificates in advance so they will be on hand when the shop opens.

An authorization number system will help prevent stolen certificates from being forged and used to acquire merchandise. It is a good idea to use a form for keeping track of certificates issued and when they are used. A sample gift certificate registry form is shown in Figure 7-7. Certificates should list an expiration date one or two years after the date of issue. Check with your state to find out whether gift certificates are exempt from state sales tax, and indicate on the certificate whether tax is included.

Many customers enclose the gift certificate in a card, so they will not need any packaging. But consider offering an alternative, such as a fancy tube with gold star glitter in it, for those who want something fancier. Some lingerie stores go all out to make their gift certificate packaging attractive, because a significant percentage of their gift certificates are reportedly never redeemed. Even certificates that are redeemed usually cost stores less than it might have cost them to box and wrap a large gift.

> Strictly Discs, a Madison, Wisconsin, shop specializing in new and used compact discs, presents their special square gift certificate inserted into the cover compartment of an empty CD box.

Special Orders and Layaway

Can you imagine walking into a discount store and asking the store clerk to order something for you that the store normally doesn't stock? Most specialty stores, on the other hand, will do special orders for their customers whenever possible. Suppliers may make this service difficult by

Figure 7-7 Sample gift certificate record.

GIFT CERTIFICATE RECORD

authorization number	purchased by	amount	recipient/s	date purchased	date used

having high minimum orders and minimum packs on specific items. Before promising to get an item you don't normally stock, make sure that the customer is serious about buying it, perhaps by requesting a deposit. Check with your supplier about availability and minimums as soon as possible, and keep the customer informed about the status of the order.

In addition to special orders, customers sometimes request items we are out of and expect back in or something we don't have a source for but will try to find. We use a two-part, 4- by 6-inch carbonless carbon file card for all these requests (see Figure 7-8). The bottom, heavier copy goes immediately into one of two sections of a file box: "on order" or "not on order." In this way, a customer calling to check on the request can be told the status of the order by anyone on the staff. The top copy goes to the buyer for that department and is stapled to the purchase order when the item is ordered. At the time that the order is placed, the file copy gets marked and moved from "not on order" to "on order."

When a requested item comes in, we notify the customer by telephone or by using a preprinted postcard of our shop. The item is then put

Figure 7-8 Sample customer request card.

```
                    CUSTOMER REQUEST
    NAME (CIRCLE ONE: MR./MS.)_____

    ADDRESS_____DATE REQUESTED_____

    _____NOT NEEDED AFTER_____

    PHONE (H)_____(W)_____

    ITEM REQUESTED_____PRICE_____

    _____

    SOURCE_____STAFF NAME_____

    NOTIFY CUSTOMER IMMEDIATELY IF UNLIKELY TO ORDER WITHIN A MONTH? ___ YES ___NO

    ANY DEPOSIT PAID?___(IF SO, PLEASE LIST ON BACK)  ITEM TO BE PUT ON HOLD?_____

    DATE  ORDERED_____B.O.?_____ARRIVED_____HOLD UNTIL_____

    NOTIFIED BY _____MAIL____TELEPHONE_____LEFT MESSAGE_____DATE AND
                                                                    STAFF NAME
```

Print on two-part carbonless carbon form (4 × 6-inch), with the card stock bottom copy to go in the special order file box and the top copy to the merchandise buyer.

Figure 7-9 Sample on-hold slip.

ON HOLD

CUSTOMER:_____

PHONE: _____HM_____WK

DATE PUT ON HOLD: _____

TAKE OFF HOLD ON:_____

ITEM/S_____

_____

PRICE/S_____

THIS MERCHANDISE IS:

☐ FROM STOCK

☐ ON LAYAWAY

☐ A SPECIAL ORDER

☐ AN OUT-OF-STOCK ITEM NOW
BACK IN STOCK

on hold for two weeks, with a slip attached to it giving the customer's name, telephone number, and other information (see Figure 7-9). Large stores might need to file items being held for customers alphabetically. When the "on hold" period has expired, we try to recontact customers to find out if they still want the items.

We use a green 4- by 6-inch card for items that customers ask us to hold for them from stock (see Figure 7-10). Sometimes customers phone for an item and want it held; sometimes they select it in the store and are not ready to buy it right away. If they wish to make time payments on an item, we put it on layaway, using a special two-part form, with copies for us and the customer, to show payments (see Figure 7-11). Encouraging regular payments on layaway purchases helps prevent customers from holding items for months and then changing their minds. When a customer does decide against a layaway item, we feel that we must refund the deposit in full, although we have been deprived of the opportunity to sell that item for the entire time it was being held. One woman routinely put a shopping bag full of Halloween, Easter, and Christmas items on layaway and then called after the holiday to say she didn't want the merchandise. We finally had to tell her that we could no longer hold items for her.

Figure 7-10 Sample customer hold card.

CUSTOMER HOLD

NAME (CIRCLE ONE: MR./MS.)_____

ADDRESS_____DATE PUT ON HOLD:_____

_____HOLD UNTIL:_____

PHONE (H)_____(W)_____

ITEM/S_____PRICE/S_____

_____

STAFF MEMBER_____

☐PAID IN FULL ☐NOT PAID ☐DEPOSIT PAID:____

Print this form on card stock (4 × 6-inch).

Figure 7-11 Sample layaway form.

LAYAWAY

STORE NAME
ADDRESS
PHONE
FAX

NAME_____

ADDRESS_____

CITY AND STATE_____

PHONE_____(HOME)_____(WORK)

SALESPERSON_____

DATE_____TO BE PAID IN FULL BY_____

ITEM/S AND PRICE/S_____

_____

SALES TAX_____   TOTAL DUE_____

Date Paid	Merchandise Amount	Sales Tax	TOTAL PAID	Staff Initials

PLEASE BRING YOUR COPY OF THIS FORM WHEN MAKING PAYMENTS. THANK YOU.

Print on two-part carbonless carbon paper.

EVALUATING CUSTOMER SERVICE

Good customer service is giving your customers what they want. And how do you know what they want? By asking. If a customer compliments you on your store, thank the person and ask if he or she has any suggestions for how you could improve it. If a customer complains about something, look at the complaint as an opportunity to learn how to do things better. Make it easy for your staff to pass customer complaints and ideas on to you. As the owner or manager, you should personally follow up on all customer problems immediately, by telephone or by mail. Thanking a customer for bringing a complaint to your attention is often enough, but you may want to enclose a gift certificate to encourage an unhappy shopper to give the store another try.

Keep a notebook handy to list items that customers regularly ask for that you don't have, and try to fill in the gaps. Having the widest possible selection of merchandise on hand is one form of good customer service. Customers like to shop at stores where they can count on finding what they are looking for.

Some shops use a mystery shopper to check up on customer service. The mystery shopper goes into the store anonymously and asks for sales assistance, makes a purchase, or brings in a return, and then submits a written report about the quality of the experience. The concept of mystery shoppers is too much like hiring a spy for my liking, but I'm sure much can be learned from their reports.

Many stores have a suggestion box for customers. Whole Foods, an innovative health food and grocery store based in Texas, has made its suggestion box the source of an ongoing dialogue with customers by publicly posting all suggestions with a written reply from a staff member. Even children's suggestions are answered respectfully by someone in the store and put up on the bulletin board.

A more formal way of finding out what customers want is by conducting a customer survey. This can be done briefly at the checkout counter, if it is limited to a few questions—for example, "How did you hear about our store?" "Did you find everything you were looking for?" and "Is there anything we can do to serve you better?" A longer survey can be sent to your mailing list, with a small gift to reward those who complete it, or filled in while a customer is shopping in the store. Other possible questions include asking where customers live, what radio and

TV stations they like, and what newspapers and magazines they read—invaluable information in planning your advertising.

Any survey done in the store should be completely optional, because some people don't like to answer questions and others may be in a hurry. Those who do answer your survey will tend to say what they think you want to hear, so you must take into account that the survey will not be entirely objective.

Consider offering postage-paid comment cards for customers to mail back to you with suggestions or complaints. Although the customer name and telephone number should be optional, be sure to respond to the comments of every customer willing to provide that information. Some businesses set up a toll-free or local telephone line with an answering machine for customers to use for comments. Provide cards listing the telephone number in the store for shoppers to take with them.

For the ultimate amount of customer feedback, consider forming a customer council. We did this when we were planning a major expansion and found that our best customers were pleased to be consulted and happy to give us an evening or two of their time. We presented the group with specific questions to discuss and invited our staff to join us for the session. Refreshments were served, and the customers were rewarded with a gift to thank them. As a bonus, the local newspaper found the idea so novel that it featured the story on the business page.

CAN YOU DO IT ALL?

When employees make suggestions, they realize that we can't implement them all. Customers also have ideas that we may choose not to act on. We know, for example, that if we asked customers what hours they'd like us to be open, they would probably want us open late every evening. We are able to operate a successful business without being open every night, so we choose to meet their needs in other ways. We offer the services we feel are most important to our customers and are economically feasible for our shop, realizing that in the future we may have to change in order to stay competitive. But the cornerstone of customer service, polite attention to the customer's needs, always remains the same and is essential to the success of every specialty shop.

8

ADVERTISING YOUR SHOP

"Advertising doesn't cost," the old saying goes. "It pays." The short-term dollar-for-dollar return on money spent for advertising may not be apparent, but in the long term, the money you invest in promoting your shop should be rewarded with increased sales.

Do you need to advertise? If you are running the gift shop at the top of the Empire State Building, probably not. The best advertising in the world will not inspire the average customer to make a special trip just to visit a small store that far off the beaten path. In fact, location alone is enough to draw customers to shops in tourist destinations and in some other well-traveled, high-traffic places. For a dry cleaner like the Whistle Stop Cleaners, situated right inside the busy commuter train station in Fairfield, Connecticut, location and signage are the biggest draw.

Most specialty shops, however, do need to advertise in order to attract new customers and to encourage existing customers to return. Good advertising increases awareness of your products and enhances your store's image. It should help differentiate your shop from the competition, especially the discount stores and category killers that advertise nothing but low prices. Use your advertising to let the public know about your style, service, selection, and knowledgeable staff.

There is no limit to the many different forms that advertising can take, from a Yellow Pages ad to a banner towed by an airplane. Signage, window displays, shopping bags, brochures, and public television underwriting can all be considered part of your advertising program. Think of advertising as a challenge to your creativity and imagination. How many different ways can you find to express the appeal of your store and your merchandise to the buying public? What is the image of your store that you want all your advertising to project?

ESTABLISHING AN ADVERTISING BUDGET

Most traditional forms of advertising are fairly expensive, so you must spend your advertising dollars wisely, especially at first. Experience, based on the types of advertising that produce the best results for your store, will help guide your future decisions. (There are also numerous low-cost or free promotional opportunities. They are discussed in the next chapter.)

An advertising budget normally ranges from 3 to 5 percent of total sales, but can be as high as 10 percent. Retailing marketing consultant Jeffrey L. Greene suggests that four factors be considered in setting the budget: (1) traffic, (2) marketplace awareness, (3) competition, and (4) price sensitivity. If you have high traffic, are well known in your market, have few competitors, and place little emphasis on price, you won't need to spend much on advertising. Conversely, if you are in a low-traffic area, are not well known, have many competitors, or want people to shop with you because of your low prices, you will need to do more advertising.

A new store needs to advertise more aggressively than one that is well established. Some sources recommend doubling your advertising budget for the first year you are in business. Of course, unless you are opening a franchise or branch store, you will have little way of predicting what this first year's sales will be. Doubling an advertising budget based on a hypothetical sales figure can be dangerous. A leather goods store on our street spent $10,000 on television advertising soon after opening, producing only $12,000 in sales. Had sales been $100,000, this might have been a wise investment. As it turned out, the store went out of business within a year. Check with other stores your size to get an idea of their advertising budget and the types of advertising that work best for them.

If your business is seasonal, budget more of your advertising money for the months when you are busiest. It is always tempting to run big ads to bring in business during slow times and to try to increase sales of slow items by advertising them. But as a rule, you should use your advertising to sell what's selling and when it's selling.

How to Spend Your Advertising Money

There are countless ways to spend the dollars you've allocated to advertising. If you've never done any advertising before, you may be surprised at how little you get for your money. An ad you barely glance at as you read your morning paper may have cost hundreds of dollars. It pays to give careful consideration to getting the most mileage from your advertising money.

Advertising can help make new customers aware of your store, including where it is located, what it sells, and the services it offers. This is *image advertising*, and it is useful for building prestige and trust among existing customers as well as reaching new ones. A motto, or *tag line*, used in conjunction with your store name and logo can help create a memorable impression in this type of ad. Try to define your store in a few well-chosen words. The Imaginarium, for example, uses the tag line, "A Toy Store Kids Can Handle." If you use radio or television, your tag line can be part of a jingle to help listeners remember it.

A second type of advertising is *product promotion*, which highlights individual items. Many products, especially national brands, do their own product advertising. Suppliers with an advertising program sometimes allow a store name to appear in their product ads or underwrite store advertising featuring their products by providing an advertising allowance.

The third type is *special event* or *sale advertising*, encouraging customers to come in during a specific time. There has been such a proliferation of sale advertising from department stores and discounters that consumers have become a bit jaded. A sale has to offer a deep discount or an unusual twist to get today's shoppers excited.

TARGETING YOUR MARKET

Who are you trying to reach with your advertising? This is the first question to ask in order to focus your advertising dollars. A fashion store for teens would do better to approach its customers through a popular radio station than the newspaper. The older, wealthy shoppers that a home design store needs to reach are more likely to read a glossy city magazine. Try to establish a profile of your typical customer, just as you did when planning your first buying decisions. Imagine an average shopper walking through your front door. Is this person male or female? How old? Where is he or she most likely to live or work? These demographics will help you develop a target market for your advertising.

In addition to your primary target market, you may wish to focus some advertising on specific segments of your customer base or your merchandise selection. We run ads for Hanukkah menorahs in the local Jewish community newspaper, because we know this is a good way to reach our best customers for these products. Your store may appeal to several such small niche markets, as well as to customers who belong to a specific population group, such as the elderly, Hispanics, or African Americans, who may not be reached effectively through the store's general advertising program. Don't forget to allot some of your advertising budget to targeting these important segments of the market.

Research the best way to reach each targeted group. Before you open, you can solicit suggestions from your focus group. Once your store is open, you can do an informal survey of which media your customers favor. Make a list of local radio and TV stations, regional magazines, and daily and weekly newspapers. Ask customers if they'd be willing to check off their favorites, but be sure to be gracious if they'd rather not participate. Offer a small treat or gift to thank those who fill in the form.

CHOOSING THE MEDIA YOU USE

Once you have determined *who* you want to reach through your advertising, three additional questions will help you decide what direction you want to concentrate on.

1. *What is the message you wish your advertising to convey?* Radio may be a better choice for timely information about a special event, whereas print advertising or television is better if you need to show an item. Stores selling complex home exercise equipment might do better with a short video "brochure" showing the features of their products than with a traditional mailing.

2. *What type of advertising is most appropriate to your store?* The choice of medium should be in keeping with your store's image. Don't do coupons or advertise in the local shopper if you are concerned about mak-

ing an elegant impression. Stores that appeal to a narrow segment of the population, such as a weaving supply store, can use direct marketing to customers interested in textile arts. This medium would be more effective than radio ads aimed at the general public.

3. *When do you want your message to reach the target audience?* You might consider using a billboard, or a drive time radio program, to influence shoppers to stop at your video store on their way home from work. If you are selling wedding rings, a newspaper bridal supplement early in the year may be the best way to reach couples in the market for rings for their summer weddings. Time your advertising to create a sense of urgency, encouraging shoppers to take action soon.

Most retailers use a combination of several media in order to get thorough coverage. Whatever you decide, it is important that you commit to a long-term program and give it enough exposure to make it effective.

Once you have a clear idea of the "who, what, and when" goals of your advertising, you can work more productively with the sales representatives from the various media. In large communities there are so many radio stations and print options that meeting with these reps can take a lot of time. Instead of listening to a canned sales pitch, type up a list of your advertising goals, and ask media reps to give you ideas for reaching them. For example, you might state that your main goal is to promote your store's name recognition among males aged thirty to fifty, and to increase sales of sporting goods to this target market over the next three months. A radio station with primarily female listeners would not have much to offer you, but a cable TV sports program might propose an attractive package.

USING AN ADVERTISING AGENCY

Professionally designed advertising tends to look much more sophisticated than the advertising most retailers create on their own. The creative staff of an advertising agency includes graphic artists who can design effective print advertising and writers who can create memorable radio and television spots. The agency's account executives are familiar with all the media in your market and can help you select the ones best for you. The agency can also help you develop and implement a consistent advertising program. Projecting a consistent image throughout all your advertising is a key factor in successful advertising.

But most small stores can't afford to use an advertising agency, at least not initially. Advertising agencies usually charge a high hourly rate, or per project fee. They also earn a commission on your ads from the media they use, which is sometimes credited toward what you pay. Nevertheless, you should meet with an agency or independent advertising consultant to see whether their services will be a good investment. You might decide to have an advertising agency work on a specific project with you, such as designing a logo or preparing a media campaign for the store's grand opening. As your store grows, and perhaps branches out or establishes franchises, you may choose to have an advertising agency handle all your advertising.

STRETCHING YOUR BUDGET THROUGH CO-OP ADVERTISING

Manufacturers benefit when retailers promote the vendor's products through store advertising. In order to encourage stores to promote their merchandise, suppliers sometimes offer to pay for part of the advertising through ad allowances, or *co-op money*. The manufacturer will usually pay 50 to 100 percent of the actual cost of advertising featuring its product if the ad meets certain criteria, such as the inclusion of the supplier's logo. Often the amount of advertising allowance available is based on the amount of merchandise purchased. Purchases are usually added up, or *accrued*, over a set period of time. One reason department stores are able to advertise so aggressively is that they earn huge advertising allowances through volume buying during each accrual period.

If a manufacturer will approve an ad that is in keeping with your image and if the ad is worth enough to your store to pay the other part of the cost, by all means take advantage of any advertising allowances your manufacturers offer. Millions of dollars of co-op money go unused each year, and it is worth investigating whether some of this money can be put to use to stretch your ad budget. Be cautioned, however, that the process of claiming advertising allowances, usually issued in the form of a credit from the manufacturer, can be time-consuming. Tapes or samples of the ads, called *tear sheets*, along with invoices and other forms, must be submitted. Be sure that the ads you place are large enough to justify your effort in claiming the co-op dollars.

Manufacturers may also be able to help your advertising efforts by providing *ad slicks*, glossy copies of ready-to-use ads, plus brand-name logos and product illustrations for creating your own ads. Some suppliers have premade radio and television spots available. If the supplier's ready-made print or broadcast ads are in keeping with your image, personalize them by adding your store name, location, and hours. The advertisement in Figure 8-1 was provided by the manufacturer, Vera Bradley Designs, and personalized by adding the store name and a few words of additional copy.

Figure 8-1 Co-op advertising example.

Joint Promotion Saves Money

If your shop is located near other stores, you can stretch your advertising dollars by cooperating with them to promote your shopping area. Customers who visit one store are likely to visit another. Bring more shoppers to your neighborhood by pooling some of your advertising money to produce general ads, especially in magazines or other media aimed at visitors, and to create a shopping guide to your area. Our store originated the Monroe Street Shopping Guide, a two-color brochure that is distributed in local hotels and visitors' centers, as well as to convention groups and our local colleges. Ads in the guide pay for the printing costs, but every business is listed and described, whether it contributes or not.

Individual ads have more impact when blocked together with ads from other shops in the same area. A newspaper or magazine will sometimes contribute the space for a unifying "banner" across the top of the page. Radio and television advertising can also be made more affordable by developing a general ad for the shopping area, with a different store being featured in the middle of the ad each time it is run. This type of spot is called a *doughnut*, because of the "hole" in the center.

Shopping centers usually require a certain amount of joint advertising, and management will develop the advertising campaigns. Other shopping areas can benefit from the merchants' forming their own association to improve the area and develop some special events, such as an annual street fair or holiday open house. With many merchants sharing the cost, purchasing banners, flyers, radio spots, and newspaper ads to promote these events is not expensive.

You need not limit cooperative advertising to neighboring merchants. Look for creative opportunities for what is known as *fusion advertising*, with the customers of one business getting a special gift or discount if they patronize another. Offer to give out coupons for a free dessert at a local restaurant, for example, if the restaurant will give its patrons a discount offer for your store.

THE WORLD OF PRINT ADVERTISING

For years there have been predictions that print on paper will be made obsolete by the electronic media, but that hasn't happened yet. By far the most common form of advertising small retailers use is print advertising, followed by direct mail. Newspapers—daily, Sunday and special weekly papers—continue to be used extensively by small businesses, in part because they are less expensive than most broadcast media such as radio and television. Yellow Pages ads, direct mail postcards, brochures, catalogs, magazines, and even business cards are all options for printed advertising.

Be sure to post copies of all printed advertising in your store where your staff can see them. Employees should always know what is being advertised and where to find the merchandise. You may also wish to make signs in the store based on your ads. If an advertisement has run in a prestigious publication, feature a copy on a sign board that says "as seen in [name of magazine or newspaper]."

Designing Newspaper and Magazine Ads

Take a look at the ads in your local paper. You'll probably see that many of them tend to be crowded, confusing, unimaginative, or otherwise visually unappealing. As a creative retailer, one of your jobs is to design ads that are as pleasing to the eye as your store displays are. And if you want customers to find your store entertaining, make your ads entertaining. Well-done cleverness and cuteness can make the reader smile, creating a warm feeling toward your store before the customer has even come in. Figures 8-2 and 8-3 show some examples of creative print ads.

Some of the many excellent books on designing your own print advertising are listed in the Bibliography at the end of this book. You may also be able to get help from the commercial art program at your local technical college, or from a freelance graphic artist. We have worked for many years with Chris Clementi, a talented artist who does product illustrations and occasional ad designs for us. She has the wonderful ability to take a vague idea and make it come to life on paper. We found Chris by advertising for a freelance artist in the classifieds and reviewing the portfolios brought to us by the artists who responded to the ad.

Most print media provide free technical assistance in designing ads. Some of their artists are better than others, of course. It can't hurt to see what they come up with, and perhaps take their concept to your own artist to be refined. You can also ask the paper or magazine to create a layout from your idea.

The Elements of a Good Print Ad

Good print ads, as illustrated in Figures 8-2 and 8-3, usually feature a headline that catches the reader's attention or announces the benefit to

Figure 8-2 Instead of just showing dozens of pairs of sale skis, this clever ad subtly draws the reader's attention to its message through a witty, visual pun.

(*Agency: Arnold Finnegan Martin, Richmond, Virginia; Art Director: Pat Harris.*)

Figure 8-3 This ad makes excellent use of white space and an attention-getting headline to celebrate the definitive design style that sets Room Service apart from its mass merchandise competitors.

(Agency: Martin Williams Advertising, Minneapolis.)

the consumer; factual *copy*, or text, that invites action; and a balance of the *white space*, or open areas, copy, and graphics that is pleasing to the eye. The graphics should be appropriate to the type of merchandise being sold. As a rule, photographs sell better than illustrations, but a drawing is usually faster and less expensive to produce than a commercial photograph. There are also many books and computer disks of copyright-free clip art that can be used in ads at no charge. To create a Christmas ad, for example, you might select a clip art holly border, write your own copy, and illustrate it with a clip art drawing of a wreath. Be sure to add your symbol logo and tag line, if you use them, and your store name in its logo typestyle, along with the address, telephone number, and store hours.

The use of open areas, or *white space*, can make an ad stand out, or headlines can be printed in white against a black background, called a *reverse*, to catch readers' attention. If you are producing a black-and-white ad, check to see whether a single additional color, called *spot color*, can be used to highlight sections of the copy or headline. Develop a recognizable look for your ads, perhaps featuring a special border and a distinctive but legible typestyle, or font. Given a choice, run smaller ads frequently rather than a few large ads on an irregular basis.

All print ads should be carefully proofread by at least two people. Always allow time to receive a *draft*, or proof copy, of an ad so that corrections can be made. Watch for odd hyphenations of words that are too long for one line and for errors in spelling, prices, and store hours. One mistake that seems to slip by frequently is automatically listing hours for Monday through Friday without noting, for example, that you will be closed Thursday that week for Thanksgiving. Since some stores actually *are* open on holidays, be sure you don't inconvenience your customers by implying that you will be if you won't.

Advertising rates for newspapers and magazines are based on the size of the ad. Newspaper ads are usually measured by the *column inch*, which refers to the width of a printed column for that publication and a standard inch in height. Magazines often sell ads based on a percentage of the page, such as a half-page or quarter-page. If you want to select the location of your ad—for example, in the sports section of the newspaper or on the inside front cover of a magazine—there is normally an additional charge. Check with the sales representative about savings available when you agree to sign a contract for multiple ads over a period of time. The *open rate*, or one-time rate, is almost always considerably higher than the *contract rate*.

Don't overlook the classified ad sections as an inexpensive location for small ads, run on a regular basis, to remind the public of your business name, location, services, and hours. Often display ads can be placed in the classifieds at a much lower rate than in the main body of the newspaper or magazine, and studies show that the classifieds are read carefully by customers in search of bargains, employment, new homes, and certain types of products such as cars and trucks.

Newspapers and magazines often also have the ability to deliver a separate advertising piece for you, either bound in or loose (like all those color supplements that drop out of the Sunday paper when you pick it up). With this service you can reach every subscribing household in a certain area, or *zone*, or reach the entire circulation of the periodical. Consider using this method to distribute a simple 8½- by 11-inch flyer, an advertising supplement provided by one of your manufacturers, or your store catalog.

TELEPHONE DIRECTORY ADVERTISING

The Yellow Pages should be a central part of your advertising plan, especially if yours is a destination shop that customers would be willing to look for. Visitors and newcomers are especially likely to turn to the Yellow Pages, as are potential customers seeking a specific item. Be sure to have at least a simple listing, called a *line listing* (as opposed to a larger display ad), under all the various subject headings a consumer might consult when looking for your products.

Your Yellow Pages ad should be fairly simple and straightforward, because you don't need to work hard to catch the reader's attention. Include all the facts that customers want to know: location, store hours, credit cards accepted, telephone, and perhaps fax number. If you offer brand names or special services, mention these in your ad as well. And list any awards you have won or trade or professional organizations you belong to that will make your store seem more credible than the competition.

Examine what your competitors are doing in the category that best fits your store, and consider using a slightly larger size or spot color to make your business stand out. Keep in mind, however, that the billing for Yellow Pages advertising will be monthly, not annually, and select an ad you can afford. In most communities, Yellow Pages ads are invoiced by the telephone company, but the Yellow Pages portion of the billing should be disbursed under advertising, not utilities, in your bookkeeping system.

When planning a store opening, keep in mind that a new telephone book usually comes out only once a year, and the deadline for inclusion may be as long as four months before publication. If you miss the deadline, you will have to wait a full year to be listed. Consider placing a "coming soon" ad in the telephone directory if it will be printed before your store opens. An answering machine can be used to give current opening date information to any customers who call before the store is up and running.

Don't overlook your white pages listing as an opportunity to make a positive first impression on customers. Many telephone directories allow for a bold print business name in the white pages, and some can accommodate spot color or even a logo. We list our store hours in the white pages, realizing that many customers look up our telephone number to call to ask when we are open.

Yellow Pages sales representatives from neighboring communities and various national business telephone directories may approach you. Don't mistakenly agree to an ad in one of these books, assuming it is your local directory. Advertise in an alternative Yellow Pages only if you feel this will be an effective way to reach new customers.

ADVERTISING IN THE STORE

The most obvious goal of advertising is to bring customers into the store. But an important part of the promotional package reaches consumers once they have entered the door. Signs, brochures, flyers, and calendars of events in the store influence customers' shopping experience and encourage them to return. The way the items purchased in your shop are packaged can help promote your store after the customer leaves; in fact, a good shopping bag becomes a walking billboard. These in-store elements of your marketing plan should be as carefully planned as your media advertising and should be consistent with the image you are trying to project.

In addition to framed signs describing your merchandise, you might want to have a supply of individual cards or handouts available by the products for customers to take when they make a purchase. This is a particularly useful service if the items you carry require special assembly or care, or if there is interesting information you'd like to share about your products, such as the biographies of the artists who made them or the folk traditions the items represent. Be sure to put your store name, address, and telephone number on these flyers, and encourage customers who are buying an item as a gift to include one in the package.

Business Cards: Your Smallest Ad

Have you ever thought of your business card as part of your advertising program? Customers appreciate being able to help themselves to a business card by the cash register, and it is surprising how much information you can fit on these little giveaways: store name, location, and telephone number, plus your tag line, hours, the names of the store's owners, a fax number, and so forth. California's Z Gallery uses a clever fold-over card with lines for customers' notes on the inside cover. At Music and Memories, a music box store in Cambridge, Wisconsin, the back of the store's business card is designated as a "wish list," with room for the stock number, description, and price of the items a customer would like.

Take a stack of business cards with you whenever you display your products at a consumer show—or anywhere other than in the store. You might also ask a related business to keep some on hand. An animal photographer, for example, might be willing to give out cards for a pet food store that is willing to return the favor. There are even special business card exchanges or shuffles, where businesspeople introduce themselves to each other and trade business cards. Check with your local chamber of commerce to see if this type of event is held in your area.

Bag Stuffers, Brochures, and Other Advertising Bargains

In-store advertising can be used to encourage customers to return. Post a calendar of special events in the store, and make copies for customers to take along. Customers love to take brochures and other literature with them, especially if they are undecided about a major purchase. Check with your suppliers about any free product literature that may be available to you, and be sure to put your store name and address on each piece with a stamp or sticker. If there are no brochures available, create your own on the store computer. There are wonderful brochure-formatted papers available from Paper Direct (800-A-PAPERS) and Idea Art (800-433-2278), as well as some office supply stores, that allow you to produce a small quantity of colorful brochures very economically.

Customers often want to jot down the toll-free number of a product line or make some notes about merchandise they are considering buying. Provide 3- by 5-inch cards with the store name, address, and telephone number for this purpose, or print this information on small pads of scratch paper and invite customers to take them home.

A bookmark, a small flyer, or a larger advertising piece can be sent home with every customer by using them as bag stuffers. Staff members can insert these items in the bags ahead of time or slip them in with each purchase. We have occasionally used this technique to help a local non-profit group by "bag stuffing" a notice of a special event for them.

Packaging as Advertising

Your store packaging is as much a part of your store image as the front display window. Attractive packaging makes the customer feel good about the decision to buy from you. When a customer leaves your store carrying a bag with your name and logo on it, chances are excellent that it will be noticed by other shoppers in the area. And if the purchase is a gift, the store wrapping will become part of the presentation, creating a positive impression of your store to the recipient and any other potential customers who are present when it is opened.

Good packaging need not be expensive. A small shop or kiosk might begin by rubber stamping its logo and an attractive design on plain kraft bags and tissue. Even the smallest shop should never use generic bags with no name on them. As the business grows, one of the many suppliers of imprinted boxes and bags can help you to develop a program of matching shopping bags, flat bags, and other packaging materials. We offer both paper and an oversize plastic shopping bag to our customers. Although the plastic ones are more expensive and not as recyclable, we do see them being reused for farmers' market shopping and even picnics.

In designing your bag program, keep in mind that an attractive bag has a much greater chance of being reused. A survey by Equitable Bag cited in *Small Store Survival* showed that "strong graphic design" was a factor in 88 percent of consumer decisions as to what bag to reuse. Shops selling more expensive merchandise should consider buying distinctive packaging to reinforce their store image. Jute, vinyl, or cloth bags can be imprinted with the store logo and given away with a large purchase or used as part of a gift package. Customers almost always reuse these bags, providing free promotion for the store.

Stew Leonard's huge Connecticut produce and dairy store is famous for its promotion featuring its plastic shopping bags. Customers who have their picture taken in some exotic corner of the world carrying a Stew Leonard bag are eligible for a free bag of groceries. These entertaining photographs are displayed in the store for all to see.

DIRECT MAIL: BUILDING A LIST

In *Ogilvy on Advertising*, advertising guru David Ogilvy refers to direct mail as his "first love and secret weapon." While media advertising can reach a large group of readers or listeners, direct mail advertising allows you to target one specific customer. It also allows you to test every variable in your mailing, Ogilvy points out, by making minor changes in a piece each time you mail a batch and tracking the responses you get each time. There are two ways of using direct mail: to advertise to existing customers and to solicit new customers by focusing on a selected list of likely prospects.

How do you develop your first mailing list? When your store opens, put a guest book by the front counter and encourage everyone to sign it. You could also put out slips of paper for a prize drawing, and enter all the names and addresses into your database. This method, however, can result in quite a few "unqualified" customers, such as children, since most states do not allow stores to require a purchase as a condition for entering the contest. Screen entries for duplicates and for childlike handwriting. Take time each day to copy the names and addresses on all the checks you receive. If you conduct a customer survey in the store, ask for an optional name and address. Be sure to add everyone to your list who fills in a request card or asks to have a package shipped, taking their names and addresses from these special forms.

Put out a stack of 3- by 5-inch mailing list cards and invite customers to fill one in. In addition to lines for the name and address on these cards, provide check boxes for special interests, allowing you to subdivide your list and occasionally send out smaller, targeted mailings. Some toy stores ask for the names and birthdates of children on their mailing list cards so they can send each child a birthday greeting with a coupon or gift offer. Your mailing list card can mention that customers signing up for mailings will be eligible for a monthly prize drawing and will receive special sale offers and invitations. Encourage everyone who comes in the store to sign up. It is much less expensive to cultivate an existing customer than to solicit a new one.

Another way to start a mailing list is to offer a contribution to a nonprofit organization in exchange for the use of its membership list. A noncompeting business might allow you to use its list, although this is more likely to happen when you have a list of your own to trade. There are two ways to use someone else's mailing list: arrange for one-time usage, the usual practice when "renting," or borrowing, a list, or ask for permission to add the names to your list permanently. Rented lists are usually provided on computer disk or self-adhesive labels.

List brokers, found in the Yellow Pages under "Mailing Lists," rent out lists targeted at specific income levels, geographic areas, or topics of interest. This is an excellent way to seek new customers, especially if you choose the right list. We have rented the list of *Bon Appetit* subscribers in our area and sent them our cookware catalog, with a special coupon inviting these potential customers into the store. In addition to magazine lists, it is possible to rent names and addresses based on occupation, group affiliation, religion, and credit card use. The price for renting a list is based on units of 1,000 names and addresses and covers one-time use for a specific mailing piece. List brokers usually include a few hidden code names to find out if a list is used more than once or for a purpose other than that agreed on.

When using more than one mailing list at a time, try to track which one is most effective by using a numeric code above the customer's name and asking all those responding to the mailing to give you the code. Before your mailing piece is addressed, have the lists compared to one another to eliminate costly duplication. This process, known as a *merge/purge*, can be done by computer if the lists are in compatible formats.

Commercial mailing services have sophisticated methods for comparing lists and also for labeling mailings and sorting them for bulk mailing according to the latest postal regulations. Although there are numerous inexpensive programs that allow you to maintain your own mailing lists on your store computer, you may find that using a commercial mailing service ultimately saves you both time and money. The service can often handle every aspect of your mailing: printing, labeling, sorting, and even delivering the mail to the post office.

A general mailing list of your customers is essential and can become one of your store's most valuable assets if you use it often. It is also beneficial to be able to break this main list down into smaller targeted lists. If you sell a variety of products, you need to know which customers are especially interested in a specific area. A crafts store, for instance, might send out a mailing on cross-stitch supplies that would not be of any interest to customers who are woodworkers. Mailing list services and store computer programs make this type of tracking feasible for even the smallest store.

In our mobile society, mailing lists need to be cleaned periodically. Bulk mail is the most economical way of sending a quantity of pieces, but in most instances bulk mail is not forwarded if the recipient has moved. Check with the post office about updating your list at least once a year. It may be possible to do this electronically, especially if you are using a professional mailing service to maintain your list on computer disk. Otherwise you can indicate on your mailing that you would like to receive address corrections, and the postal service will, for a fee, return all the undeliverable pieces to you with the recipient's new address.

Catalogs—On Your Own or in a Group

Even with the advent of desktop publishing, creating a full-color catalog is still a very costly proposition. Anything less than full color is ineffective in most fields where there is competition from many other catalogs, although a two-color, or even single-color, catalog may work if your product line is truly unique.

For most stores, the only way to offer a full-color catalog is to purchase one from a single supplier, personalized with your store name, or to become a member of a catalog group that represents merchandise from many vendors.

Single-supplier catalogs are narrow in scope, but they do offer an economical opportunity to highlight one particular line. Over the years, we have sent out vendor catalogs featuring a collection of specialty foods, a line of Christmas ornaments, and a sale on kitchen gadgets. Because the suppliers know you will order all the merchandise in the catalog from them, the price for a single-line catalog is often quite low. Buying the catalog merchandise from one source makes it easy to reorder, and catalog shipments are often given priority by the vendor.

Multivendor, or syndicated, catalog groups function either as a buying service, with all orders from individual stores going through a central office and single shipping point, or as an advisory service, with the stores buying their own merchandise for the catalog directly from the vendors. Some catalog groups allow retailers a great deal of say in what goes into the catalog, and others have professional buyers who select all the merchandise.

Catalog groups offer many advantages beyond the production of a slick, professional-looking catalog with your store name on it. The collective buying clout of the group helps convince vendors to grant generous advertising allowances, often in the form of a 5 or 10 percent discount taken right off the invoice. Priority may be given in shipping orders of catalog merchandise. Some catalog groups negotiate exclusive rights to a new item before it is made available to all other stores. New products a shop tries because of the catalog may become steady sellers. Members in a catalog group often enjoy support and guidance both from the catalog company and their fellow group members.

We belong to the William Glen catalog group, which got its start in the huge gourmet cookware store by that name in Sacramento, California. When we joined the group, our shop was very new. Bill and Glen were very helpful to us, and over the years Orange Tree Imports grew up to match the sophisticated image projected by the catalog. We were encouraged to carry all the merchandise that was featured and found that many of the new lines were successful for us.

But no matter what items are featured in the catalog, our customers invariably first mention the family and staff photos that are always on the inside front cover. These pictures give the catalog such a personal feeling that very few customers realize that we don't produce it ourselves. Our name is, of course, printed on the front cover, and we sometimes do a custom front cover illustration or put our own products on the back cover. We also occasionally insert a customer coupon in the catalog, with very positive results.

Twice a year the members of the William Glen group meet to vote on what items will be featured in the catalog. Bill and Glen then negotiate with the suppliers for advertising allowances and take care of all the product photography and descriptions. We would not have the time or the money to do all this for a catalog for our store alone.

There are, however, some drawbacks. Many of the other stores in the catalog group are strictly gourmet, which means there is very little merchandise from the rest of our store in the catalog unless we do custom pages. Most of the other stores are located on the West Coast, and they seem to do better than we do with wine and seafood accessories as well as luxury items. We try to stock almost everything in the catalog, but that means that we bring in a few products, such as solid brass bottle openers on floor stands, knowing it is unlikely we will sell them.

Our catalog, sent out twice a year, takes up a major portion of our advertising budget. We use it mostly to "presell" the customers on our mailing list, telling them more about each product than we possibly could in the store. We sometimes also send catalogs to a rented mailing list to try to bring in new customers, and we give away copies in the store as well.

A syndicated catalog group works quite differently from William Glen. Syndicated catalogs are published by companies with professional buyers to select the merchandise and negotiate with vendors. The merchandise is then usually presented to the catalog stores at a general meeting, together with lectures, workshops, and the opportunity to meet with other retailers. The syndicated service may also offer store design advice and assist with mailing list management. In some cases, a large portion of the catalog merchandise is stored in a central warehouse and ordered through the syndication rather than directly from the individual vendors.

To determine whether there is a catalog right for you, check with your major suppliers to see if their merchandise is featured in any group catalogs. If you find a good possibility, request a sample copy and compare the image it projects to that of your store. Are most of the items pictured ones that you normally carry? Does the look of the catalog resemble your shop in terms of quality and sophistication?

Once you have selected a catalog, call other retailers who belong to that group and ask about their experience. Many shops report significant increases in sales when they send out a catalog, but there are also some drawbacks. You will not have complete control over the merchandise selection and pricing, the catalog will not reflect your store's unique character, and you may find that your customer base is not large enough to support the considerable volume of catalogs you will need to buy.

If you decide to produce your own catalog, be sure to get a good idea of all costs before you commit to the project. Don't forget postage, which adds considerably to the expense of any catalog mailing. Consider printing a separate price list so that the catalog will not go out of date as prices change. Check with suppliers to see if they can provide you with product photographs, and negotiate with them to give you advertising allowances to cover some of the cost of production.

The Store Newsletter

The more often you communicate with your customers, the more often they will visit your store. Computer word processing programs make it easy to produce professional-looking newsletters to send to customers monthly or quarterly. A newsletter is an efficient way of using a very small mailing list when you start out or to augment an annual catalog mailing for a larger store. The newsletter can also be an effective handout in the store, and many customers will pick up a copy as they are leaving.

Some stores send out multipage newsletters filled with new product information, letters, and special event listings, with a calendar for customers to cut out and save. Bookstores and music stores frequently include reviews in their newsletters, while others feature craft ideas, recipes, and humorous anecdotes. Many reward regular customers by occasionally making a special offer available only to newsletter readers.

Postcards

A postcard mailing can be an effective way to make regular use of your mailing list. The cards themselves are not expensive to produce, especially if you print them in a single color of ink on colorful card stock, and there is a considerable savings in postage in comparison to other mailing pieces. Check postal regulations for size and layout specifications, especially if you will be using a bulk mailing permit. We once had an 8,000-piece postcard mailing rejected by the post office because the layout failed to meet postal standards.

> Borders Book Shop provides complimentary postcards featuring a bold graphic book design in black ink on colored card stock. Customers are encouraged to use the cards by a sign offering to mail them anywhere for free.

Producing a full-color picture postcard of a store is expensive, and usually a large minimum quantity must be printed. But if you are in a tourist area and your storefront is unusual or attractive, it may be worthwhile to produce postcards of your store. Make them available for free or at a nominal cost. We printed photo cards of our store many years ago for a large mailing and still use the leftovers to communicate with customers about special orders and other requests.

Postcard decks are a relatively new form of direct mail advertising, and many firms consider them a cost-effective way to reach new customers. Groups of postcards from a variety of companies are mailed in a plastic envelope to a carefully targeted mailing list. These mailing pieces may be simple coupons or elaborate full-color cards that the consumer can mail back for more information. A response rate of 5 to 15 percent is considered very successful on this type of mailing, but at a cost of only five to ten cents per card, the investment may be well worthwhile.

OUT-OF-HOME ADVERTISING

If you limit advertising to traditional print media, you may be missing out on some opportunities you haven't even considered. The category of *out-of-home* advertising includes options ranging from sponsoring litter removal on a section of highway to painting a mural on a city wall. There are numerous ways to reach potential customers on their way to and from somewhere.

Billboards are perhaps the most obvious way to reach those who are on the road, although these signs frequently lack the wit that endeared the Burma Shave signs to America or the attractive design one expects of a good print ad. If you decide to create a billboard, do it well. Make it clever, or appealing, or even outrageous. Make it interesting to the consumer. But be sure that the design is in keeping with the rest of your advertising program.

A city bus or company truck can serve as a moving billboard, advertising your store as it travels around town. Some stores use their own truck as a stationery billboard, parking it where it will be seen by passersby. Ben and Jerry's Ice Cream has taken the lead in creating trucks that are actually moving murals by artist Woody Jackson. Seeing one of their trucks go by is always a pleasure.

Commuters on a bus or train, or waiting at a bus stop, have lots of time to read ads. Transit ads are a good way to reach certain types of customers and to convey a longer message than would be possible on a billboard. The money generated by ads inside buses and trains also helps support public transportation.

Mitchells of Westport, a creative Connecticut apparel retailer, has found an unusual way to market to the New York–bound commuters who make up an important part of their customer base. The Mitchells staff occasionally surprises those waiting for a train at one of the five nearby train stations by giving out free newspapers tagged with a Mitchells sticker and free coffee in paper cups with the Mitchells name on them. The coffee and newspapers are purchased from the train station's regular vendors so as not to create any ill will.

BROADCAST MEDIA: RADIO

The advertising images projected by radio and television are fleeting, so it is essential to commit to a campaign with a great deal of repetition in order to make the broadcast media work effectively. Radio allows you to speak personally to an individual. The result is immediate and intimate, and the ads you design for radio should reflect that feeling. Music and sounds can be used to create a mood to augment the spoken copy. This text can be professionally recorded or read by the announcer during the program. You might want to be your own spokesperson, especially if you have an interesting voice or accent. A good, recognizable announcing voice in radio commercials can help build a sense of trust in your business. A catchy jingle may also help customers remember your store's name, but you will need to repeat the ad many times to make it seem familiar to the public.

An announcer with name recognition can be paid to ad-lib about your shop. Be sure that he or she is familiar with your store and has a fact sheet to refer to with the name, address, and advertising angle. An announcer speaking from personal experience usually carries more weight with loyal listeners than a canned ad, and the announcer may speak for longer than the time you have paid for. Ad-libbed ads can also backfire, of course. Listen to other ads by the same announcer to see if he or she is good at improvising.

The immediacy of radio makes it ideal for announcing events with time value. The copy can create a sense of urgency, encouraging the listener—who may well be in his or her car already—to go to your store right away. Be sure that each ad mentions the store's name and location at least twice.

Radio ads, or *spots*, are sold in increments of 30 seconds. This may not seem like a long time, but it is long enough to read approximately sixty to seventy words of copy. Instead of buying 60-second spots, consider running 30-second spots twice as often. Select the times that your spots will run based on the listening habits of your customers, as well as your ad budget. *Drive times*, for example, are excellent for reaching men and women commuting to and from work.

If your store is busy during the first few months of the year, traditionally a slow time for retailers, you may be able to buy radio and TV time rather inexpensively. Business advertising drops off after the busy fourth quarter of the year, so stations are eager for advertisers in January, February, and March. And with the lighter advertising schedule during these times, your ad will stand out.

Many radio stations offer the option of a *live remote broadcast* from your store. The public enjoys the novelty of seeing radio personalities in action, and announcers like to meet their listeners. To be truly effective, a remote should be tied to a contest, event or special offer that will draw listeners to the store. The announcers should sound excited about being in the store and should mention free refreshments, entertainment, a sale, or other offer when they invite customers to come see them. If the store is hosting a visiting artist or celebrity, suggest that the announcer conduct a brief interview with the featured guest or with a store spokesperson.

Radio stations often run contests for their listeners, offering prizes donated by retailers in exchange for promotional announcements. These prizes tend to be big-ticket items, but you may find that the cost to you, which is the wholesale cost of the merchandise donated, makes the deal a good value in relation to the number of times your store will be mentioned on the air. Even when bartering merchandise for spots, you should be given a contract that spells out how many times your store will be mentioned and approximately when those mentions will occur.

ADVERTISING ON TV

The profusion of cable television stations has slashed the advertising rates for television, but the production costs to create even a 30-second spot remain high. Since your locally produced ad may run before or after a sophisticated spot produced by a large national advertising agency, it is unwise to cut corners when creating TV ads. If you are going to use television, obtain professional production advice from the television station or your advertising agency. You may wish to create two or more ads at the same time, so that you can rotate them during a heavy advertising schedule.

TV is the only medium that is both visual and aural. It allows you to tell a story, demonstrate a product, or communicate an image of your store or products in a way that will delight the eye and the ear. Not everyone, of course, will be watching *and* listening. Your store name, location, and tag line should be shown in writing on the screen for those of us who hit the mute button on the remote whenever ads come on.

Some of your suppliers may have professionally produced television spots available for you to use. Hummel Gift Shop in New Springfield, Ohio, provides its own distinctive announcer's voice and music to replace the canned text on the television ads provided by suppliers of collectibles. Other successful television ads for Hummel Gift Shop include commercials that appear to be news stories: staged interviews filmed in the store with owner David May discussing upcoming special events with a reporter.

Retailers such as David May who have strong, likable personalities are often successful at starring in their own television ads. Customers like to buy from someone they know, and if you are usually present in your store, encouraging the public to identify your store with your trustworthy and familiar face gives you an advantage K-Mart will never have. The downside of regular TV appearances is being recognized wherever you go and realizing that whatever you do or say reflects on your business. Individual promotion also makes it difficult to share the responsibility (and credit) equally with the store's other partners or staff members, and of course it may make it difficult to eventually pass the business on to a new owner.

Alternative Television and Radio Advertising

Public radio and television are prohibited from carrying commercials, but they are often able to give extensive descriptions of the businesses that sponsor them. Public television underwriting has actually been one of our most effective means of advertising. For years we have sponsored *The Frugal Gourmet*, as well as some of Julia Child's programs. These shows have a loyal following among our customers who are avid cooks. Ask your public television and radio stations if there are programs that might tie in well with your merchandise.

Most public television stations raise funds through an on-air auction or membership drives that feature premiums to reward those who sign up. Donating merchandise for the auction or fund drives is an inexpensive way to gain exposure on your local public television station. This year all of the merchants on our street grouped our auction donations together into a special auction hour featuring Monroe Street products, with our business owners as the auctioneers. Next year we plan to ask our staff to answer the telephones, hoping for a few good shots of our enthusiastic employees wearing their matching store T-shirts.

Check with your local cable TV company about creating your own *infomercial*, or leased-access cable show. Elaine Kennelly, owner of Kennelly Hallmark Shop in Hartford, Wisconsin, produces a 30-minute cable television show, taped in her shop one day a month, that is aired six days a week. *Elaine's World* is her own version of a home shopping network, with each show consisting of three ten-minute segments highlighting a different group of products. A local and a toll-free number are listed for viewers who want to order the merchandise she is promoting, but the main benefit is that customers come into the store daily requesting items they have seen on the show.

RIDING THE ELECTRONIC WAVES: ADVERTISING ON THE INTERNET

Not one to rest on past success, Elaine Kennelly has also started advertising her shop on the Internet. Many people feel that this is the wave of the future for advertising, because it combines the personal feeling of radio, the visual appeal of television, and the opportunities for written text of print media. Customers seeking information about your store and products through their home computer can spend as long as they like perusing the information. Internet and CD-ROM advertising can also be interactive, a possibility unique to the computer at this time. A customer can specify what information he or she would like to see and can even place an order with the store via the computer's modem.

The field of electronic advertising is changing rapidly, and it will be exciting to see where it takes us. The cost of posting a home page for your business has already fallen drastically, with inexpensive programs allowing you to create your own "home" on the Internet for less than the price of a print ad. If you are going to use this type of advertising to expand beyond your usual marketing area, be sure to invest in an 800 number, or subscribe to one of the 800 number services that will take messages for you. Electronic advertising should be of the same quality and look as the other advertising you produce for your store and should be updated frequently. Before taking the plunge, query your customers to find out if many of them are on-line, and if so, what goods and services they would suggest you promote through the Internet. A recent study sponsored by Mastercard shows that most on-line users are interested in buying computer software, event and travel tickets, entertainment, publications, and computer hardware. A much smaller percentage is interested in purchasing clothes, jewelry, or sporting goods via the Internet.

Stores eventually will be able to send customized e-mail messages to many of their customers, announcing new merchandise arrivals and special promotions. If you are able to receive e-mail now, be sure to list your e-mail address on your business card, together with your fax and telephone numbers. Both suppliers and customers may wish to communicate with you electronically.

EVALUATING YOUR ADVERTISING

Many retailers view advertising as throwing money down a black hole, because it is often difficult to see clear results from an advertising campaign. Consumers seldom mention seeing or hearing an ad, and in fact every so often a customer will mention coming in because of an ad that never existed. But it is possible to make an effort to try to track the effectiveness of an advertising campaign, beyond the obvious method of looking for an increase in either general sales or sales of the item advertised. There are several ways to track results:

- Include a coupon in your ad or in your mailing. Ask staff to keep all coupons and to write the total amount of purchase in one corner.
- For radio advertising, offer a free gift or special discount to anyone mentioning the ad.

- Track responses to a special offer by instructing customers to ask for a certain employee (who may even be fictitious) when they call or stop in.
- When doing consumer surveys, be sure to ask how the customer found out about the store.
- Query sales staff as to whether they think many new customers came in as a result of a promotional campaign.
- Use a *split run*, placing the same ad in two different delivery zones or sections of the newspaper to see which is more effective. Test slightly different versions of a print ad or radio spot to learn what works best.

ADVERTISING WHEN SALES ARE DOWN

It is tempting to save money when the store is not doing well by not advertising. That, according to advertising specialist Jay Conrad Levinson, in *Guerrilla Advertising*, is like stopping your wristwatch to save time. You need frequency and persistence in order to succeed in advertising. The store that discontinues its advertising and disappears from the public eye may soon disappear entirely.

Advertising that is well researched and designed should at least pay for itself. Even a store that has fallen on hard times should work hard to promote itself. An economical advertising program, coupled with a full array of inexpensive creative promotions and some free publicity, can help attract new customers and bring the old ones back.

ALTERNATIVE USES OF ADVERTISING

Some of the most interesting advertising is not really business advertising at all. As a store owner, you are in a unique position to run an ad that promotes a cause you believe in or makes people think. Not every piece of advertising needs to be commercial in nature. As long as ads align your store with what you strongly believe to be important and just, and do not offend important segments of your customer base, there is no reason that your advertising cannot be used as a force for good. Benetton and The Body Shop, for example, often lobby for humanitarian and ecological causes in their ads, winning the goodwill of customers who are of a like mind—though they do risk the ill will of those who don't agree with their views.

Advertising in concert and theatrical programs provides support for nonprofit groups and at the same time creates a positive image for the store as a patron of the arts. It is always worthwhile to be associated with excellence.

You can also use your advertising dollars to place small ads in church bulletins, neighborhood newsletters, school yearbooks, and other publications that benefit your community. Some stores consider these ads to be charity donations rather than advertising, but they do serve to generate goodwill toward the store—and that is really the goal of any advertising you choose to do.

9

CREATIVE PROMOTION AND PUBLICITY

"Operating a business without proper promotion is like winking in the dark," according to retailing experts Don Taylor and Jeanne Smalling Archer in *Up Against the Wal-Marts*. "You know you're doing it, but no one else does." Imaginative promotions can help specialty shop retailers distinguish themselves from their larger and less resourceful competitors, garnering free publicity and that most treasured form of advertising, customer word of mouth. Finding creative ways to attract shoppers and to entertain them once they enter the store is both challenging and enjoyable.

Promotion includes the many different ways retailers attempt to catch customers' attention: coupons, special events, sales, contests, and celebrity appearances. Promotions often tie in naturally with publicity and PR (public relations), the free media coverage of the store and any of its activities a reporter might find newsworthy. Paid advertising is part of the marketing packaging for many promotions, but some are created especially with free publicity in mind. Give special consideration to any promotion that may result in some mention in the newspaper or on the news, since this editorial coverage has more validity in the customer's eyes than any paid advertising—and it's free.

SALES, SALES, SALES

Sales are the most overworked promotional concept in retailing today. Some stores hold sales every week, celebrating mythical founders' birthdays and holidays that the public has otherwise forgotten. This approach leads to customers' refusing to shop in a store unless there is a sale. Customers also learn the patterns of when sales are held and wait for them. The dinnerware business, for example, used to feature two major sales a year, until consumers caught on and stopped buying china the rest of the year.

Most shops do need to hold a clearance sale occasionally to move out inventory that is reluctant to leave on its own at full price. We call our spring clearance "Orange's Lemon Sale," and kick off the event by giving out fresh lemons to the first one hundred customers. There is always a banner in the window announcing the Lemon Sale, prompting one of my fellow retailers to comment that he thought it was wonderful I was so willing to admit my mistakes in public. All sale merchandise is marked with a lemon yellow tag and displayed on long tables. We have found that clearance sale shoppers (a special breed) appreciate being able to look at all the discounted items in one place.

Our annual fall street festival, or sidewalk sale, allows us to clear out unwanted goods before the busy holiday season. We set up lots of tables outside and hope for good weather. We continue to lower prices as the day goes on, and much of the merchandise that is left by the end of the day goes to charity.

We used to have a permanent clearance area in the store but found that the odds and ends of clearance merchandise never looked attractive. However, an attractive sale display can be made if you feature a large quantity of a single item or an entire line. Some retailers bring in special discounted merchandise to sell on sale. These discontinued or overstock items are offered by suppliers at a low wholesale price so they can be sold at full markup, but at a price the consumer finds attractive. If you are certain that these goods will sell, special purchases for a sale can generate a bit of extra income from customers attracted by the prospect of a good deal.

A storewide discount sale is useful if you have a sudden need to raise cash. Some stores also use this type of promotion to attract new customers or to bring existing customers back into the store. The drawback to holding a "20% Off Everything" sale is that no one wants to shop in the store immediately before or after the sale. If it is a regular event, customers will wait for it, or feel bad if they miss it and have to pay full price.

Timing is crucial on a sale. If a sale runs too long, customers feel no sense of urgency and may put off coming in until they forget to do so. A limited number of days is preferable, with a prize drawing or extra discount rewarding those who come early. Some stores send out a mailing to the preferred customers on their mailing list, offering a day or two head start on any sale before it is advertised to the general public. Notices sent bulk mail do not necessarily arrive when you want them to, so send these private sale invitations out early enough that those on the mailing list will be sure to receive them several days before the "customer appreciation days" of early sale shopping.

Reduced Price Offers

Promotional pricing on individual items, or entire lines, can be used to draw customers' attention to them. Often suppliers offer special pricing on their products, allowing retailers to promote the line on sale while maintaining full markup. You can mark items with a sale price, or use a percentage off sign and take markdowns at the register. Most customers are not very quick at math, so unless you are offering something simple such as a 10 percent discount, you may wish to put the sale prices on the merchandise in addition to the sale signs.

"Before" and "after" prices are an effective way to draw attention to an attractive price. We use a white tag to show the regular price and a red tag marked "special" for the promotional price. Keep in mind that if you state that an item is "regularly" one price and is "now" a lower one, you could be required to prove that it was indeed originally the higher price. In London, Harrods Department Store brings in truckloads of special merchandise for its huge annual sale, putting it all out at "regular" price before the sale in order to stay within the letter of the law.

Variations on price promotion include "buy one, get one free," which is in essence a 50 percent discount off each item. When I was a child in Pennington, New Jersey, I loved the corner drugstore's Penny Sale. If you bought one notebook for full price, you could buy a second one for only a penny (which even then didn't usually buy much). I'm not sure that I would have been as intrigued by a "half off selected notebooks" sale, although that is really what was being offered; a second notebook for "only a penny" seemed to be a real bargain.

Gift with purchase (GWP) is another way to "discount" a specific item by selling it at full price but offering a second item with it for free.

Toiletries are often offered this way, with the value of the travel bag or other GWP sometimes exceeding that of the perfume. These promotions usually originate with the supplier, but there is no reason that a nursery, for instance, can't offer free flower seeds with a special garden tool set. Customers love the idea of getting something for nothing.

Percentage-off sales, in which customers get a discount off retail prices, are usually fairly straightforward, but there is room for creativity in conducting this type of sale if you wish to introduce an element of chance. Shoppers select their purchases knowing only that they will receive a discount ranging from 10 to 50 percent. At the register, customers open an item in which a slip of paper has been hidden revealing their discount. These slips can be hidden in helium-filled balloons, plastic Easter eggs, or even fortune cookies. Carry the balloon, egg, or fortune cookie theme through in your advertising and window displays, making the sale part of a coordinated special event.

T Q Diamonds, of Madison, Wisconsin, made an offer that appealed to the gambling nature of their customers: every gift purchased in the store between Thanksgiving and Christmas would be free if it snowed more than 3 inches on New Year's Eve. Owner Timothy Quigley reported a sales increase of 50 percent over the previous holiday season. Oh, and it *did* snow on New Year's Eve, although not a full 3 inches—but his gamble was covered by a special insurance policy from the World Wide Weather Insurance Company, just in case.

Price Promotion in Ads

The majority of all advertising for department stores and discounters is centered around price, and few specialty stores can compete with the giants on price alone. Ads for individual products should sell the features and benefits of the item, and perhaps also mention service, location, or other factors that might draw a customer to your store. Having said this, I hasten to add that you probably *also* need to mention price, and the price should be reasonably close to what a big store would charge. The fact is that most customers want high value, quality service, and the lowest price. Not all items in your store need to be at the same low price as a discounter's, but the items you advertise should be competitive.

PROMOTIONAL METHODS AND IDEAS

There are many ways other than holding a sale to bring new customers into the store and to encourage existing customers to return. To select the best approach for your shop, it is important to think about whom you are trying to reach in your promotion and what will motivate him or her to make a special trip to your store.

You may find that different promotions are necessary to reach various parts of your target market. As long as your efforts are in keeping with your store image, and aren't all aimed at the same consumer, there is nothing wrong with running several promotions at the same time.

Coupons

Coupon promotions are an excellent way to test the response to store advertising, since they require customers to bring in physical proof that they have seen an ad. Coupons can be distributed in many ways: through direct mail, in print ads, as bag stuffers, via the Welcome Wagon program for newcomers, or even door to door (as long as you don't use the mailbox, which postal regulations restrict to U.S. mail). But coupons are not for every store. They are not upscale enough for very sophisticated shops and may be ineffective for stores depending mostly on transient tourist or walk-by traffic.

A number of services specialize in delivering coupons. In many areas there are companies that issue coupon books, such as the national Entertainment Book, which are sold to consumers by nonprofit groups. If you are in a tourist area, you might suggest that merchants, restaurants, and motels put together a tourist packet to be mailed to visitors calling or writing for information. Coupons can also be sent out together with offers from other businesses in a *marriage mail packet*, so called because it combines the advertising from one firm with that of several other noncompetitive businesses, allowing everyone to share the cost of the mailing. Coupons are an effective way of bringing existing customers back into the store. At the time of purchase, give customers coupons to be used during their next visit (as seen in Figure 9-1), or offer a free gift with a cash register receipt from the previous month.

In order to make a coupon work well, the offer must be attractive enough to motivate a customer to make the trip to the store and to bring it along. A 10 percent or greater discount storewide, or on popular items, or

Figure 9-1 Chickadee Depot "bounce back" coupon, which helps boost first-quarter sales by bringing holiday customers back.

Thank You Certificate
$5.00 OFF

your purchase* of $25.00 or more at

Chickadee Depot™
Wild Bird Supplies, Garden & Nature Gifts

**3236 University Avenue
in the Shorewood Shopping Center
Madison, WI
Offer good January 15 through
April 15, 1996.
*Good on any merchandise except
sale items, binoculars and bird seed.
No cash value, offer limited to one certificate
per person per purchase and or/visit**

© October 1995 Chickadee Depot, Inc., Madison, Wisconsin

a special free gift or service are all enticing coupon offers. The cost of any giveaway items should be considered part of the advertising budget. If coupons for a free sample bar of Crabtree & Evelyn soap cost $50 to print and distribute, and 200 bars wholesaling for $1 each are given away, the total cost for the promotion is $250. The cost per customer brought into the store is $1.25, which probably would compare favorably to the response to other forms of advertising at the same cost.

A coupon need not be a plain, flat piece of paper. Hardware, crafts, and used book stores have created effective coupons by printing their advertising on brown paper bags and inserting them in the local paper with an offer that everything that fits in the bag will be 20 percent off. Printing special bags does require a large order to be cost-effective, but shops with several branch stores may be able to make use of this idea.

If you include a coupon in a printed newspaper or magazine ad, be sure to request special placement on an outside edge so that customers can tear it out easily. It is also important to proofread coupon copy carefully to be sure that customers will not misunderstand the offer. Coupons should always mention your store name and address and have an expiration date, including the year.

Keep all coupons turned in by customers, making a notation in the corner of the total amount of the customer's purchase. This information will allow you to measure the effectiveness of the promotion.

Valued Customer Cards

The cost of maintaining a current customer is considerably less than that required to obtain a new one, and many stores make their regular customers feel appreciated by offering them special benefits. Some bookstores, including national chains such as B. Dalton, sell an annual discount card to their regular customers for a nominal fee. The card provides a discount on all books purchased during the year, encouraging shoppers to make their investment in the card pay off by buying all their books from the same source.

The latest development in valued customer cards is the *smart card*, or fidelity card, being used by some grocery chains. These cards look like credit cards but are not used for payment. When scanned at the register, the card provides the customer with coupon-like savings on advertised products, check cashing privileges, and in some cases frequent shopper points toward prize awards. The merchant is able to compile a useful database on its customers from the smart card application form and from the data captured with each purchase, allowing the store to target special promotions and advertising at its best customers.

Frequent Buyer Programs

Retail stores have discovered another way of increasing customer loyalty: programs that reward shoppers for the amount they spend in the store. These *customer loyalty programs,* modeled after the airlines' frequent flyer programs, usually require that the customer keep track of purchases. It is more customer friendly, but also more complicated, for the store to keep records for each customer. The store might offer to keep a copy of the frequent buyer cards on file, so that purchases are noted on both copies in case one is misplaced.

At Stitcher's Crossing, a Madison, Wisconsin, embroidery and hand-craft store, regular customers receive a plastic key ring tag that gets punched each time they make a purchase. Many other stores have a wallet-size record that can be marked each time a purchase is made. Larger chains, such as the Hallmark stores, issue plastic cards that look like credit cards and can be electronically encoded with purchase amounts.

Another way to run a frequent buyer program is to ask customers to bring in their receipts when they total enough for an award. A special small envelope can be provided for shoppers to use for saving cash register receipts.

What will you call your frequent buyer program? In an effort to sound chummy, J. C. Penney established a "Bra and Panty Club." When I received my membership card, I asked the sales associate what sorts of things go on at the Bra and Panty Club meetings. She didn't seem at all amused.

Rewards for frequent purchases range from "buy twelve pair, get one pair free" and "free pair of socks with the fourth pair of shoes" at a shoe store to a 50 percent discount on any one collectible figurine when purchases total a certain amount at a fine gift shop. Awards can also include items that promote the store, such as T-shirts, tote bags, mugs, and other items bearing the shop's name and logo.

> At Canterbury Booksellers, in Madison, Wisconsin, the "Book a Night at Canterbury Inn" program offers frequent buyers a free night in Canterbury's opulent bed and breakfast. A night in the Clerk's Room is the reward for $500 in book purchases, and a night in The Miller's Room is free with purchases of $800. Members of their annual Canterbury Card program receive an upgrade on any room certificate they earn.

Frequent buyer programs sometimes require that the reward level be achieved within a certain time period. A time limit encourages shoppers to come in more often, but some customers find the limitations inconvenient. The goal of a frequent buyer program is to create happy, loyal repeat shoppers. Make the program easy to understand and simple to use so that as many customers as possible will want to participate.

Discount Cards

It is growing increasingly common to offer a storewide discount to senior citizens one day a week. In order to promote this benefit, we provide senior citizens who shop in our store with a special card that mentions our senior citizen day, the discount amount, and a few low-markup items that are not included in the discount. By asking customers to show the card in order to get their discount, we eliminate having our employees ask customers how old they are. We also have an opportunity to add their names to our mailing list. A sample senior citizen discount card is shown as Figure 9-2.

We use a similar discount card to encourage restaurants to shop with us by offering them 10 percent off on all items purchased for professional use. A special discount card offers culinary students at the local technical college a discount on their cutlery purchases. A hospital gift shop might offer a special discount to the hospital's employees. Other stores offer special discounts to companies buying corporate gifts. Targeted discount cards can be given to qualified individuals or businesses in the shop or

Figure 9-2 Sample senior citizen discount card.

STORE NAME

SENIOR CITIZEN DISCOUNT CARD
This card must be presented before your purchase is rung up.

is entitled to a 10% discount on all merchandise except clearance sale items on

SENIOR CITIZEN TUESDAY.

used as part of a promotional mailing aimed at a special segment of the store's market.

Collectors' Clubs

The Bra and Panty Club may not enjoy getting together for meetings, but many other groups of collectors do. Stores that deal with hobbies or collectible gift lines can develop a loyal following by helping to organize collectors' clubs. If there is room, meetings can even be held in the store. Your store can provide light refreshments and door prizes.

> The Hayloft, a complex of gift and clothing shops near Peoria, Illinois, offers special "club plans" for frequent buyers of its collectible lines. Shoppers must reach a minimum dollar level in purchases before being eligible to join the free "club plan," which entitles shoppers to special offers as well as free merchandise when various levels of purchase are achieved.

The members of a collectors' club should be encouraged to determine the course of the organization, with some guidance from the store and the vendor for the collectible line. Meetings might feature guest speakers from the supplier, new products introductions, and members' sharing their own collections. Our local teddy bear collectors' club also does charitable work, donating teddies for the police to give to children who have suffered a trauma.

Many bookstores offer book discussion groups a place to meet, lists of suggested books, and a discount on the group's choices. Be sure to offer book group and collectors' club members some special benefit in your store, and keep in touch with their membership through your mailing list.

SPECIAL EVENTS TO ATTRACT CUSTOMERS TO YOUR STORE

A special event is often an effective way to create a sense of excitement in your advertising, encouraging customers to come in during the one day, or several days, that the event is being held. Special events are also fun for staff members, providing them with the opportunity to do something a little different with displays and hospitality.

Product Demonstrations and Seminars

Retailing as entertainment can mean just that: live music in the store or a magician who entertains shoppers' children. It can also refer to a myriad of creative activities that bring customers into the store and enhance their shopping experience. Even shoppers in a hurry enjoy stopping for taste samplings of specialty foods. And those who are shopping as a recreational activity are attracted to stores that offer something more than just sales and a display of products.

The Mall of America in Minneapolis is filled with every conceivable type of shop, but the ones that are most memorable are those that feature constant demonstrations of their products. At Bare Bones, a shop selling products and toys relating to the human body, a staff member stands near the entrance with a rubber eyeball or other unusual product in order to catch the attention of the hundreds of shoppers passing by. At The Scientific Revolution, employees in lab coats offer to demonstrate any item a customer is interested in. This hands-on approach encourages customers to handle and then purchase the merchandise.

Product demonstrations can be held at random times when the store is likely to be busy or scheduled for specific times and promoted through advertising. Larger stores may be able to schedule several demonstrations at the same time, increasing their chances of good traffic. Ask your staff members to demonstrate products, or ask your vendors to recommend someone who specializes in this type of work. Sales reps often enjoy the opportunity to get feedback from the buying public by demonstrating items in their line.

There are as many different types of demonstrations as there are products. Here are examples of a few:

- Cooking
- Crafts, sewing
- Cleaning techniques
- Food sampling
- Skin care and makeup
- Home decorating tips

- Care or polishing of metals
- Use of hand tools
- Children's story hours
- Gardening techniques
- Fashion accessorizing
- Musical instrument clinics

Having someone demonstrate an activity in your store window always attracts attention. Resort shops know how visitors, especially young ones, can be mesmerized by watching someone make taffy or fudge or create blown glass animals. Stores in other areas draw customers by featuring craftspeople—weavers, spinners, calligraphers, or painters—at work in their windows.

In addition to live demonstrations, consider making use of a small TV/VCR unit to show informative videos about your merchandise. Ask vendors for promotional videos about their products, preferably in continuous-loop format so you won't need to remember to rewind. Keep the volume low so that those not interested in listening are not distracted as they shop.

Guest Appearances

Other special events in the store might include appearances by artists, crafts people, or authors. The guests can answer customers' questions about their work, pose for pictures with their fans, and sign autographs. If you invite a celebrity to your store, be certain that you can attract enough interested customers to make the appearance worthwhile for the guest visitor. Give some thought to providing a comfortable, attractive place for the celebrity to sit, and have a staff member on hand to fetch more product, a new pen, or a drink of water. Those who are on long publicity tours appreciate any thoughtful hospitable touches that make them feel especially welcome in your town and in your store, such as a home-cooked meal, a gift certificate to a local coffee house, or a small fruit basket in their hotel room.

Suppliers or publishers sending artists and authors on tour to promote their products should provide you with publicity materials well in advance of the event. They also usually send an agreement spelling out your share of the expenses. If you decide to bring in a celebrity guest on your own, you will, of course, need to pay for transportation, hotel, meals, and perhaps an appearance fee. Check with retailers in nearby cities to see if any would like to have the same person in their store, so that you can share the airfare costs. You might also be able to contact a celebrity scheduled to perform a concert or play in your area, and arrange for the person to make an in-store appearance to promote a product or charity in which he or she has an interest.

Costumed Characters

Families with children love the photo opportunity that a costumed character offers. The classic "pictures with Santa" promotion is still a must for almost every large mall in America, as is having the Easter bunny in residence in the spring. A specialty shop can distinguish itself by offering something a little different, such as an appearance by a children's storybook character or a life-sized version of a stuffed animal. Suppliers sometimes rent or loan costumes based on their licensed characters, such as Cherished Teddies by Enesco or Hello Kitty by Sanrio. You might consider an appearance by a local sports team mascot or your city or state's beauty pageant winner.

Costume shops can provide full body costumes, such as a cow for June Dairy Month (a major event here in Wisconsin) or a nutcracker for a Christmas promotion. Wearing one of these costumes is not as easy as it looks. Our toy buyer, Nanci Bjorling, offered to lead a children's parade dressed as a troll during the heyday of troll collecting. The rubber headpiece turned out to be quite hot, but of course she couldn't take her head off in front of the children.

Remember that the person in the costume can't take a drink of water or usually even speak while in character. Limit appearance time to an hour, or build in breaks where the person can relax in private. It is also very important to have an assistant on hand to handle inquisitive children and to help the costumed character move around, especially if the costume limits vision.

Some of the new superstores entering the specialty shop field have permanent photo opportunities as part of the decor. In the Warner Brothers stores, for example, children can get their picture taken next to a larger-than-life Bugs Bunny made out of durable resin. Shops in tourist areas should consider whether there is an outdoor display relating to their area that visitors would enjoy photographing. Be sure to have a sign with your store name placed so that it will be included in the picture.

Conducting Contests

The creativity of my customers never ceases to amaze me. We have held many contests over the years, and only once, when we held a rather vague "create a Christmas ornament" contest, have we been left without enough entries to make an interesting display. This past year we repeated the gingerbread house contest last held in 1988, and although the entries were few, they were magnificent. We have also sponsored wooden nut-cracker, miniature Christmas tree, guess the jelly beans, and children's art contests. Our chocolate dessert contests provided the refreshments for four gala chocolate festivals benefiting local music and dance organizations. Our annual egg art contest, with a special category for the best Ukrainian egg, is now in its eighteenth year.

The cost for running these competitions is extremely low. The contests are promoted through flyers posted in the store and mailed to past entrants, as well as one or two print ads. We send press releases to the local media, which usually result in at least one mention in the paper. Entrants fill in a form when they bring in their creation and are given a receipt. For the gingerbread house contest, we also gave each person a $10 gift certificate to thank them for entering.

Contest entries are all numbered so no one can see who made each one. They are then judged by a volunteer committee of staff members, sometimes assisted by one of our sales reps or another outside guest. We give out as many prizes as possible. We keep a supply of inexpensive prize ribbons, imprinted with the store name, on hand at all times for this purpose. Winners also get merchandise prizes and gift certificates, with a $50 or $100 shopping spree often serving as the grand prize. All entries are displayed in the store or in the window. Shoppers love to see what other customers have created, and we have received a great deal of free newspaper and television coverage of our various contests.

Shops can also band together to hold competitions. Our shopping street was enlivened one Halloween by a window painting contest, and an art contest for local preschools provided dozens of pictures to display on various storefronts during a spring street fair. Shopping center stores can band together to hold events such as a celebrity look-alike contest or an Easter egg roll in the mall area. On State Street, a pedestrian shopping mall in Madison, a contest for the best holiday window display encourages every store to do its festive best.

Young customers enjoy guessing games, especially variations on the old "guess the number of beans in the jar" contest. We tried this with jelly beans once and accidentally broke the jar when we took it out of the window. I'll never forget the challenge of counting slightly melted jelly beans, interspersed with shards of glass, in order to determine the winner. The next time we did this we used little rubber dinosaurs—and counted them on their way *into* the jar.

Most states have strict regulations about raffles requiring the purchase of tickets, but allow stores to conduct free drawings, or sweepstakes, for prizes. A prize drawing can be used to compile a special interest mailing list during an event such as a celebrity artist's appearance. Ask the supplier sponsoring the appearance to donate a door prize, or have the artist autograph an item from your stock to be given away. If businesspeople are an important part of your target market, have a drawing that customers enter by dropping their business card into a bowl. Add all the names from your trading area to your mailing list.

Open Houses

Inviting customers to a one- or two-day open house sounds both hospitable and homey. For many stores, the only actual event taking place during an open house is the serving of refreshments, and perhaps a percentage off on a certain line, or item, in the store. To make an open house more memorable, include live music (we favor quiet instruments such as harp, flute, or dulcimer) and gifts or favors for everyone attending. Some stores have drawings for door prizes or offer a special item for sale that is available only during the event. Guests can be treated to a crafts demonstration, or have items signed by a visiting celebrity, or watch a video presentation about some of the shop's merchandise. A greeter with a guest book can make visitors feel welcome—while ensuring that everyone's name is on the store's mailing list. Staff should dress up for the event, and you should use fresh flowers and other touches to dress up the shop as well. An open house should always feature light refreshments, such as punch and cookies or wine and cheese—but avoid sticky foods that might cause messy fingerprints on the merchandise.

Offering a percentage of sales to a charity is an excellent way to attract free publicity for your open house. Ask the charity to allow you to use its name and mailing list to spread the word about your event. Be sure to keep the charity's staff informed about your plans so they can answer any questions that come to them. Invite prominent citizens who are supporters of the charity, and encourage them to bring their friends and associates. Send out a press release about the event, and invite any members of the press who might like to attend.

There are many types of open houses: a men-only shopping night, a two-day event highlighting a certain product line, a private evening for members of a club, or a seasonal open house officially launching the Christmas holiday season. We held two bridal open houses, with wedding cake from a local bakery and flowers from a neighboring florist, to announce our entry into the wedding gift market. A hospital gift shop might target staff nurses for a private reception, giving each a small angel pin as a little gift. Art galleries traditionally use an open house event to promote a new exhibit, serving light refreshments while patrons enjoy mingling, admiring the work, and chatting with the artists.

The Grand Opening

The debut of a new shop or a branch store is a joyous occasion. The celebration of a grand opening is an opportunity to announce the store's arrival and let the public know what type of promotion, hospitality, and service the shop plans to offer. It pays to do it right, because you can only do it once.

Most people wait a few weeks before inviting guests to visit them in a new home. The same rule of thumb should apply to inviting the public to the store's grand opening, because there are always some glitches when a shop first opens. Wait until most of the merchandise has arrived, the staff has gained some experience, and the displays are set up the way you'd like them to look. When you feel you have things under control, then it is time to throw your store's first special event.

A grand opening is often done in two parts: a private evening affair for friends, neighbors, fellow retailers, professional advisers, and suppliers and a two-day or one-week event open to the public. You could also invite the members of the press, or influential city officials, to a special open house soon after your store has opened. Entertainment, refreshments, and special promotional pricing will help attract a crowd. Special signage and advertising should be planned to promote the event, including invitations mailed or delivered to neighboring households.

Themed Events

Bloomingdale's has perfected the idea of an all-store merchandising and marketing event that lasts for several weeks. These promotions are an essential part of what is called "the Bloomingdale's Blitz." A theme, such as products from China, is used to create displays and demonstrations throughout the store. New merchandise is brought in, or even custom made, for the event. Music, food, art, and entertainment throughout the store tie in with the theme. The result is a unique and exciting retail event that fascinates and attracts curious visitors as well as serious shoppers.

A smaller specialty shop can't put on an event as grand as one of Bloomingdale's, but the concept of putting together a longer, multifaceted event based on a season, a merchandise category, or a country is a good one. Work with several vendors to select a product mix that ties in with the theme, and ask them to back you up with product samplings, special offers, and demonstrations throughout the event. Arrange for window displays, refreshments, and entertainment to fit the theme. If your event focuses on merchandise from one nation, contact that country's trade consulate or embassy and ask for posters, brochures, and other promotional materials. We promoted Danish, Norwegian, and Swedish goods with a Scandinavian festival supported by the various embassies and tied in with a silent auction of items donated by our suppliers to benefit the Scandinavian Studies Department at my alma mater, the University of Wisconsin.

Events Outside the Store

Not every retailer has the imagination to look beyond the four walls of the shop for promotional opportunities, but those who do find new ways to reach customers and interest them in their products. Bookstores often sponsor book fairs in schools, bringing in children's books on consignment and giving a percentage of sales to the school or parents' organization. Gourmet specialty shops offer food tastings at international food fairs. Interior design shops decorate rooms in charity designer showcase homes or lend props to other stores to display in their windows. Dinnerware stores display their china and silver at bridal fairs, and hardware stores set up booths at home improvements shows.

There are two types of out-of-store events: those that are strictly promotional, such as exhibits and displays, and those that seek to sell merchandise. For promotional events, insist on attractive signage to identify the merchandise from your shop. Send along a supply of your business cards, brochures, and store catalogs. For out-of-store events that involve selling goods, you will need a travel kit with the essentials of day-to-day retailing: a cash register or cash box, change, pens, charge card slips and an imprinter, signs, scissors, tape, bags for the merchandise, and literature promoting your shop. The literature you hand out should include a coupon or other incentive to bring the shoppers into your store to see your full selection. Check in advance to see if you will need to bring your own tables, table coverings, carpeting, lights, and chairs. Take enough merchandise and props to create an attractive display that will represent your store well.

Over the years, we have set up temporary shops in a number of locations, including a cat show, a baby fair, an antique show, and an art fair. It's a lot of work to transport goods and set up the display, but it's also fun to isolate one segment of our merchandise, such as cat-related gifts, and present them to a closely targeted audience. Several of the events we've been involved in have had a charity tie-in, which is something we always look for in promotions.

PUBLICITY AND PUBLIC RELATIONS

Paid advertising is often an integral part of marketing a special event in the store, but one of the advantages of sponsoring a creative promotion is that there is a good chance that it will garner some free publicity. There are two advantages to this type of press coverage: you don't have to pay for it, and it has greater credibility with the public than the advertising you *do* pay for. The disadvantages are that you can't ever count on getting free press coverage, and you have little control over the content of the coverage you do get. Most newspapers, and radio and television stations, maintain a policy of keeping commercial advertising and editorial coverage separate, so spending a lot of money on ads is unlikely to have any effect on how much feature coverage you are able to generate.

Because free publicity is a gift, it pays to be very nice to anyone from the press. Many years ago an article about our shopping area failed to mention one merchant, and she called the newspaper and read the poor reporter the riot act. I'm sure that the next time that newspaper wanted to do a feature on a specialty shop, hers was not the store they called. We are contacted from time to time by reporters working on a seasonal shopping story, or by a TV station needing a kitchen to film a segment on new trends in cooking, and we always do our best to cooperate, even if we don't end up being mentioned by name.

When you are contacted by the media, cooperate in every way, keeping their deadlines and other restrictions in mind. Do what you can to make it easy for them to get the information and footage, or photographs, that they need. Keep in mind that some days, such as Sundays, are slow news days, so your chances of getting some television or radio coverage are much greater than on a busy weekday. Even if you haven't sent out an official press release in advance, you may be able to get a reporter and camera person to come on short notice to cover some interesting event at your store if the station is short of feature stories for that day's news.

If you are to be interviewed for television or radio, ask if you can get a general idea of the questions you'll be asked a few minutes before the interview begins. Tell the reporter how you would like the store's name pronounced and try to get him or her to mention the location, as well as any other key points that you feel are important. Speak clearly and briefly. Very little of what you say—just brief sound bites—will be used, so choose your words carefully. Never say anything to a reporter that you don't want publicized, even if you are speaking off the record.

The Press Release

A press release announces an event, a unique new product line, important personnel appointments or promotions, an in-store visit by a celebrity, or other newsworthy information, to the media. The more human interest there is in your story, the more likely it is to be used. Remember that a press release should not sound like ad copy.

Press releases should be sent to TV newsrooms, magazines and all local newspapers, including the smaller papers in nearby towns. Shorter press releases are appropriate for community calendars and other radio coverage. Be sure to send out press releases at least two weeks prior to an event, and even earlier than that if you hope for coverage in a monthly magazine. All press releases have similar basic elements:

- *To:* The name of the publication or station, and the editor or other contact person
- *From:* The store name, address, telephone and fax numbers; and the name and title of the store's contact person for the media
- *The date of the press release.* If the item can be printed right away, add, "For immediate release." If the news is not to be announced until a certain date, indicate "For release on . . ."
- *The facts about the product or event.* For events, be sure to answer the questions who, what, when, and where. State all key facts in the first sentence. Write as if you were writing an article, not an ad. Limit your release to one page, and be sure to mention the most

important information in the first paragraphs. If the story has to be shortened, the final paragraphs will usually be dropped.

* *Enclose good black-and-white photographs, or mention that they are available.* Be sure to indicate the store name and telephone number on the back of all pictures, together with a caption and the photographer's credit line. Include a signed release for any individuals in the photo, especially if they are customers or other nonemployees. To avoid duplication, send photographs that will not appear in your paid advertising.

When writing about an unusual new product, you might also enclose a sample. This can also be an effective way to grab the attention of a media person for a special event—for example, delivering a small box of chocolate along with a press release about a chocolate festival. Keep in mind that photographs and samples usually are not returned.

When you send out a press release, consider enclosing a general fact sheet about the store. This information probably won't be used by the press, but it can't hurt to supply it. The fact sheet, press release, and any photos can be sent together as a press kit in an attractive folder with the store name on the cover.

Press releases and kits can be mailed or delivered. It pays to know in advance the name of the best person to contact at each publication or station and to make sure the information goes directly to that person. Follow up with a telephone call a few days later if you wish, asking if the release has arrived and if there are any questions you can answer.

Looking for a Publicity Angle

The key to getting in the news is to do something newsworthy. Shops that are frustrated by a lack of free publicity often don't have an angle to get the press interested. Brainstorm with your staff about special events, services, or products that set your store apart from others, and send out press releases until you are successful at garnering some coverage. Don't forget that business reporters are often eager for stories about shops with an unusual approach to management or merchandising or for information about stores that have recently expanded or changed. There is also nothing wrong with sending out a press release to announce a significant charity donation you are making or a service project that your staff is involved in.

Human interest and humorous stories are often considered news-worthy. We once called a local columnist to tell him about the "nonsense file" we keep, with clippings about the silliest products offered to us over the past twenty years. Unfortunately some of his readers misunderstood the story, and we received numerous telephone calls asking the prices of items we'd never carry, such as Styrofoam wind chimes ("if you love the look but hate the sound") and video aquariums. Add local newspaper and magazine editors to your store mailing list so they are always aware of what is happening at your shop. This is an easy way to be sure the press hears from you regularly, but it shouldn't take the place of formal press releases.

Duane Barmore, owner of Chickadee Depot, garners free publicity by offering to be interviewed in the media about his area of expertise, wild birds. You can become known as an articulate spokesperson in your field by volunteering to speak to community groups on subjects relating to your merchandise. Bring along samples of what you sell, and don't forget to bring catalogs, product literature, and business cards. When we give talks, we usually also bring a little gift for everyone attending and a coupon offer to entice each person into the store. Invite a member of the press to at-tend your talk, or send out a letter to the media mentioning that you are an experienced speaker on a topic sure to be of interest to their audience.

Positive Press Relations

The press does you a favor by mentioning your shop, especially if the feature is complimentary. (Thankfully, specialty shops are not usually subject to the same type of reviews as restaurants. A few negative com-ments in the press can quickly kill a fledgling eatery.) Remember to ex-press your gratitude to the reporter or publication, and mention that you'd be happy to talk with the person again at any time.

Post framed copies of any positive articles about your store, along with any popularity awards, such as "Best Antique Store," you may have won. You should mention these awards in your ads, and you might con-sider borrowing an idea from movie ads and quoting a newspaper article in your advertising, especially if a reporter has said something brief and beneficial about your shop. The fact that the compliment comes from an unpaid outside source lends it greater authority, just as any article or news feature seems more trustworthy to the public than the advertising you pay for.

10

GOOD WORKS ARE GOOD BUSINESS

The positive public relations generated by being a good corporate citizen often far outweigh the amount of advertising that could be bought with the number of dollars spent. Donating merchandise and sponsoring fund-raising events are very visible ways of doing good, and those actions form a natural part of most specialty shops' public relations campaigns.

Retailing also offers the opportunity to make a positive contribution to the local and global community through wise buying choices, good environmental policies, and even thoughtful hiring practices. Generosity and good business ethics can greatly enhance your store's reputation as a business leader, and most customers are eager to patronize stores whose spirit and community involvement they admire.

CHARITABLE DONATIONS: WHAT TO GIVE AND WHO TO GIVE IT TO

On some of the slower days of winter, I think requests for donations sometimes outnumber the customers wanting to buy things. Retail stores are easy for nonprofit groups to approach and are undoubtedly asked to give more often than the average insurance office or electrical contractor. Fortunately retailers are also more visible to the public, so we are in a position to gain more by supporting causes in which our customers are involved and by helping to sustain the community our business depends on.

When someone approaches us for a donation, we always start by asking a few questions:

- Who will benefit?
- How will the money or item be used?
- If the donation is for a fund-raiser, when is it?
- Is there any special benefit for donors, such as a free program ad?
- Have we donated before—and if so, what did we give?

We have a policy of giving to most arts, environmental, and social service organizations. Since we're not big sports enthusiasts, we tend to say no to team sponsorships. We also don't usually give to individual churches or religious groups, although we always make an exception for any charity in which one of our employees is actively involved.

In a small town, it may be very important that you donate to the major service clubs, local schools, churches, and the Little League. In a larger community you may feel freer to choose to focus on environmental causes or to support the opera. The choice is yours; however, it helps to have a policy in place so that you can give a quick and polite response to those soliciting donations.

Every good cause is happy to receive cash, but this is rarely the best choice of donation for a retail store. If a performing arts group is soliciting funds, you can usually buy an ad in the program instead of making a cash donation. Don't just hand over a business card to be reproduced; a program ad should be as attractive as the rest of your ad campaign. Program ads tend to be standard sizes, so it is practical to have a few designed and camera ready for this purpose.

Other charities might be able to use your monetary donation to purchase uniforms or T-shirts, which could be printed with your name or logo. If you donate money toward a fund-raising event, perhaps you can be listed on the invitation as an underwriter or host.

When you make a cash donation, get a receipt from the charity, and post the amount to the donation account in your bookkeeping system. Most cash donations to nonprofit organizations are tax deductible. Merchandise donations, however, do not get deducted from the donation account, because when you take your next physical inventory, the value of your inventory will have been lowered by the cost of the goods donated. It is still a good idea to ask for a receipt for merchandise donated, especially if you are tracking the causes of inventory shrinkage.

One of the advantages of having a shop is that you can generously donate merchandise with a high retail value, and the cost to you is whatever you paid for it wholesale. For this reason alone, it is usually advantageous to give goods rather than cash if the charity has a way to convert the merchandise into money. Many nonprofit organizations hold raffles and auctions to raise funds. When we are donating goods that will be bid on, we first try to ascertain if the merchandise will be displayed or just listed. A showy item representing our shop is the logical choice for auctions where bidders will see the goods, especially our local public television auction, which nets us free TV exposure. In most other instances, we give a gift certificate, which will bring the high bidder into our store to shop.

We also get many requests for door prizes, but I'm not wild about giving door prizes, because they rarely have a direct effect on the financial success of a charity event. Still, we give small gift certificates and items as door prizes when we can. We were able to provide almost 500 table favors for the YWCA's Women of Distinction luncheon over the past three years, thanks to three of our favorite suppliers. Each donated small perfume, bath gel, or hand lotion samples for the event, at no charge, and we added labels with the name of our store.

You may want to give your customers a chance to support a fundraising project by bringing donated items to the store or making contributions to a monetary fund. Some stores also involve customers in the

The Book Angel Project at Pooh Corner, a children's bookstore, encourages customers to pick a paper angel with the name of a needy child off their tree. Nonprofit agencies have provided the children's ages and interests as well as their names, so patrons—and their children—can select a book they think the child will like. Pooh Corner offers a 10 percent discount on all books purchased for the project and wraps them in festive paper with the angel as the gift tag. A star with the donor's name then replaces the angel on the tree.

planning of a major charity event by allowing their customers to vote on which organization should be the recipient of the money raised.

Wholesale suppliers are often very generous when asked to donate an item to be used as a raffle prize or auction item. When asking for a donation, allow plenty of lead time, and be very specific about the nature of the cause and what you hope will be donated. If you work through a sales representative, you may find that the rep has out-of-date samples of products that he or she is willing to donate. Our reps know that we are happy to find a worthy home for any merchandise they want to dispose of, including one-of-a-kind greeting card samples that my Girl Scout troop for many years sent to nursing home residents during the holidays. Follow up any donation with a written thank-you note to both the supplier and the sales rep.

It is fun to find toys and other small items from our suppliers to order as prizes for children's carnivals and seasonal events. We even have a large wooden lollipop tree game (shaped like an orange tree, of course) that we loan to school groups, complete with lollipops and prizes. The cost to us is minimal, and the parents in charge of arranging for games and prizes really appreciate it.

Finding Good Homes for Unwanted Goods

No matter how low you mark clearance goods, you will never get rid of the very last item. Yet even a pathetic-looking pile of picked-over sale items in most cases can be put to good use by someone. Resist the temptation to throw it all in the trash, and sort through the remainders looking for items that you can recycle or donate to charity.

Some stores are hesitant to donate merchandise with their name on it to local charities. I once stood in line behind volunteers from a local theater's garage sale who were humorously discussing some of the less desirable items our shop had given them. You may want to avoid this by transporting unwanted merchandise to a different part of the state. Another option is to remove all the tags or require the charity to do so.

Use your imagination when finding a home for unwanted goods. Can some of the items be used by an after-school program as crafts supplies? Could a kindergarten class use them to play store? Would a nursing home find them useful as tray favors? Charities that sponsor flea markets, garage sales, or resale shops are often happy to receive odds and ends, but avoid the temptation to donate shopworn or unsalable merchandise to those asking for donations for auctions and raffles. If a cause is going to showcase your donation, give something you are proud of.

FUND-RAISERS AND BENEFITS

As a retailer, you are in a unique position to hold fund-raisers of your own, either as an effort to help a charity in which you believe strongly or to give a boost to a store promotion such as a grand opening. When you decide to do something to help a charitable organization, be sure to contact its office or board of directors so it can assist you. The organization will probably end up fielding telephone calls about the event, so keep its staff well informed.

One of the most popular ways of doing an in-store fund-raiser is to pledge a percentage of all sales, or sales of a particular item, to the cause—perhaps for one day during regular store hours or at a special event during a time you are normally closed. Dozens of retailers participate in Madison's citywide AIDS benefit day, and our street for many years held a nursery school benefit evening, with the shops only open to the parents and friends of the local schools. In either case, the hope is that shoppers will spend a bit more than they would have otherwise, so that the 5 to 15 percent donated to the charity is offset by an increase in sales. If you are doing a benefit for a charity, ask if it will send a notice to its members and other supporters announcing the event. This is an excellent way to attract new customers. We also invite the group to have representatives in the store the day of the benefit, thanking people for shopping and giving out information about their organization.

At San Francisco's Imaginarium toy store, nonprofit groups are invited to hold an after-hours shopping benefit in which the shopper gets a 10 percent discount *and* the school gets a 10 percent cash donation. J. T. Puffin's, a toy and gift store in Madison, Wisconsin, helps local nursery schools and day care centers acquire new playthings and educational materials by recording the purchase amount whenever a customer mentions the name of his or her child's school between September and December. J. T. Puffin's then donates a merchandise gift certificate to the school valued at 10 percent of these sales.

For a grand opening, you might choose to have a gala evening bene-fit with special refreshments and entertainment. If you want to allow vis-itors to shop, you can pledge a percentage of sales, but otherwise you can either make a generous cash donation in honor of the occasion or have pa-trons buy admission tickets, with all the proceeds going to the cause.

For several years we sponsored a chocolate festival as a fund-raiser for local arts organizations. The bountiful chocolate buffet featured culi-nary creations that had been entered in our two chocolate cooking con-tests. The entrants in the amateur competition were rewarded with numerous prizes donated by our suppliers. In the category for profes-sional chefs, restaurants, and bakeries, the prizes were framed certificates to display in their place of business, and of course these certificates men-tioned our shop as sponsor. At the chocolate gala, little girls dressed as chocolate kisses sold Hershey's Kisses with numbers under them that could be redeemed for small prizes, such as chocolate bars, also donated by our suppliers.

When a Ronald MacDonald House, for the families of critically ill chil-dren, was being built in Madison, we supported it by publishing *The Orange Tree Imports Cookbook*. The book includes recipes from our staff and our Cooking School instructors, and the proceeds furnished one of the guest rooms at the house. (To be truthful, we still have cookbooks on hand, but we went ahead and made the full donation the year the house was built.)

SELLING GOODS THAT DO GOOD

Many years ago, we started selling UNICEF cards at Christmas, with 100 percent of the sales benefiting the United Nations Children's Fund. Obvi-ously we lost some sales of our regular boxed Christmas cards to those buying UNICEF cards, but we felt strongly about supporting this cause. Today many of our most popular lines of Christmas cards and calendars are published by nonprofit organizations such the Sierra Club, the World Wildlife Fund, and the Audubon Society—and we earn full markup on the merchandise. We still feature UNICEF cards, of course, but carrying these other lines is a painless way to support other worthwhile causes and to allow our customers to feel good about their purchases.

Many of our other suppliers have selected a charity to work with and are pledging a percentage of sales on certain items to these organizations. The amount of money that ends up being donated is generally kept confidential, but in the case of companies like Department 56 and Enesco, both suppliers of collectibles, gifts, and seasonal items, their corporate donations are in the millions.

Local groups have come to us with calendars, note cards, and Christmas cards that they have produced, and we usually carry these in the store at no markup in order to support their work. Since we are more aware of merchandise trends and marketing than they are, we also offer to advise them on the items they are producing. Unless the production cost and artwork is all donated, nonprofit groups can easily end up losing, rather than making, money on the merchandise they produce.

Taking a Stand—What You *Don't* Sell

What you decide not to sell is also a reflection of what you and your business stand for. If you believe that war toys and play guns are harmful to children, then your toy shop should boycott that category. Selling cigarettes is a profitable business, but if you want to discourage smoking, your pharmacy or grocery store should not offer them.

Many other buying decisions are less clear. Should a bookstore offer works that it considers to be racist or offensive to women? The University Bookstore in Madison had a book on its shelves from a small press on how to shoplift. Where should the line on free speech be drawn? Should your shop buy products from manufacturers that may exploit their workers, knowing that if you don't, these workers will be unemployed? Should you boycott countries that have human rights policies you find objectionable, even though your dollars will help the innocent people who live there?

All of these decisions require careful consideration and some difficult deliberations. You might involve your staff members in discussing these issues and in establishing a policy that reflects your store's philosophy and image.

ENVIRONMENTALLY SOUND RETAILING

When Earth Day and the environmental movement captured the imagination of the public in the 1980s and 1990s, the retail industry jumped on the bandwagon, creating thousands of T-shirt designs with rain forest slogans and entire stores dedicated to Mother Nature.

The irony, of course, is that Mother Nature would undoubtedly prefer to be left out of the retailing world. There are frankly very few products sold in the name of saving the environment that actually do any good, because consumption itself is usually a negative. Unless a store sells nothing but items such as bulk foods and natural fiber clothing, chances are that it is encouraging people to buy things they don't really need. But this does not mean that shopkeepers have no means of sharing in the responsibility for the future of our planet.

In *The Ecology of Commerce*, Paul Hawken, founder of the Smith and Hawken gardening catalog and shops, challenges small businesses, including retailers, to conduct their businesses according to this economic golden rule: "Leave the world better than you found it, take no more than you need, try not to harm life or the environment, make amends if you do." While admitting that much of what consumers will buy is unnecessary, he argues that there is virtue to be found in marketing items "of clarity and simplicity, products that cut through the clutter of our lives and allow us to perform the daily acts of living in a more satisfying way." These items should be "objects of durability and long-term utility whose ultimate use or disposition will not be harmful to future generations."

The consumer, unfortunately, is not always willing (or able) to pay for lasting quality. Although it makes sense to offer a range of prices to satisfy all customers, a retailer should not knowingly carry items such as poorly made plastic toys with a short life span of play value and a long life span in a landfill.

Durability is not always a factor in buying decisions, of course. A clothing retailer, for instance, knows that no fashion will last forever. Most clothes are, however, easily reusable and eventually recyclable into scrap fiber. Some types of fabrics, such as natural, undyed cottons, do less harm to the environment in their manufacturing process than synthetic materials. Educating the consumer about these factors can lead to an environmentally informed decision, although the percentage of customers making choices based solely on environmental factors is still quite limited.

A clothing store can encourage customers to recycle used clothing by donating items to those in need. Other types of stores can take trade-ins of furniture, working appliances, and additional items that still have a useful life ahead of them.

Some bookstores use the trade-in concept to add used books to their selection. Patrons are given store credit for the used books they bring in, which stimulates sales at the same time that it keeps books from being thrown away.

Carmen's, a ladies' specialty store known as The Coat Store of Madison, sponsored a charity coat event for over twenty-five years. Customers received an allowance of up to $30 toward a new coat for every coat that was brought in. Thousands of good used coats were cleaned and repaired at Carmen's expense and given to those in need.

Many retail businesses are natural recyclers. Antique shops, vintage clothing stores, and even baseball card dealers keep products flowing back through the economy rather than creating new goods. But those that must purchase new goods to sell can still give consideration to the ultimate disposition of these products once the consumer tires of them.

Where Will Your Merchandise Go?

Countries such as Germany and Japan are starting to insist that manufacturers plan for the disposal of a product, or at least its packaging, when they manufacture it. In the United States, we have a long way to go. Inexpensive trash removal that carries the problem of discarded merchandise out of sight often alleviates any pangs of conscience we might have when buying a new product to replace an old one. But where do old appliances, computers, or broken pieces of furniture go when they die? Even if they can be incinerated, the fumes may contribute to air pollution. And we are kidding ourselves if we think that the manufacturing process involved in creating many of the new goods we sell does not contribute to the destruction of the environment.

The environmentally conscientious buyer takes reuse, recyclability, easy disposal, and safe manufacturing procedures into consideration and selects products that do the least harm. Biodegradable plastics, for example, are better than other plastics because they will eventually disintegrate after being thrown away. But unfortunately these issues are rarely clear-cut; few standards have been set for what qualifies as biodegradable and recyclable. One manufacturer of plastic garbage bags, for instance, claimed that its were biodegradable, when in fact they just broke up into small but long-lasting particles. Evaluating these factors for every product used or sold in a store requires a commitment few people are willing to make.

As we move toward more international awareness of the importance to us all of considering environmental factors, manufacturers will undoubtedly make it easier to compare the environmental impact of various products. Meanwhile, spending your buying dollars with companies that clearly express concern for the natural world will encourage others to imitate their environmentally sound practices.

Educating the Buying Public

Retailers have a unique opportunity to educate customers about the choices they can make regarding factors such as the durability and usefulness of the products they buy. A mission of Whole Foods, a creative housewares and health food market, is to educate customers about the origins and uses of all the products it sells, with entire file drawers full of free information.

Product selection can also help customers make educated choices. When offered beautiful stationery products that happen to be made of recycled paper, customers often select items that will have less of a negative impact on the environment than those usually offered by mass merchandisers. There is still some question as to whether customers are willing to pay more for environmentally friendly products, but for about the same price, they often appreciate this feature.

The Product Packaging Dilemma

Even shops selling goods that are consumable, such as foods and toiletries, have to face the dilemma of packaging these items. At the same time that we have become concerned with reducing packaging for the sake of the environment, additional packaging has been encouraged in the interest of safety and hygiene.

Unless you are a very large operation, you will have little control over how items come packaged to you. You can try to specify that you want an item not packaged, in case the supplier has the ability to provide the merchandise that way. But very few items are offered with optional packaging, because manufacturers and importers prefer standardization. They also like to package items to reduce breakage in shipping and to promote awareness of their own brand name. Many stores want to receive items packaged because the larger size is thought to discourage shoplifting. This was the rationale behind the shrink-wrapped cardboard "long-box" on compact discs, which were eventually eliminated after musicians such as Canadian singer Raffi protested their wastefulness.

A package can also provide information about the product that will help sell it to the consumer and give directions for the item's use. It can allow an item to be hung, or *pegged*, for display. It can enhance the appearance of the merchandise, and preserve the freshness of perishables. And yet in many cases we have to question the long-term effects of packaging that will outlive its contents by decades.

In evaluating whether to buy merchandise that comes packaged, take these factors into account:

- Is it necessary for this item to be packaged? (If not, is the same item available elsewhere unpackaged?)
- Is it overpackaged?
- Can the packaging be reused or recycled?
- Is the packaging biodegradable, or can it be incinerated?
- If an item doesn't come packaged, will customers expect the store to put it in a box when they buy it?

Do You Have a Box?

Customers often expect a gift item to be put into a box so that it can be wrapped, and certainly no one would want to struggle with gift wrapping a stuffed kangaroo without boxing it first. But many items come already boxed, and it is a waste of resources—environmental and financial—to take an item out of its box and put it in a gift box. Instead of doing this, we offer to gift wrap over the manufacturer's box for free.

For items that don't come boxed, we provide gift boxes. Many packaging suppliers offer gift boxes made at least in part from recycled paper. These boxes are often attractive enough to require only a ribbon and bow, saving on the gift wrap paper that would have been used to overwrap it. Some stores use decorative paper gift bags, made of recycled paper, as their store wrapping.

Almost all stores use bags for customers' merchandise. Most manufacturers offer bags made at least in part of recycled paper, and of course paper is easily disposed of. Paper bags do, however, take up considerably more storage space than plastic ones. Thin plastic merchandise bags are especially popular throughout Europe, along with heavier plastic tote bags.

"And on this wall, I have my Irma grocery bag collection."

The Danish grocery chain Irma has developed a wonderful solution to the proliferation of plastic carrier bags: it charges customers a small fee for each bag, encouraging their reuse, and uses the money to support the work of artists whose creations are featured in full color on the sides of the bags. Customers are much more likely to reuse a bag that is a work of art.

Packaging for Shipping

On a windy garbage day, one used to see swirls of Styrofoam "peanuts" being chased by broom-wielding shopkeepers in the alleys behind neighborhood shops. This wonderful, lightweight packing material was a shipper's dream: easy to use, clean, and with a safe cushion for all the different kinds of merchandise being shipped in cardboard cartons.

But these "peanuts" have a tendency to escape from trash containers, and, more unfortunately, they have a tendency to last forever in landfills. Merchandise coming in our back door was almost always packed in "peanuts," and merchandise going out the front door hardly ever was. The result was a buildup of packing materials that far surpassed our store's ability to reuse them in shipping mail order purchases out to our customers. Happily, we were able to find a small ceramics manufacturer and a pack-and-ship operation that are only too happy to get our Styrofoam "peanuts" for free, so we now leave them stacked in cartons or bags for pickup by one of these companies.

Some of our suppliers have started using new packaging materials that look like Styrofoam but dissolve in water. Others are experimenting with actual popcorn, which can either be dissolved or eaten by animals. This doesn't take into account the fact that mice are sometimes a problem for shops, but it is an original and organic solution to the packing dilemma.

Minimal Impact Retailing

The catalog of REI, a national outfitter for outdoor sports, suggests that customers practice "minimal impact" camping and hiking. As a retailer, you can also try to minimize your impact on the environment by making intelligent choices about how your store is operated. In addition to making wise choices when buying merchandise, the environmentally aware shopkeeper makes informed decisions regarding such variables as energy usage, paper, and recycling.

A retail store usually requires an immense amount of lighting every hour that it is open. These lights generate a lot of heat, placing heavy demands on air-conditioning during hot weather. In cooler months, energy is needed to heat the store, with constant heat loss from customers' opening the door to outside air. The only positive side is that retail stores seldom have as many windows as a private home, so heat loss through glass is usually minimized.

There are lighting choices that use less energy than incandescent bulbs and have a longer life expectancy per bulb. Energy-saving fluorescent fixtures can be used where spotlighting products is not important, and low-wattage halogen bulbs can be used to provide intense spotlighting. Check with your local power company for information on the best way to save energy when designing lighting for a store.

Ceiling fans, setback thermostats at night, and other energy-saving tips used by home owners can apply equally well to retail shops. Some stores in cold climates save heating energy by using a revolving door, or a small entrance vestibule requiring customers to come through one door and close it before entering the second door. These entranceways keep blasts of icy air from coming into the store with each customer, but they are cumbersome for the disabled, parents with strollers, and customers carrying packages. You will need to provide an alternative entrance if you have a revolving door, or automatic door openers on double-doored vestibules.

Recycling in the Store

Recycling the aluminum soda cans from your staff lounge may have a very small impact on the environment, but recycling the mountain of cardboard and paper your shop generates can make a big difference. We are fortunate to have public recycling of cardboard, newspapers, and magazines in Madison, but the city requires that all cardboard cartons be flattened, cut to a certain size, and tied together, which is impractical for the weeks when we receive several hundred boxes. We choose instead to pay for private pickup of the cardboard boxes we can't reuse and our office paper trash. We have to remove Styrofoam peanuts, plastic bubble pack, and other nonpaper items, but this sorting process is much easier than flattening and bundling.

A store that generates a lot of office paper might consider investing in a shredder to convert this trash into packing material for outgoing shipments. We reuse the cleanest cartons in which we receive merchandise to send out shipments of customers' purchases. They may not look as spiffy as brand-new boxes, but they are usually quite serviceable.

GIVING SOMETHING BACK

One of the benefits of success in retailing is the ability to contribute something to the well-being of the community that sustains the store. There are many ways to do this: through ecological action, support of the arts, partnership with the schools, and volunteer activities. You can act locally or on a more global scale.

To have a positive environmental impact on your own neighborhood, look for an opportunity to plant trees or restore an older building that otherwise would have been torn down. On a larger scale, you might choose to support conservation groups such as the Sierra Club by selling their licensed products, or by holding a fund-raiser for an organization involved in environmental issues around the world. Just by taking responsibility for the impact your shop has on the environment, you help ensure the future of the community in which you hope to do business for many years to come.

Become a Patron of the Arts

Your support and advice can make the difference between success and failure for a craftsperson or artist. Galleries have traditionally played an important role in the work of artists, promoting their work to collectors and handling business transactions so that the artist is free to create. Many well-known artists owe their rise to fame to an art dealer who truly believed in their work.

The role of patron is not limited to art galleries. Almost any shop can purchase some merchandise that is handmade by a craftsperson or artisan. Even if these purchases are made through an importer or wholesaler, the income eventually will reach the artists, making it possible for them to continue to ply their craft.

The income derived from handcrafts can have a significant impact on the life of a person living in poverty. By buying a product that someone has made, you may be helping that person support his or her family and community. Shops such as Self-Help carry only items made by artisans in Third World countries who need a dignified way to make a living. Many of the crafts they sell are traditional arts from the area, so their shops are helping to preserve cultures that might otherwise disappear.

One World Market in Durham, North Carolina, has taken to a new level the idea of using buying dollars to help people. In addition to purchasing handmade products, it has given a grant of $1,000 to Candlemakers of Hope, a crafts co-op made up of women trying to help themselves escape the grip of poverty. Thanks to One World, Brenda Johnson of Candlemakers of Hope can now say, "A few months ago we were welfare mothers looking for a break. But now we are actually struggling businesswomen with viable contacts and inventory—and we are beginning to see the light at the end of the tunnel. That light is a candle and it is burning bright."

If artwork and handmade crafts do not fit with your merchandise mix, consider helping artists by using their work as part of your store decor or displays. At Una Mundo, a card and gift shop in New York, the work of part-time employee Tim J. McCarron was used to decorate the walls. The result was public exposure for the artist, leading to a show at the National Arts Club.

Many theatrical and musical groups ask retailers to advertise in their programs, a good way to get your shop name associated with excellence in the performing arts. We also serve as a ticket outlet for local groups, which brings customers into the store. When a group asks us to sell tickets, we have them fill in a form that lists the details of the event, ticket prices, how many tickets we've received, and who is authorized to pick up money or bring more tickets. We sometimes receive a pair of complimentary tickets in thanks, and we give these to our staff.

Public television underwriting is considerably more expensive than a program ad, but can be an effective way to "buy" television advertising for your store. Surveys of our customers indicate that many of them are supporters of public television, so it makes good sense for us to be underwriters. We look for shows that have a relationship to what we sell, and there are customers who drive to our shop from adjoining states because they have seen our name as a sponsor of *The Frugal Gourmet*.

Partnerships with Schools

The students of today are the employees and customers of tomorrow. There are several ways your specialty shop can play a positive role in your community's schools. You can offer to speak to classes about retailing or about some of the merchandise you carry. You can invite groups to tour your store, including a behind-the-scenes look at what is involved in running a business. Every year we host a group of elementary school students studying ESL (English as a Second Language). I particularly enjoy trying to show each student some merchandise from his or her home country, and I ask them questions about the items to give them some practice in speaking English. One year I showed them some black pasta and asked them to guess what is used to make it that color. Squid ink is the correct answer (which is why I've never eaten any, I must admit), but this question really had them puzzled. They knew Americans had strange eating habits, but they couldn't quite think what we would eat that was black. Finally one little boy raised his hand and shyly asked, "Ants?"

Many high schools have work-study programs in which students are placed in local businesses to gain real-world experience. If your operation could offer some challenging work to high school students, call your nearest high school for details about this program. Work-study students sometimes continue in their jobs after graduating, so this could be a source of future employees. There may also be a program in retailing at the high school, running the school store, or the concessions at sports events that could use your help as an outside adviser. Consider sponsoring an entrepreneur club after school, encouraging students to learn about small business and free enterprise. Their math and reading skills, as well as their self-confidence, will benefit from starting and running their own business projects.

High schools and middle schools are always looking for incentives to motivate students to come to school, stay in school, and do well academically. In Spring, Texas, merchants offer discounts to students who achieve good attendance, complete their assignments, and do well in class. The stores at East Towne Mall here in Madison provide thousands of dollars worth of merchandise and gift certificates to the middle and high schools in the area, to be used as incentives for student achievement programs.

> Pegasus Games, a unique shop in Madison, Wisconsin, with the motto "Games You Never Outgrow," encourages high school and middle school students to do well academically by offering a 10 percent discount on any one purchase to students with a 3.0 or higher grade point average. Students with a perfect 4.0 GPA get 20 percent off. "We hope to instill the idea that gaming is for after the studies are done," says co-owner Lorece Ferm Aitken.

COMMUNITY LEADERSHIP

You may not have the influence of a celebrity spokesperson like Robert Redford, but by virtue of being a retailer, you have more status in your community than many less visible businesspeople. You can choose to use that position to help the entire community, as Gift Gallery/Northridge Pharmacy of southern California did. When the town was devastated by an earthquake in 1994, the owners turned their shop into a rallying point for the community. They set up a first aid station and provided replacements for critically needed prescriptions for all customers at cost. Those who could not pay were given them for free. As the community started to recover, the pharmacy put up a mural in place of its broken windows, encouraging other businesses to stay and rebuild.

Your store can serve as a focal point for a special interest group such as writers, feminists, runners, or even model train buffs. You can provide these groups with leadership, materials, lecturers, and a place to meet. In exchange, they are likely to become loyal customers. At GAIA Bookstore in Berkeley, California, the customers even held a fund-raiser to keep the store open when a new chain bookstore threatened its existence.

Mentoring other businesspeople can be a way to help your community. Many years ago, we helped organize the first merchants' association in our area. In addition to stretching our advertising dollar by doing joint promotions, we encourage and support each other, to our mutual benefit. As an experienced retailer, I am happy to be able to meet with individuals, especially other women, who are thinking of starting a retail or a wholesale business and offer them some guidance.

Hiring That Helps

The Americans with Disabilities Act mandates that businesses make jobs available for those with physical disabilities. In many situations, this is no sacrifice on the part of the employer, because staff members who need some assistance are usually just as valuable as those who don't. We often assume, however, that most jobs in retailing are too physical for someone in a wheelchair or require more communication than a person who is blind or deaf can easily handle. But I have been waited on by a deaf employee at Wal-Mart and have seen someone stocking merchandise from a wheelchair there. Perhaps the rest of the retail world will learn a lesson from this discount giant and give physically disabled employees more opportunities.

There are also individuals who need meaningful work in their lives who cannot perform the same jobs as others. If you need someone to do routine clerical tasks, stocking, or housekeeping duties, consider contacting an agency that places mentally, emotionally, and physically challenged individuals in businesses. The agency often provides customized training and a job coach to help the client succeed at work. It will also help make the rest of the staff comfortable with the employee.

Tasks that arise from time to time, such as stuffing envelopes with sales literature or attaching labels to hundreds of table favors for a fund-raising event, can be performed in a sheltered workshop. Check to see if there is a facility in your community looking for projects for its clients. There are many ways your payroll dollars can be used to help those in need.

GIVING TIME

If your shop decides to support a particular cause, your staff may want to be involved. The best way to ensure their participation is to have staff members participate in the decision about what charity to support, but involvement beyond duties directly related to the shop should always be optional. Employees may already have projects of their own—or may not share your enthusiasm for the one you select.

Adopting a cause can be a good way to build team spirit among staff members. One year we bought gifts for a large family in the rural South through the Box Project, a nonprofit organization that assigns donors to a specific family in need. Many staff members brought in wrapped gifts to supplement those purchased by the store. Other shops sponsor a staff team to participate in a fund-raising run or bike-a-thon, or they get together a group to answer telephones during the public television station's pledge drive.

If there are times when staff members are not usually busy, you could "loan" interested employees to a good cause while paying their salary. Wisconsin Harvest is a local nonprofit organization that picks up leftover food from restaurants and bakeries and delivers it to meal sites. Businesses can adopt a once-a-week route and ask any employee who is willing to take an hour to do the pickup and delivery. You might consider sponsoring an employee interested in volunteering at a local school to tutor, or at a nearby meal program to help serve lunch to the hungry.

THE REWARDS OF GIVING

Good deeds do not usually go unnoticed. Chances are that you will receive some public recognition for your efforts, and there is no harm in seeking this recognition by sending out press releases or mentioning your work in ads or in-store materials. Your efforts may well inspire other retailers and individuals to get more involved in supporting good causes. You will also make your customers feel that they are part of something worthwhile when they shop at your store, and they will reward your generosity with their loyal patronage.

11

MANAGING DURING TOUGH TIMES

On a good day, retailing is more fun than work. When you arrive in the morning, a few customers are already waiting outside, eager to buy, your staff is cheerful and ready to help them, your store window displays are eye catching and attractive, and you know the merchandise your customers want is all in stock. In reality, some days are like that. And some are not.

The retail business is made up of people, buildings, money, and merchandise, and something can go wrong with all of them. Employees may steal, quit, or neglect their duties. The government may decide to audit you. Your roof may leak, or the front door may fall off (this actually happened to us the week before Christmas two years ago). Customers may shoplift or switch their alliance to the new discount store on the edge of town. Your main supplier may go out of business. Your boxes and bags may arrive late. The money may run out. Your store may catch on fire. Chances are not all of these will happen to you, or at least not all at once, but it is wise to plan for when things do go wrong, because eventually something will.

INSURING AGAINST AND PREVENTING CRIME, DISASTERS, AND OTHER PROBLEMS

No business can afford to be without some form of insurance, and your insurance agent should be a member of your advisory team from the start. If you can't trust the agent not to sell you more insurance than you need, perhaps you should find a new person to deal with. Ask for recommendations from the other businesses in your area for an insurance agency experienced in the retail field.

Basic business insurance includes liability coverage protecting the individuals who come in contact with your store: staff, customers, and other visitors. It also protects against loss in the event of fire, with extended coverage available against storms, explosions, riots, and other disasters. Policies often have separate coverage for window breakage, signage, and company-owned vehicles.

In choosing coverage and deciding on the amount of the deductible, determine how much you are comfortable covering yourself in the event that something happens. If you can absorb a $200 replacement cost on a broken window, for instance, then it makes sense to get window coverage with a $200 deductible. This will be cheaper than insurance with a lower deductible. If your signs are not worth much money, skip the added cost of signage insurance.

The lease on your store will probably specify how much liability insurance you are required to carry. It will also specify who will pay for fire insurance for the building and whether you need additional special fire liability insurance in case a fire starting in your part of the building damages other premises. Be sure to check which parts of the store you are responsible for insuring. In some strip malls, for example, you may need insurance coverage for the windows but not the door.

Stores located in areas prone to flooding, hurricanes, or earthquakes may find it difficult to get insurance to cover these natural disasters. Check to see if there is a government-sponsored program in which you can participate, or try to get a policy with a high deductible and put aside the amount of the deductible as "self-insurance."

Insurance written to cover the replacement value of your store's inventory and fixtures in case of fire actually insures only part of your loss. You will also lose money by not being able to be open for business. This is the reason for *business interruption insurance*, which compensates you for the temporary loss of income due to fire or other natural disaster. This type of insurance gives you time to get your business back on its feet and allows you to pay your employees during the time you are closed. There are different types of business interruption insurance, and some pay benefits based on your past net profit—which can be a problem if your business is not very profitable. Ask your agent for details about what policies are available to you and which one would best suit your needs.

If customers routinely leave items with you for repair or resale, be sure to look into property damage liability insurance. Customers will appreciate knowing that their diamond ring, or antique table, is insured in the event that something happens while it is in your store.

Company-owned vehicles must be insured; if staff members use their own cars to run business errands or make deliveries, check to see what coverage is available for them. Even if they have their own auto insurance, you may be liable in the event of an accident. Investigate the driving record of anyone who will be entrusted with a store-owned vehicle, and insist on courteous and safe driving by those representing your business.

Will insurance cover you in case of theft? If your store is broken into while it is closed, damage to the building and stolen merchandise should be covered by theft insurance. Robbery, in which force or the threat of force is used, can also be covered. But shoplifting, that all-too-common form of shrinkage that takes place during open hours through theft by customers or pilferage by staff, is unlikely to be paid for by insurance. Your only insurance against this type of theft is prevention.

Shoplifting Prevention

The major retail chains spend millions of dollars to prevent theft. For most small shops, the best solution is a simple one: attentive customer service. Greet every customer entering the store, and make the person feel welcome. A certain percentage of shoplifting occurs because the thief feels angry at the store, sometimes because of the lack of personal attention. Don't make it easy for a shoplifter to steal something by leaving areas of the store unattended. Check back periodically with shoppers who are browsing so they know you are aware they are still in the store.

It is much better to deter a shoplifter than to try to catch one. Confronting someone and accusing him or her of taking something is always awkward, and in many cases, the law prevents you from stopping someone unless he or she has clearly attempted to leave the store with merchandise not paid for. Consult with your local police about what you legally can and cannot do when you catch someone stealing, and pass this information along to your staff.

Movin' Kids, a Madison, Wisconsin, children's shoe store, was the victim of an unusual type of retail theft. A large shipment of expensive boots was stolen from right in front of their eyes when a trucking company that did not require drivers to carry deliveries inside unloaded several cartons on the sidewalk in front of the store. After it was signed for, a car (which may have been following the truck) drove up, loaded all the cartons in the back, and sped away.

Teenage (and preteen) shoplifting is a serious problem, and word gets around quickly if your store is considered an easy mark. Stores carrying products appealing to teens need to take special precautions and to make it clear that anyone caught shoplifting will be dealt with seriously. As with potential shoplifters of any age, the best solution is prevention. Don't treat all teenagers as potential thieves, because most are not, but don't tempt teens to steal by putting desirable items in a blind area or by ignoring teen customers in the store. Greet everyone entering the store, and offer attentive but not suspiciously overbearing service.

From time to time we call the parents of a young child who has pocketed something, or a parent will bring in a child who has taken something from our store. I usually ask the adult and child to come with me to an area where we can talk in private, and then I explain to the child that shoplifting is stealing. If the parent agrees, I ask the child to give back the item *and* to pay for it—the opposite of getting something for free by taking it. We also ask that for one year, the child not come in the store without an adult. This policy seems fair and is kinder than calling the police, yet we almost always lose the family as customers, because the parents are embarrassed to return.

One young shoplifter actually suggested that we get convex mirrors to deter theft from some of the less visible parts of the store, and we reluctantly took him up on the idea. Other stores may find that surveillance cameras are an effective deterrent, and these cameras are available in an inexpensive dummy form that may fool some amateurs.

Professional shoplifters are much harder to deter, and they often work in pairs or teams to distract the sales staff so they can steal. There is little you can do to combat this type of crime except to call the police as quickly as possible. Be certain to warn neighboring businesses if you think professional shoplifters are at work in the area.

Large-ticket items and goods such as jewelry, leather goods, and stereo equipment that can easily be resold by shoplifters may require special shoplifting-prevention devices. A number of systems are available that require a magnetic encoded tag or ink-filled device to be removed when the item is purchased. If someone leaves the store without having the tag removed, an alarm sounds, and when an ink-filled tag is removed at home, the garment is ruined. Unfortunately employees occasionally neglect to remove or deactivate the sound-alarm tags, embarrassing legitimate customers who set off the alarm when leaving the store. When the alarm sounds, approach the customer calmly and first offer to correct the situation, rather than assuming the hapless individual is a thief.

Small, very expensive items should be kept in locked, or at least closed, cases. Keep in mind, however, that items in cases do not tend to sell as well as those that customers can handle. A shop with all of its merchandise behind glass does not appear inviting to customers who want to browse.

Discuss shoplifting with your staff members so they can be alert to suspicious behavior. If a customer appears to be looking around nervously, a sales associate should ask if he or she needs help, and then stay near the customer, dusting shelves or straightening displays. Watch for individuals with oversize coats, especially in warm weather, and large shopping bags or backpacks. If you are concerned about shoplifting, you could require that bags and backpacks be checked while shoppers are browsing.

> Chicago's late, and lamented, Guild Bookstore used a deck of playing cards cut in half diagonally to create unique claim checks for customer bags checked at the counter. A wooden clothespin was used to attach one half of the card to the bag, and the customer was given the other half to hold until ready to leave the store.

Crime from Within: Employee Theft

No one wants to believe that someone on staff would steal, but national statistics point to employee theft as a major problem for retailers. Although there are unscrupulous individuals who will steal given any opportunity, most people will not try to harm a business they love. It is important that employees feel involved in the business and that they feel appreciated. As with shoplifting, retail theft by an employee can be a way of expressing anger.

If you are concerned about employee theft, Ruth Jacobsen suggests in *Your Own Shop* that you flatten all cartons you are throwing away and not allow staff to park by the loading area or to leave by a back door. Large quantities of merchandise can be taken very quickly by someone backing a truck up to the loading dock and filling it with goods. You might also require that staff purchases be rung up by a manager, and do spot checks of staff parcels and backpacks when employees are leaving work. Take a periodic physical inventory of any area you suspect may be subject to theft rather than waiting for the annual inventory. Employees are often in a position to know what merchandise wouldn't be missed until inventory time.

Controlling the number of people who have access to the building after hours is also a good idea if you are concerned about theft. Some security alarm systems can provide a record of who left the store last and of anyone who enters after hours. Each employee is provided with a personal code to disarm and arm the system.

It is important to realize that the store's merchandise is often very tempting to employees. A generous store discount will encourage staff to acquire the items they want without resorting to dishonesty. We offer our staff all merchandise at 10 percent above wholesale, and we also have a "free box" with merchandise they can help themselves to. These items are usually slightly flawed products for which we've received credit from suppliers or display items that are no longer salable.

Retail businesses are also in danger of losing large amounts of money from embezzlement, or theft from the till. You might consider having a background check done before you hire bookkeepers or managers who will have access to the store's checking account. Review the shop's bank statements and other financial information regularly, and be alert to irregularities. Match credit card invoices to the business expense receipts turned in by employees who hold cards. Check telephone bills periodically for unusual charges on long-distance calls.

Watch for suspiciously low sales or high refunds when certain employees are working the sales floor, or frequent redemptions of credit slips and gift certificates, which may mean someone is pocketing the money. Insist that customers always get a cash register receipt so that no one can ring up a lower amount than the actual sale, or no sale at all, and keep the proceeds. Cash registers were in fact originally called the "Incorruptible

Cashier," because every time the drawer was opened, a bell rang. According to language historian Bill Bryson (*Made in America*, Morrow, 1994), this is the original reason for using odd amount prices such as 99¢. The need to give some change on all purchases meant the register's bell would sound during every single transaction.

Cautionary procedures may help catch the occasional dishonest employee, but the best deterrent to theft from within is to make all staff members feel that they are a valued part of the business. Let your employees see that you always deal honestly with suppliers and customers, setting a high moral standard for your store. Unfortunately, circumstances beyond your control may sometimes lead an employee to steal. When this happens, you must cope with both the loss and the bitter feeling of having been betrayed by someone you trusted.

Crime Prevention

Some loss from shoplifting is a fact of life for most retailers, but we all fervently hope to avoid more invasive crimes such as burglaries and holdups. Most police departments will offer advice on crime prevention that is specific to your store location and layout. We have invited the detective who specializes in this field to address our staff on security issues. Although it is frightening to discuss all the possible ways one can become the victim of a crime, we were able to use what we learned to make the store a safer place. Here are some of the safety pointers:

- Try to have more than one person working on the sales floor at all times.
- If someone demands money or threatens you, always give the person what he or she wants and try to get him or her to leave. Avoid being taken along as a hostage if at all possible.
- Do not keep excessive amounts of cash on hand. Consider a safe if you need a place to store money before depositing it.
- Vary the time that deposits are taken to the bank and the route that the person making the deposit takes to get there.
- Trust your instincts. Call the police if someone seems suspicious.
- Do not go into a basement or storeroom alone after closing in case someone is hiding there. You could restrict access to these areas by having a locked door or one that buzzes when it is opened.
- Empty your display window of valuables at night.

- Leave the cash register drawers open and empty when you are closed.
- Leave a few lights on at night so that suspicious activity will be visible from the street.
- Have a safe place for employees to keep their purses while they work.
- Consider installing an alarm system. (This may reduce your insurance rates, so be sure to notify your agent.)
- Be sure your doors, windows, and locks are secure and cannot be jimmied easily.

Ensuring Personal Safety

Providing a safe environment for your customers and staff is the best way to prevent as many accidents as possible. Look around your store for safety hazards in your displays, such as unsteady racks or sharp hooks at eye level. Be sure your entrance is well lit and kept clear of ice and snow in the winter. If your staff leaves by a back exit, make sure that it is also well lit and free of trash and other hazards.

We provide individual personal alarms for staff to borrow if they have to leave alone late at night. We also sometimes pay for taxi rides home for those who work late. In some cities, this may be the only way to get employees to work after dark. Consider setting up a contract with a taxi company or car service if your staff will be making regular use of this benefit.

Fires, Storms, and Other Catastrophes

Several times a year the fire department inspects our store for compliance with fire codes. Although we may grouse, we appreciate the fact that the firefighters want to be sure we have safely marked exits, doors that can be opened easily in an emergency, and stairways and aisles that are clear of merchandise. They also require that we have fire extinguishers on hand that are in good working order, and in fact each extinguisher must be inspected and certified annually. Be sure your fire extinguishers are well marked and that your staff knows how to use them.

Smoke alarms are a good idea for stores located in a neighborhood where someone would hear the alarms if they went off at night. Smoke detection systems can be set up as part of your alarm system, connected to a central monitoring office. Sprinkler systems are costly but effective in halting the spread of a fire. Check with your insurance company about rate reductions on fire insurance if your store has a sprinkler system installed.

Your store's computer equipment needs special surge protectors to prevent it from being damaged by an electrical power surge or lightning strike. Backup copies of all important computer files should be made at least weekly and stored off the shop premises or in a fireproof safe. Copies of deeds and important financial documents should be kept in a safe deposit box. Take photographs of your store and any major fixtures or expensive inventory items in case you ever need to place an insurance claim. Store these pictures somewhere other than the shop in case of fire.

Every part of the country has its weather-related hazards: hurricanes, flash floods, mud slides, dust storms, earthquakes, and so forth. In Wisconsin, ours are blizzards and tornadoes, so we have established procedures for closing the store and taking shelter in the event of a tornado watch. Customers are invited to take shelter in the basement with us, a glimpse behind the scenes that they often find quite interesting. We keep a battery-operated radio and flashlights in the waiting area so we will know when it is safe to go upstairs. If members of your staff are likely to have to take emergency action in the face of a natural disaster, make sure they know what to do.

All stores should have emergency telephone numbers posted by the telephones and a well-stocked first aid kit on hand. In the event of a minor injury to a customer, a little first aid and a lot of concern, including a follow-up telephone call, can prevent the episode from escalating into a lawsuit. Managers should know the basics of first aid, and everyone should know where the first aid kit is located. We offer our full-time staff the opportunity to take CPR training on store time, although we hope this is a skill they'll never need to use.

When Disaster Strikes

It is every retailer's nightmare to hear fire sirens and realize that they are headed toward your shop. If your store is ever subjected to a catastrophe such as a fire or explosion, your first concern, after making sure employees and customers are safe, should be to secure the premises, blocking off any hazardous areas and getting broken windows and doorways boarded up. Once you have taken care of these safety issues, you must decide if you want to stay in business. If you do, it is essential that you get the store up and running as soon as possible. Assure the public through the media that you will be back in business soon. Set up temporary office space so that you can communicate with suppliers. Keep staff on the payroll as much as possible, working to get new merchandise and fixtures ready.

You may find that the publicity from the crisis eventually will work in your favor. Little Luxuries, of Madison, Wisconsin, was a relatively new and unknown gift shop when it suffered extensive damage from a fire in the restaurant next door. The media mentioned that the staff had just finished repainting the store when disaster struck, a human interest touch that caught the public's attention and earned its sympathy. Sales the year after reopening were double what they had been the year before.

CUSTOMERS CAN BE TROUBLE

The customer is *not* always right. Individuals experiencing unhappiness in some other aspect of their life sometimes take it out on easy targets, such as the sales staff of a store. Others may try to appear powerful and controlling by dominating the retail transaction, insisting on special pricing and services. Returns seem to bring out the worst in people, and customers with returns often enter the store with a combative attitude as if expecting a battle.

Whenever possible, the best way to disarm problem customers is by listening to what they say, empathizing with their complaint, and asking, "What can we do to make this right for you?" A cheerful refund for a return, for instance, gives the customer braced for an argument little to complain about. But there are people who seem to need to complain or who appear to enjoy making others unhappy.

The fact is that some of these customers are not worth keeping. They take their toll on staff morale and upset other customers. From time to time we have had to send a letter to individuals like this refunding their money (things always come to a head over one item, it seems) and suggesting that since we don't seem to be meeting their needs, they try the mail order catalogs and alternative shops we list for them.

The majority of problem customers don't fall into this category. Most people respond well to a sincere effort to solve their problem and a generous dose of empathy. When someone called recently to complain about another customer's getting waited on before her, I could honestly say that I would have been irritated too. I tried to find out the details of when it happened and who was involved, and asked her what action she wanted me to take to be sure it didn't happen again. I also thanked her for calling the problem to my attention. A customer who complains gives you the opportunity to make things right, but customers who are angry and don't call probably tell their friends about it.

When you feel that your customers are being unreasonable, compare them to Jeremy Dorosin. He was so unhappy with two espresso machines that he purchased from the Starbucks coffeehouse in Berkeley, California, that he spent $10,000 of his own money on newspaper ads demanding an apology. The chain had already offered to replace the $469 worth of machines with more expensive models. Despite a subsequent offer of a refund and the replacement machines, Dorosin wanted Starbucks to spend $247,182 for an ad apologizing to him in the *Wall Street Journal.*

Vandalism

Parents constantly worry about their toddlers breaking something in the store, but most of the damage to merchandise and displays is done by adults. The era of the "you break it—you bought it" rule has passed in most retailing environments, but customers are still afraid to admit that they have accidentally broken something. We usually find broken items hidden in our displays rather than being brought to us by the customers who broke them. If an item is accidentally broken by anyone, adult or child, we absorb the loss. Items that are very valuable or fragile are kept in a closed case. We sometimes put a sign by fragile items requesting that customers ask for assistance if they would like to look at it more closely. If an item looks very fragile but is not, it pays to put a sign by it inviting customers to handle it. Merchandise that can be touched always sells better.

There is a big difference between accidental breakage and vandalism. A customer once informed me that a teenager was stomping on bath oil beads in our cutlery department, and this clearly was no accident. When I insisted that the girl clean up the mess, she informed me that she was only responsible for squishing *some* of them. Her friends had apparently made a quick escape.

Graffiti can be a headache for retailers, especially in urban settings. Prompt removal of graffiti is thought to be the best deterrent to future damage. There are surface treatments that can be applied that will make graffiti removal easier. Most police departments can give retailers advice about dealing with this problem.

PERSONNEL WOES

Someday I will accept the fact that all of my staff can't be happy all of the time, but nothing upsets me more than personnel problems. Sometimes one individual is grumpy and sets the tone for the rest of the staff. Sometimes the entire group is unhappy about a work-related issue, such as salaries or work schedule. And sometimes it is necessary to confront an employee about his or her inadequate performance or behavior, which is never easy to do.

Staff morale is vital to the health of a retail operation, and nothing upsets a customer more quickly than an unpleasant encounter with a crabby salesperson. I prize enthusiasm and a strong spirit of cooperation above all other virtues in an employee and have been known to encourage whiners to look for work elsewhere because they have a negative impact on the rest of the team.

Creating job satisfaction is a continuing challenge. Studies have shown that employees are not just looking for money when they work; they also want a feeling of doing something meaningful and being appreciated. Many retailers find it difficult, or even embarrassing, to praise their staff constantly. One reason may be that they don't feel appreciated themselves. When Bob Greene, the author of the excellent *1001 Ways to Reward Your Employees*, spoke to store owners and managers at the American Booksellers Association convention, his audience made it clear that few of them felt anyone had expressed appreciation for *them* recently. If you own your business, you need to look to your own need for self-esteem. If you employ one or more managers, be sure they often hear from you that you think they are doing a good job.

Encouragement can take many forms, as Greene's book shows. Recognition plaques, trips, gift certificates, and even cars, such as Mary Kay's famous pink Cadillacs, are ways to keep your staff fired up and content. My personal favorite is his suggested reward of offering a tattoo of the store's logo, although no one on my staff has taken me up on it yet.

"Just put the store logo somewhere between 'Mom' and the bald eagle."

When problems do come up, take them seriously. Be available to meet immediately with any staff members who have a concern. The issue may not seem urgent to you, but if it is important to them, they will appreciate that you make it a priority. Listen carefully, and if necessary repeat back what you understand them to be saying. Ask for suggestions for solutions, and promise to do what you can. If appropriate, make a note about the conversation and any follow-up in the employee's personnel file.

Communication is a great antidote to festering discontent. Allow staff an outlet for their frustration at regular staff meetings or smaller conferences. Have a suggestion box if you feel there are complaints that employees would be hesitant to bring up in public. Encourage everyone to propose constructive solutions when a problem is brought up. Never belittle anyone's concerns, or discuss an issue involving only one or two individuals in front of the group.

If there are employees on your staff who don't get along, try to schedule them so they are not working side by side. Take into account that employees experiencing personal problems may require some leeway in their job duties. It may be difficult to accept the fact that all staff members are unique, complex individuals, with distinct personalities and problems. Try to treat everyone with respect and understanding.

WHEN YOUR BUSINESS IS IN FINANCIAL TROUBLE

Once you've gotten past the turbulent and exciting first years of owning a shop and have started showing a profit, you might expect that retailing will settle into a comfortable pattern of growth. This is often the case, but sometimes factors beyond your control send sales or profits into a downward spin. Suddenly you may find it hard to meet your payroll or to pay your suppliers. Merchandise that used to sell quickly begins to languish, tying up capital unproductively.

As soon as you see sales declining or expenses increasing, try to evaluate the reasons. Call a meeting of your staff or a group of trusted advisers and ask them to brainstorm about possible factors. Is the economy slowing down? Is your location declining in popularity? Has increased competition taken a bite out of your sales? Is your product mix no longer in tune with what customers are looking for? Is your pricing not competitive, or are your margins too low to earn a profit?

Having evaluated these factors, take time—preferably away from the store—for a long, unemotional look at your options, which include:

- Closing or selling the store
- Becoming part of a franchise
- Moving to a new location
- Refocusing your merchandise selection
- Adding new customer services
- Giving your storefront or fixtures a facelift

Be sure that your display techniques are up to date, your staff well trained, and your customer policies competitive. Consider diversifying your product mix or adding a related side business. To augment the seasonal nature of the nursery trade, for example, Family Tree Garden and Gift Center in Carbondale, Illinois, added a large selection of bird feeders and bird seed. Canterbury Booksellers in Madison, Wisconsin, developed a lovely bed and breakfast to complement their bookstore, including a gift certificate for a free book with each night's stay.

Surviving a Cash Crunch

If your business is short of money, you have two options: increase your debt by seeking additional loans and investments, or raise cash by quickly selling some of your inventory and assets. Banks don't generally like to be approached for loans in an hour of crisis, but if you have a preapproved line of credit with your bank, you can draw on it when you need to. In addition to traditional loan and investment sources, consider asking vendors to lend you money by extending the due date on their invoices. If you do take advantage of delayed dating terms, be sure you are doing so with the express approval of your vendor. "Leaning on the trade" without prior agreement is unfair and transfers your cash flow problem onto someone else's shoulders. Wholesalers too have payrolls to meet and rent to pay.

If you are unable to pay your vendors on time, be sure to notify them of the delay, and tell them when payment can be expected. Keep in regular touch with those you owe money so your staff won't be on the receiving end of angry telephone calls from your creditors. If at all possible, come up with funds to make regular partial payments on the amounts you owe.

You may find that you have some sources of personal funds you hadn't considered using. A second mortgage on your home may generate funds if the house is not part of the collateral you pledged to get your original funding. You might be able to borrow against a life insurance policy. In a pinch, retailers have been known to use credit cards to pay for inventory and even expenses. The interest rates on some credit cards are much higher than others, so shop around and consolidate your purchases onto one card with a low rate. Consider a card that will give you a discount or points toward a frequent flyer program. Be sure to pay the credit card debt off as soon as possible.

An inventory reduction sale can raise funds in just a few days. Offer a flat discount, such as 20 percent off on everything in the store or an attractive reduction on expensive items. As long as you are making some profit on the merchandise sold, you can raise the cash you need and then replace the inventory with fresh goods. Excess merchandise is often a source of cash flow problems, so it would be wise to review your buying policies if you are often short of funds.

Is there some other way your store can raise funds? Perhaps you have some office space that you can lease out. You could also lease space on your selling floor to an independent vendor, for example, a florist. Department stores have done this for years, with areas such as the shoe department being run by a separate business.

Cutting overhead can help solve a cash flow problem—perhaps you could reduce the hours you are open or cut back on buying trips. If payroll is your major expense, you may have to make the painful move of laying off some of your staff. Be honest with your employees if you think layoffs may have to happen. Reassure those who are laid off that the decision is not a reflection on their performance, and if you will not be rehiring them, help them look for new work. Let your employees know about any unemployment benefits they may be entitled to. And if you hope that the layoff is only temporary, keep in touch with those who are not working so that they know how things are going for the store.

When times are bad, resist the temptation to eliminate essentials such as advertising. You want your old customers to know that your business is still alive and well, and you need to continue to attract new customers. Project an image of success and confidence, no matter how tough things are going.

RESPONDING TO BAD PUBLICITY

One book on retailing suggests that as a cute marketing gimmick, you hire people to picket your store with signs that say something like "Prices Too Low." Most of us, especially in politically correct cities such as Madison, would rather avoid even the appearance of controversy. Negative publicity, which is often unfair, can do a great deal to damage the reputation of a store.

When confronted with any situation in which you need to work with the media, do your best to be upbeat and cooperative. Keep in mind that reporters are working under a deadline and need your timely response. When replying to their questions, avoid "no comment," which to the public means you are hiding something. Be honest, and after consultation with your lawyer, admit blame if it is appropriate. If someone has been injured, show compassion for the victims even if you are not at fault.

Thriftway Market in San Francisco was faced with picketing from a grocery clerks' union that wanted to organize the small shop's employees. In order to make sure that the public knew its side of the story, the store used window signs including enlargements of letters of support from fellow merchants and even copies of its payroll records. The signs mentioned that more information was available inside, where staff had well-written flyers available telling the store's side of the controversy.

Once you are certain that the public is also aware of your side of the story, patience is the best remedy for negative publicity. Eventually the public's attention will turn elsewhere.

KEEPING AN UPBEAT ATTITUDE

As Michael Antoniak says in *How to Open Your Own Store*, "We all have lousy days. Your customers may want to share theirs with you, but they don't want to hear about yours. It's not always easy, but you must smile and be polite even on the worst of days. Maintaining good relationships with your customers is a dance of perceptions." Customers want to associate with success. No matter how poorly things are going, you must resist the temptation to complain.

That doesn't mean that you should keep the stress of dealing with problems to yourself. Rather, be selective about when and where you discuss what is going wrong. One of our young employees once asked if we had any other "boss friends" we could talk to. Luckily we do. It often helps to trade stories with other small business owners and managers. Not only do we get to complain without worrying about upsetting our customers or staff, but we sometimes find that other retailers have solutions to the problems that are bothering us. I strongly encourage you to cultivate a spirit of camaraderie rather than competition among your fellow merchants. You can also look to community organizations for businesspeople, such as the chamber of commerce, a women-in-business group, or service clubs such as Rotary, for opportunities to meet others dealing with the challenges of running a business. Seminars such as those offered by the Small Business Development Center can be wonderful places to meet other owners and managers.

Stress is a factor in everyone's life, but when you are in charge, it is important that you have ways of coping with it that will not harm your business or your staff's morale. Eat regular meals, get some exercise, and get enough rest. Probably the best antidote to the stress of retailing is to get away from the store. Go on real vacations, not just buying trips. "My advice is for retailers to plan into their schedules several vacations a year," suggests Potpourri Designs owner David Grimes, "even if they are only three- or four-day-long weekends. This is virtually the only time when you can get a perspective on your business—from a distance—and at the same time, restore your soul a bit."

It is important to develop other interests and friends outside the shop's four walls. Do some volunteer work, and pursue a hobby. Stanley Marcus, chairman emeritus of the Neiman Marcus stores, said, "Despite my great love and devotion to the specialty store retailing field, I don't regard it as the most important activity of mankind, and I don't mind saying so. I take my business seriously and work extremely hard at it, as I would at any other endeavor which attracted my interest, but I can still take a good philosophical look at it and its relative importance in the world scene."

Try not to carry your worries home to your spouse all the time, and be sure to make time for your family and friends. After all, business is only one small aspect of your life. If you make it the only focus of your existence, it will be hard to keep a healthy perspective when things do occasionally go wrong.

12

LOOKING TO THE FUTURE

When our shop was about seven years old, we had to decide if we wanted branch stores or children. It was a tough choice, since we loved retailing and found our lives very full with the day-to-day challenges of running our shop. I want to assure Erik and Katrina that we have never regretted giving the nod to babies instead of branches; however, we do realize that the future of Orange Tree Imports would have been very different had we opted for additional stores.

There are many crossroads in the lifetime of a specialty shop. When you first open, you are not concerned with whether the store will outlive you or whether you will eventually have five—or fifty—branch stores. If things do not go well at first, you need to decide whether to stay in business at all, and if you are going to stay in business, what to change in order to improve sales. If everything does go well, you need to decide whether you will stay the same size, expand, change your product mix, move, or open branch stores. Retail stores need to change constantly in one way or another in order to stay alive. A store that doesn't change at all may eventually be referred to by that most dreaded of all commercial real estate terms: an occupied vacancy.

RIDING THE WAVE OF SUCCESS

Success can be as hard on a business as failure. When a store experiences runaway sales increases, management and buyers may have difficulty keeping up. Cash reserves and staff energy can be strained. It is better to plan for gradual growth than to wish for runaway success, which can result in an excess of debt and poorly planned expansion.

If a store achieves runaway success due to a passing fad, such as trolls, pogs, or any other collectible craze, the public may lose interest very suddenly. One of my employees once asked why I didn't stop buying an item when it was at the peak of its popularity and about to die. The answer, of course, is that you can see the peaks only in hindsight.

The key to handling a fast rise in sales is caution. Don't invest too heavily in inventory if you think a trend may pass. Reorder often, or place future dated orders that you can cancel. Make sure you are taking extra markup to protect your bottom line from disaster if the fad passes.

Many, and maybe most, specialty stores are based on trends that may not remain at the same level of popularity forever. The country look, for example, dominated gift shops in some parts of the country in the early 1990s. As styles change, these shops will have a choice of diversifying or closing. The decision to close a store should not be viewed as a failure. In order to be successful, a store does not have to survive forever. In many cases it is enough to have taken a good idea, created an exciting shop, and enjoyed however many years of success it could sustain.

SMALL CAN BE BEAUTIFUL

A shop that is very successful from the start may be tempted to add branch stores early in its development, a move that is sometimes fatal. To take a concept that seems to work well in one place and open more shops can be tempting. After all, the joint buying power of several stores does allow for better pricing and more efficient use of the buyers' time. But other expenses increase with each branch added: the initial cost of more fixtures and inventory, plus the monthly expenses for rent, utilities, insurance, and payroll. A branch store usually requires a manager, and the manager's salary will be higher than that of most other retail employees. The financial strain of each branch, plus the added demands on the owner's time, can be detrimental to the health of the original store. If a branch is located too close to the original store, it sometimes is said to cannibalize the sales of the original store by drawing on the very same customers.

Confining yourself to one store does not mean restricting growth entirely. We have tripled in size at our single location and achieved an annual sales volume of close to $1.5 million. Even with just one store, we are large enough to provide a number of different jobs for our thirty-six employees and to employ ten of these staff members full time.

When considering additional branch stores, the first question you should ask yourself is why do it. If you are interested in an increase in profitability, you may be disappointed. If you are looking for new challenges for yourself or opportunities for advancement for your staff, consider whether there are options for growth within your current location. It is sometimes better to run one store passionately than to have your attention diverted to several locations.

MULTIPLE STORES: GROWING YOUR BUSINESS

The reasons that compelled you to get into retailing to begin with may influence your decision to open a second, third, or fourth branch: an ambition to create a new and exciting store, a desire to fill a need in the marketplace, an eagerness to promote merchandise you have a passion for, and an interest in creating new jobs.

One particularly compelling reason for branching out is to provide opportunities for advancement for staff members. Although we have been fortunate to have staff members stay with us for over fifteen years, the fact of the matter is that working for a single-location store does not offer much of a career track, especially if it is a family business that will most likely be passed on to the sons or daughters of the owners. If you decide to open a branch store to provide a new management position for a loyal employee or a family member, be sure the person plans to stay with the job. Consider offering a financial stake in the success of the branch to encourage the person to make a long-term commitment.

Managing multiple stores requires special skills and systems. Some functions, such as bookkeeping, adapt well to being centralized at a main office or in the "mother" store. Others, such as personnel management and day-to-day operations, need to be entrusted to a manager or management team in each location. Good communication with the individual store managers, and on some occasions the entire staff of each branch, is essential to the success of a multiple store operation.

A computer network can be used to convey sales data from each branch store to the home office or main store for order placing, but buying decisions function best when there is some autonomy at each location because the customer base will vary from one area to another. Shipments from vendors can be sent to a central warehouse and then allocated to the individual stores as needed, or shipped directly to each branch (in which case separate "bill to" and "ship to" addresses need to be specified on the purchase order). Freight, payroll, and storage costs are all factors in deciding how best to divide up merchandise shipments.

Financing Your Growth

Anita Roddick of The Body Shop, and author of *Body and Soul*, has so many stores that she claims 28 million people pass by her shops around the world each month. Within six months of opening her first store, she was eager to branch out—so eager, in fact, that she pledged 50 percent of her company to an investor willing to lend her the money she needed. Ian McGlinn's £4,000 investment was worth over £140 million by the early 1990s. "Giving away half the business is considered by many as the biggest mistake I have ever made," she commented, " but I don't resent it. I needed the money, I needed it quickly, and Ian was the only one then who would give it to me."

For every success story like The Body Shop, there are many stores that don't survive rapid growth. If you have decided to open a branch store, it is time to write a new business plan and to examine the sources of funding available to finance the new store while keeping the original store running. Not many people remember that Orange Tree Imports actually started as a branch of Bord & Stol, a Scandinavian furniture store. After six months, the cash flow problems were acute, and Bord & Stol was having trouble paying the bills for the branch store. I'm sure it was a relief to the owners when Dean and I offered to buy the business.

If your business is incorporated, you could finance your growth by selling shares to employees, family, or other investors. Large retail operations might even consider going public, offering stock on the stock exchange. The CML Group, which owns such specialty chains as NordicTrack and Smith and Hawken, encourages investors to buy shares in the company by offering registered shareholders with more than 100 shares an investor card good for a 10 percent discount on merchandise in any of its stores.

Some states allow small corporations to raise funds by selling stock through a small corporate offering registration (SCOR). You could also bring in new partners for branch development, giving these investors partial ownership of one or more of the branch stores.

Franchising Your Store

An additional option available for financing new stores is franchising. If you have a strong retail operation, you could consider franchising your idea to others, who would then own their own stores but pay you an ongoing franchise fee. Franchise owners provide the capital for their own store, freeing you from the need to find the funding. One caveat, however: You would not have the same degree of control that you have over a store you own yourself.

How do you know if your store concept is right for franchising? In *Succeeding in Small Business*, Jane Applegate suggests that you ask the following questions:

- Is your business at least two years old and profitable?
- Have all the bugs been worked out?
- Will your idea translate to other locations?
- Are you patient and willing to train new franchise owners?
- Do you have enough money for the legal work, marketing, training, and other expenses?
- Can others be taught to do what you do?

What will you be offering a franchise holder? You will already have made all the initial decisions about the store name, image, design, and merchandise. You will share what you have learned from your initial mistakes, providing a store concept that has already been time tested. Perhaps you have products that are manufactured or imported exclusively for your shop, giving the franchise holders the advantage of obtaining merchandise not otherwise available to them. Volume purchasing will allow you to offer store supplies, fixtures, and goods at a lower price than a single store could obtain. In exchange for these advantages, the franchise holder will pay you an initial fee, plus whatever percentage of sales or other periodic payment you negotiate.

Jane Applegate points out that if you decide to franchise your store concept, you will be taking on a moral obligation to protect the investment made by your franchise holders. State and federal regulations governing franchising help to protect the interest of those investors. Check all the pertinent regulations and work with a lawyer experienced in franchises before making an offering to the public.

Other Ways to Expand

Branch stores are not the only way to grow your business. You might consider adding a "sister" store, one carrying a different product line, in the same area. This second shop could just be a kiosk or pushcart, which would allow you to experiment with a new merchandising concept that might work in your original store. You could also set up a second store on a seasonal basis, especially if there is a vacancy in your area.

As an experiment in large-scale mail order marketing, we ordered 5,000 of Arabia's enameled serving bowls from Finland and ran a national ad in *Bon Appetit* magazine. This venture into selling by mail taught us that it can be quite boring to sell thousands of the same item to customers you never see. We broke even and decided to stay with traditional retailing. Although we do send out a catalog complete with a mail order form, we concentrate our mailing on zip codes within driving distance of the store. Other shops may find it quite rewarding to have a mail order business to supplement their retail store. In addition to traditional catalogs and media ads, it is now possible to advertise your merchandise on the Internet or via CD-ROM disk. Felissimo, a creative New York gift and home accessory retailer, promotes its merchandise nationwide through an interactive CD-ROM shopping service called "To Market." If your store has unique items that are difficult for shoppers to find locally, explore the possibility of outreach marketing.

With more manufacturers getting into retailing their own goods, it may be time to turn the tables and have more retailers get into manufacturing. Constant contact with customers gives you the advantage of knowing what the public wants. If you see a need, look into whether you can have the product made for you at a reasonable cost. If this custom merchandise is successful at retail, consider selling it wholesale. Ask the sales reps who sell to you for advice on selling to other stores, and consult your accountant about whether the wholesale operation should be considered a separate business.

As a sideline, I design, produce, and market T-shirts and other licensed merchandise for The King's Singers, a wonderful English a cappella group. This project is part of Orange Tree Imports, but it has its own categories in our bookkeeping system, which allows us to track the success of the line. The King's Singers merchandise will never be a source of great profits for our store, but undertaking a new project from time to time helps keep retailing exciting for me.

Fillamento, a San Francisco contemporary home furnishings store, recently opened a wholesale showroom in New York highlighting thirty-three of the artists and craftspeople whose products are featured in its award-winning California store. Owner Iris Fuller comments, "I needed a new challenge, and I knew I didn't want to do a second store. The wholesale line gives me an exciting opportunity to help promising artists and to do more merchandising, which is my real love."

Direct import items that sell well in your shop could also be a way to enter the wholesale market. Gage, Incorporated, an upscale gift shop in a resort area of Wisconsin, began direct importing a line of Italian candles for its own store. The line sold so well that it arranged to be the American importer of the candles, and this successful wholesale business supplements its somewhat seasonal retail operation. Wholesale customers appreciate knowing that the products have been market tested in Gage's own store.

MOVING ON

The high rate of retail "failures" does not reflect the fact that sometimes a shopkeeper decides to close the store for reasons other than lack of business success. Many shops do close because of financial reasons, of course, especially if they were started with insufficient capital to keep the doors open for the first year or two. But you may find that your store concept goes out of fashion, that you want more free time, or that the local economy takes a downward spin. You don't have to be open for decades to have had a successful shop. It is a major accomplishment to have brought your dream to reality.

If you decide to leave retailing, you can either sell your shop as a going business or close the store. Either move will have a major impact on your staff, and it is important that they be kept informed of your plans. No one deserves to go to work one morning and find an "out of business" sign on the door. Incredibly, this does happen.

Selling Your Store

When you sell a successful shop as a going business, your goal is to arrange for such a seamless transition that will be almost unnoticed by customers. But if the store has been faltering, the announcement of new owners can bring with it the promise of a fresh start and a new direction.

To find a buyer for a retail business, start with those who know the business best: your employees and family members. If one individual can't come up with the financing to buy the business, perhaps two or three could join together to do so. You may have a loyal customer who is so devoted to the shop that he or she would like to consider owning it. A neighboring business owner may be looking for a new opportunity. In 1986 we expanded our store for the second time, buying the shop next door when the owner retired, and connecting our two businesses. Perhaps one of your competitors, even one located in another community, would like to own your store.

You may wish to sell your business and stay on as a buyer or manager. Your new role relieves you of the worries of owning the shop and is one way to solve a severe cash flow crisis. The new owner, whether a corporation or an individual, will bring new ideas, new funds, and new energy into the business. If you find you are burned out on management duties or stretched to the limit of your financial resources, you may be able to keep the shop you love open and take on a different role yourself by selling it to someone else. Allow yourself a retirement option, however, if you find you don't work well with the new owners.

In order to sell your business, you will need to have all your financial records in order. The buyer will want to know how profitable your shop has been, which is a good reason to keep accurate, honest records. In addition to paying for the furniture, the fixtures, and the wholesale value of the merchandise, the buyer may be willing to pay a premium called "goodwill" for the positive reputation of the store. The more profitable the shop is, the more you can ask for in goodwill. You can also request a payment for promising not to open a new store that will compete with the one

"And remember, Mrs. Smithers likes all her packages in the paisley gift wrap. . ."

you are selling. This *noncompeting clause* is usually valid for a certain number of years and an agreed-on geographic area.

There are brokers who sell businesses, much the way a realtor sells buildings. These specialists will know of any individuals looking to buy a retail business, especially out-of-towners wanting to relocate to your community, and can also help you place a value on your shop.

As part of the sale of the store, discuss which staff members may be kept on by the new owner. Encourage the new owner to benefit from the experience of your employees by retaining as many of them as possible. You may also offer your services as a consultant or buyer for a certain number of months, or even years, after the sale.

Going Out of Business—Making a Gracious Exit

Although it is gratifying to see the store carry on without you, the fact is that you may walk away with more money if you go out of business than if you sell to a new owner. This is especially true if you have not shown a profit, and there is no goodwill to be paid. Unless you are selling your building with the business, there is little to be gained by a buyer in obtaining a shop full of merchandise that has not been selling well enough to be profitable. And without the premium of goodwill, there is little advantage to you to selling all of the goods at wholesale or below.

A going-out-of-business sale will in fact often start by offering the goods at very close to full retail. The first weeks, or even months, the storewide discount may be 15 or 20 percent off. The wider public attracted by the store closing ("sale vultures," we sometimes call them) will be drawn by the promise of bargains, and a considerable amount of merchandise can be moved at greater than wholesale value. As the sale progresses, the discount will need to be deeper, but very little will probably remain by the time the markdown is 50 percent or more.

Be sure to put signs on your fixtures indicating that they will be available for sale when you close. There are always new retailers looking for an inexpensive way to outfit their store. Leftover fixtures could be offered to resale shops or other charities, along with any merchandise left the day you close.

In big cities, it is not uncommon to see small businesses with "going out of business sale" signs in their windows for years. Local regulations designed to prevent this kind of dishonesty may require that you obtain a "going out of business permit" before you can use that phrase in your signage and advertising.

There are companies that specialize in assisting businesses in closing, and we get mailings from them in discreetly unmarked envelopes almost every week. Some of these companies make their profits by bringing in their own closeout merchandise to supplement your stock. They have marketing gimmicks and games that they use to promote the sale, which may be a relief if you don't have the energy to run the sale yourself. But when one of our neighboring businesses brought in a company to close their store, their regular customers found it unsettling to be dealing with these rather slick outsiders, with their complex and somewhat misleading promotional schemes.

If you decide to go out of business, you may be tempted to walk away from some of the bills not yet paid, especially if you are closing because the store is losing money. Suppliers complain that they lose thousands of dollars each year when stores close. The practice of leaving wholesale bills unpaid is no different than a customer paying for merchandise in the store with a worthless check. If you have ordered and received merchandise, you are required to pay for it, even if it takes a long time to do so. Remember that the sales representatives who wrote orders with you will not get any commissions on goods not paid for and that other retailers (and ultimately the consumer) will have to pay higher prices for merchandise to make up for any amount not paid by a store going out of business.

A store closing is a time of loss for those who loved the store, and especially for those who worked there. Be sure to offer assistance in finding your staff new positions. Don't be surprised if they take job offers before you have finished your going-out-of-business sale. It can be distressing for them to see the store empty out and start to look shabby, which it will as the merchandise selection is reduced. Staff members need to protect their own future and should take whatever opportunity comes their way. You may need to contact a temporary agency for salespeople for the last weeks of the sale.

LIFE PLANNING ISSUES FOR SPECIALTY SHOP OWNERS

The future of a store is often linked with the life plans of its owners. When the owner decides to retire or relocate, or if someone key to the business dies, major changes will usually occur in the store's operations. Planning for the transition brought on by the retirement or loss of the owners can help ease the transition for everyone involved.

The Importance of Having a Will

Do you and your business partners have a will? Few people would intentionally throw the business they love into utter chaos, but in fact the sudden death of the owner can have just that effect. Without the guidance provided by a will, there is no way to know who is going to own and run the store and pay the business's creditors, or what is to become of the employees and the shop full of merchandise. We are all mortal and need to face the fact that death could occur at any time. If your business is thriving, you will want to plan for it to be able to carry on without you some day.

When a spouse, family members, or other partners are involved in the day-to-day store operations, it is usually not difficult to decide who to list in your will as the successor. Check with your lawyer about ways to avoid heavy estate taxes after you have established who you would like to have inherit the shop.

Without a likely family member or partner, you may find that there is no one you would like to have inherit the business. In this case, you will need to ask your lawyer, or the executor of your estate, to arrange to sell the shop as a going concern or to liquidate the merchandise and assets. Provisions can be made in your will to authorize the person of your choice to keep the shop running until the estate can be settled. Keeping the store's staff and customer base intact for a possible new owner will make the transition much smoother. Key-person life insurance, with the store as the beneficiary, can be a great help in paying off debts that are due or covering the salary of a manager to handle day-to-day store operations.

When we wrote our first wills, we did not have children. We decided that if we both were to die, we'd want our employees to have the first opportunity to bid on the business, followed by family members and then the general public. Now that we have two children almost at an age when they could run the store, we would want them to have the opportunity to keep the business going if they so choose.

Planning for Retirement

Corporate and government employers can often offer their employees retirement benefits and pension plans that are the envy of those of us in small business. As an independent retailer, you need to save for your own retirement, and the earlier you begin planning for retirement, the better things will look when you finally decide to hang up your price gun.

The retirement plans available to you depend on whether you are a sole proprietorship, partnership, or corporation—and whether you offer a plan that covers all of your employees. Your accountant and lawyer can advise you of your options, which may include setting up a 401(k) or other pension plan for your staff, or contributing to a personal independent retirement account (IRA) each year.

A pension plan for your staff members may be important to them, although if your employees are mostly high school or college age, retirement seems so distant that they would rather have more money now. Employee pension plans are often set up on a *vesting schedule*, which rewards longevity by increasing the amount that belongs to the employee with each added year of employment. If a staff member leaves before being 100 percent, or fully, vested, the remainder of the money goes back into the retirement fund, to be shared by the remaining staff members. Lawyers, accountants, insurance agents, and financial advisers can provide information on pension plans. Watch for administrative costs, which can be costly on a small 401(k) plan, especially when the laws change and the plan must be redone.

The equity you build up in your business will also be part of your retirement savings, but unless you plan to sell or close the business when you retire, you may find this asset to be less liquid than other savings. If the business can afford it, you could draw out some of your money or arrange to stay on the payroll as a part-time consultant after you retire. Check to see what course of action will be most advantageous from a tax standpoint, especially after you begin to draw social security benefits.

Family Business Succession

For family-owned businesses, part of the process of planning for the future may include deciding which family members will take charge of the store when the owner retires. This planning process needs to begin several years before retirement in order to ensure a smooth transition that is fair to all involved, including employees who are not family members. Don't give these employees reason to resent family members who come into the business. Keep family and business relationships separate, insisting on the same high standards of training and performance for all staff. Consider asking to be called by your name, rather than Mom or Uncle Joe, when in a business setting. Make it clear to other employees that there will be no favoritism in assigning schedules and responsibilities.

It was once said that if you hope your children will take over your business, watch what you say at the dinner table. If your children hear only complaints about your customers, suppliers and staff, they may not be interested in getting involved. Even if children do like the idea of running a shop, I think they should be encouraged to follow their own interests first. After they have gotten an education and experienced the outside working world, they will be better able to decide whether the family business is right for them.

There are many difficult decisions to be made when it comes time to pass the leadership of your store on to a successor. If you have more than one child, you will want to be fair to them all. If none of your children wants to be actively involved in the business, you will need to find someone else to run it or own it. And keep in mind the serious tax issues involved in having someone inherit your business. Depending on your business structure and other factors, the taxes may be so high that the store will need to be sold to pay them. Consult with your lawyer far in advance of retiring to facilitate a successful transition.

RUNNING THE MATURE BUSINESS

If you are not ready to retire and your store is doing well, you still can't sit back and let the business run itself. As Mary Kay Ash, founder of Mary Kay Cosmetics and author of *Mary Kay on People Management*, says, "You can't rest on your laurels. Nothing wilts faster than a laurel rested upon." Retailing is a dynamic and ever-changing field. If you don't keep up with your competition, you will fall behind.

When you first go into business, you will be fascinated by visiting other stores, reading trade magazines, and studying books on retailing. As the years go by, it continues to be important that you keep up this search for new ideas and remain open to suggestions for change. In northern California, I visited a large family-owned gift and stationery shop that looked as if it had been frozen in time in 1965. Although the merchandise was new, the dated fixtures relied heavily on old-fashioned pegboard. The light fixtures and even the color scheme were vintage sixties. Tradition and loyalty are keeping the business alive, but it seems doubtful that this store will survive if it faces any significant new competition.

One way to keep your attitude toward retailing fresh is constantly to set challenging goals, such as providing the highest-quality fresh produce or creating as many new jobs as possible, that will keep you striving. Invite staff to help write a mission statement for your store, such as the one in the first chapter, reflecting goals you all can work toward.

You should always be asking yourself how you can do things better. There is no aspect of your shop, from your cash register procedures to your gift wrap selection, that can't be improved or changed. Continue to read and to study what other retailers are doing. Listen to motivational tapes and go to seminars. Try to avoid the twin evils of burnout and boredom by having outside interests and by getting away from your shop regularly. If you make the store the sole focus of your energy, you won't be able to sustain that level of involvement for the long haul. Remember why you went into retailing, and do what you can to hold onto that vision and passion over the years.

RETAILING FOR THE FUTURE

The future of retailing may look very different from retailing today, although the rumors that catalog and computer shopping would make stores obsolete seem to have been premature. Certainly, specialty shops have continued to change over the years (a book on small store retailing from the mid-1960s voted the corset shop "most likely to succeed"), but the basic premise of offering shoppers a variety of goods, attractively presented and available to be purchased on the spot, has not. Customers enjoy the opportunity to see and touch the merchandise they are considering purchasing. Shopping can also be as pleasing a sensual experience as visiting an art museum and as entertaining as going to a movie. It is up to the creative retailer to make sure that the customer experiences an enjoyable social interaction and a presentation of merchandise that is a visual delight.

Instead of viewing the electronic and catalog shopping world as a threat, today's retailers can use these media as tools for promoting their shop and their goods. The Internet can be used as a way to reach new customers near and far. Mail order catalogs can be used to bring in new shoppers, presell merchandise to existing customers, and market to customers outside your geographical area. Catalogs on CD-ROM combine the two technologies, allowing customers to view merchandise on their home computer and then to place their orders electronically or by telephone.

Just as listening to a symphony on the radio is not the same experience as sitting in a concert hall hearing the orchestra perform, shopping by mail or modem will always lack something. Going shopping allows customers to surround themselves with merchandise they may never have seen before and to consider buying items they didn't know they wanted. Shopping is an activity many families and friends enjoy doing together. A good specialty shop is also a place where customers can learn more about a special interest, such as doll house miniatures, and can meet others who share the same hobby.

As a retailer, you have a unique opportunity to share your excitement about the merchandise you carry with everyone you come in contact with. You can have an important influence on the lives of your customers, provide meaningful work to your employees, and have a positive impact on the world around you. Your specialty shop should be more than just a means of making a living; it should be a creation you are proud of and one that you continue to perfect.

GLOSSARY

account number: A code number assigned by a vendor to each of its retail accounts.

accounts payable: In bookkeeping, the account showing the amounts owed to others, usually for goods and services.

accounts receivable: In bookkeeping, the account showing any funds due to the store, usually from customer charge accounts.

accrual: In advertising, the amount of advertising allowance available based on a percentage of accumulated purchases during a certain time period.

acid-test ratio, quick ratio: A rough indication of a business's ability to meet its financial obligations, determined by dividing current liabilities by current assets, such as cash, inventory, and receivables.

actual cost: On invoices, the billed cost less any discounts.

ad (or advertising) allowance: Reimbursement, in the form of cash or merchandise

credit, for a portion of the cost of advertising a vendor's product.

ad slicks: Advertisements and illustrations for ads provided to retailers by the vendor, usually on glossy paper and camera ready.

advance order: A purchase order placed far in advance of the ship date. These orders help vendors forecast their needs, so incentives such as "early buy" discounts are sometimes offered. See also **program order**.

advisory board: A voluntary group of business peers, customers, and other mentors willing to assist you in making major business decisions.

allowance: See **ad allowance; freight allowance**

anchor: A department or discount store, usually over 50,000 square feet, large enough to draw a significant number of customers to a shopping center.

anticipation: A discount for early payment offered on a vendor's invoice. Invoices sometimes specify "no anticipation" to prevent stores from taking discounts not authorized by the vendor.

as ready: On a purchase order, specifies that the merchandise should be shipped when available.

BO: Abbreviation for "back order."

BOM (beginning of month): The inventory at the beginning of a month.

back order: Merchandise not available when the first part of an order is sent, to be shipped separately at a later date. Abbreviated as BO.

bait and switch: An illegal advertising tactic in which customers brought into the store by a low-priced offer are intentionally steered toward a more expensive product.

balance sheet: A financial statement showing the total assets and total liabilities of the business, totaled to give the business's net worth.

bar code: A universal product code that can be machine read, showing the distributor's number, as assigned by the Uniform Product Code Council, and identifying the individual item so that a price can be assigned to that item in the store's Point-of-Sale system.

big box stores: Very large, no-frills discount stores.

big-ticket, large-ticket items: Expensive products.

bill of lading: A receipt given by a trucking company to the shipper, stating the nature and quantity of the goods being shipped.

book inventory: The dollar value of the inventory, as stated in accounting records.

bottom line: The profit or loss line on the income statement.

bounced check: A check refused by the bank because of insufficient funds in the account; also called **NSF** (not sufficient funds) checks.

bread and butter merchandise: Basic items that should never be out of stock.

break-even point: When expenses equal income; the business is neither earning nor losing money.

breakage allowance: Permission to deduct a certain amount from the invoice for any items broken in shipment.

breakage insurance: A cost added to the invoice for insurance against breakage in shipment.

bulk rate: (1) Lower rates on ads earned by agreeing to purchase a certain amount of advertising; (2) lower postal rates available when mailing a large number of pieces at the same time, provided they meet certain criteria.

bundling: Pricing two or more items together as a unit. Can be used to offer customers a savings or to add markup without customers noticing.

business plan: A written budget and statement of intent outlining a plan for creating and sustaining a new business.

buying group: Independent stores banding together to purchase merchandise in quantity in order to get better prices, terms, and selection.

buying offices: Professional buyers located in major market centers, or overseas, who place wholesale orders on behalf of client stores.

COD (cash upon delivery), COD charges: A payment method whereby the shipping company collects payment for the merchandise when delivering the goods. Some vendors specify that only cash or a bank cashier's check (not a store or personal check) is acceptable as a form of payment. An extra fee, called a COD charge, is almost always added for COD service, and is usually paid by the recipient.

COGS: Abbreviation for "cost of goods sold."

call system, up system: In stores with salespeople on commission, a way of rotating who serves the next customer.

call tag: Authorization to return merchandise, with the receiver, usually the vendor, paying the freight. For example, a manufacturer might send a UPS call tag for the return of some defective merchandise. When the goods are boxed and ready, the call tag is placed on the box as the shipping and address label, and UPS picks up the parcel and returns it to the supplier.

camera-ready art: Ads or other items to be printed that are already assembled in a form that can be used without further alteration by the printer.

cancel date, cancellation date: The date after which you no longer want a merchandise order to be shipped. You have the right to refuse any goods sent after that date.

cancellation notice: Notification from a vendor that products unavailable to ship will not be held on back order.

capital: (1) The money raised to invest in a business; (2) the equity the owners of a store have in their business.

carrying charge: Interest on unpaid balances.

carrying cost: The expense of having money tied up in inventory items, as well as providing storage and display space for them. An item purchased at wholesale for $100 may have a much higher carrying cost if it remains unsold for a long time.

case pack: A full carton of a single item, sometimes specified as the minimum quantity that can be ordered of that item. Vendors allowing less than case pack orders (broken case packs) sometimes give a lower price on full case packs.

cash against documents (CAD): An importing term, referring to the payment for goods being due when proof of shipment documents are presented.

cash discount: A discount on an invoice when the bill is paid upon receipt of the goods or earlier than the due date. Somewhat of a misnomer, since payment is almost always made by check.

cash flow: The need to generate enough cash from sales to pay the bills.

cash wrap (cash wrap counter): The checkout area where customers conduct transactions and have their purchases put in bags or boxes, or gift wrapped.

category killer: A single store or chain large enough to dominate the market in a certain category of merchandise, such as toys or books, discounting prices and selling in quantities that saturate the marketplace.

category management: A recent approach to buying, used by large chains, in which product groups are managed as a unit, using extensive computerized data and with the active cooperation of major vendors, customized on a store-by-store basis.

charge-back: Retailer deductions from a vendor's invoice for breakage, freight allowance, advertising, shortages, etc. Some stores try to take advantage of suppliers by taking unauthorized, and unjustified, charge-backs.

chart of accounts: In bookkeeping, the breakdown of expenses and income into various categories.

cherry pick: Carefully selecting the best items in a line of merchandise, often ordering just a few items instead of a broad assortment.

circulation: The number of copies of a newspaper or magazine that are distributed. The number of readers may be considerably larger than the actual circulation.

classification: An assortment of related merchandise grouped together within a store. Also called a *category* or *department*.

clip art: Graphics, symbols, or other illustrations that may be used for some purposes without paying for the rights or obtaining permission from the artist.

closeouts: Discontinued merchandise sold by wholesale vendors at a discount. Closeouts often represent a good opportunity to add greater markup as well as offer the goods to customers at a more attractive price.

collectibles: Merchandise limited in its availability, which sometimes increases in value if later resold by the customer on what is called the *secondary market*.

color separations: The way in which color photographs are prepared for printing.

column inch: The unit on which print advertising rates are based. The width of a column inch varies from one publication to the next, but the height is a standard inch.

commission: A salary paid to a salesperson based on a percentage of the sales made.

common area: Shared public areas in a shopping center, such as the hallways, rest rooms, and parking lot. See also **lease terms**.

common carrier: Long-haul trucking company using semi trucks to transport large shipments of goods to various delivery points. Also called an *LTL* (less than truckload) shipper.

comp: (1) A mock-up of a proposed ad; (2) a complimentary ticket or other item, often provided to promote an event.

confirmation copy: An acknowledgment of the receipt of a purchase order, confirming the prices and quantities ordered.

consignment: Goods displayed in the store but not paid for unless sold. The ownership of consignment goods does not pass to the shop until the items are sold.

container: A large, standardized shipping unit for overseas freight shipments by boat or airplane.

contract rate: The rate charged by a publication for its advertising, depending on the

amount of advertising to be purchased over a period of time.

cooperative: A business owned and controlled by its users.

cooperative advertising: Advertising costs shared by a vendor and the retailer.

copy: The verbal text of a print or broadcast advertisement.

corporation: A form of business, with one or more shareholders forming a state-chartered organization that functions as an independent entity.

cost: The wholesale price of merchandise.

cost averaging: Basing the retail price on the median of two different wholesale prices, usually the standard price and a promotional or discounted price.

cost of goods sold (COGS): A calculation of the total wholesale cost of merchandise that has been sold, taking into account shipping costs and markdowns.

cottage industry: A crafts operation or other business operated out of the home.

counter cards: (1) Freestanding in-store signs, often with easel backs; (2) greeting cards sold individually.

credit references: Data provided to new vendors by a store in order to apply for an open account with favorable payment terms.

cross merchandising: Displaying complementary but unrelated items in one place, such as red striped mugs, towels, and hats, in order to prompt multiple purchases.

D & B: Dun & Bradstreet, a credit reporting firm providing ratings based on statistics provided by the business and its vendors.

DBA: A term used to identify the business name an individual is using to "do business as" (e.g., "Joe Smith, DBA Smith's Florals").

DOI: Date of invoice

dated order: A purchase order with a specific ship date required.

dating: Delayed payment terms, usually a special arrangement in which seasonal goods are not paid for until close to the time the merchandise will be sold.

dead merchandise: Items no longer selling well.

debit cards: Similar to credit cards, except that debit cards immediately deduct the amount of the purchase from the card bearer's bank account.

deep and narrow: To order a small selection of items, but in large quantities. The opposite is *shallow and wide*, meaning to carry a broad selection with only a few of each item in stock.

deferred billing: For customer charge accounts, an offer to delay the payment due date in order to encourage immediate purchases.

delivery date: The date merchandise ordered should arrive in the store.

demographics: Statistics describing various features of a group of people, such as where they live and how much they earn.

depreciation: The decline in value of major assets, such as furniture and fixtures.

direct imports: Merchandise imported by a store directly from the country of origin.

direct mail: Advertising and promotions mailed or faxed to a targeted group.

discount: Selling merchandise at a price reflecting less than standard markup. A *discounter* is a store selling merchandise below normal price levels and usually offering reduced customer service.

discounting (of an invoice): Taking a cash discount, often 1 to 2 percent, in exchange for paying an invoice earlier than the usual due date.

display ad: A print advertisement that uses graphics or pictures.

distributor: See **middleman**.

double-entry bookkeeping: A system of checks and balances in which every entry is listed as both a credit and a debit. Single-entry bookkeeping is like a personal checkbook register, without the balancing of debits and credits, which helps ensure accuracy.

doughnut: In radio advertising, an ad that allows a blank space for the announcer to speak. A spot for a shopping district, for example, might have a general message at the beginning and end, with time for copy about a specific store in between.

drop ship: To have merchandise sent directly from the supplier to the customer, bypassing the store.

dump: A disposable freestanding display provided by the vendor, usually featuring a single type of merchandise.

EDI (electronic data interchange or interface): A direct link between the store's point-of-sale cash register system and the computer of a major vendor. This system allows for automatic reorders when the store's inventory falls below a predetermined level.

EOM (end of month): (1) An invoice payment term that means the bill is due at the end of the month in which the shipment was made; (2) EOM inventory refers to the inventory value at the end of a month.

ESOP (employee stock ownership plan): A program that allows employees to buy stock in the business or to receive stock as part of their compensation.

end cap: The short end of a freestanding gondola display, often used for rotating displays highlighting certain products. In large stores, the end cap displays are at the end of the aisles, attracting customers' attention to the products in that area.

equity, equity financing: (1) The value owned in a business or property, beyond the amount owed to other parties; (2) financing a business by giving a certain amount of interest, or ownership, in the business in exchange for the investment.

ex works: "From the factory," as in "all shipping is ex works."

exclusive: (1) The promise that the same line of merchandise won't be sold to a nearby competitor; (2) the promise that a certain item won't be sold to any other store or mail order catalog during a certain time period; (3) an item available only through one supplier (as opposed to being trade goods).

expense: Money paid out to run the business, such as rent and utilities, but not to purchase merchandise to sell.

extend: To extend a purchase order is to multiply the quantity ordered times the price per item, and then to add these extensions together to get the total amount of the order.

extended terms: Added time before an invoice will be due.

FFA (full freight allowed): See **freight allowance**.

FICA (Federal Insurance Contributions Act): Social security taxes.

FOB (free on board): The point at which shipping costs begin to be the responsibility of the store rather than the supplier. Usually used to designate the city or town the shipment will originate from (e.g., FOB New York).

factor: A bank or finance company that provides funds to a manufacturer or importer by "buying" its accounts receivable. Payments from retailers are then usually payable to the factor rather than the vendor.

fidelity card: See **smart card**.

first cost: On imported goods, the cost before shipping and customs fees are added.

fiscal year: The twelve months that make up the business's financial year for tax purposes; often, but not always, the same as the calendar year.

fixed assets: Long-term assets, such as buildings, furniture, and fixtures.

floor limit: The maximum amount of purchase for which a merchant can accept payment by credit card without first obtaining an authorization number from the credit card company.

flyer, flier: In advertising, a single-page handout or circular.

focus group: A small group of current or potential customers willing to get together for a discussion about one or two specific issues relating to the business, such as marketing plans and merchandise selection.

foot traffic: The average number of pedestrians passing by the store on a given day.

football: The price of an item is said to be footballed around when it is subject to frequent changes, especially due to discounting and competition.

franchise: A licensing agreement in which the franchisee buys the rights to own and run a store in a specific geographic area based on a concept developed by the franchiser. Usually franchise fees cover the use of the business name and logo and assistance with buying, store design, and marketing.

freight allowance: Credit from the vendor toward the cost of shipping goods to a store. *Full freight allowance* means that the supplier will pay the entire shipping cost up front or reimburse the store for all shipping fees. A *percentage freight allowance*, such as 2 percent, is figured on the value of the goods, not on a percentage of the freight costs.

freight claim: A request for reimbursement from the shipping company for merchandise lost or broken while in transit.

freight collect: The trucking company collects payment for the shipping fee on delivery.

frequency: The number of times a potential customer may hear or see an advertising message.

furniture and fixtures: The display fixtures, office furniture, and other major furnishings of a store.

future dating: See **dated order** and **dating**.

GWP (gift with purchase): A free item (often provided by the manufacturer) given to a customer with the purchase of a specific piece of merchandise.

gondola: A freestanding, rectangular display with shelves or hooks on the two long sides and room for special displays on the ends, or end caps.

goodwill: An amount paid in purchasing a business that is based on the consistent profitability, or earning power, of the business.

gray marketeer: Someone who purchases brand-name and collectible merchandise overseas, or transships it from an authorized dealer domestically, and sells it to stores at a discount without the permission of the company holding the rights to the products.

gross: (1) The gross profit, or gross margin, is the net sales less the cost of goods sold. This is the profit before operating expenses are deducted; (2) a gross of an item is 12 dozen, or 144 pieces.

guaranteed sale: A vendor's offer of merchandise with a promise to take back unsold goods, usually after a specific time period, in exchange for a refund or credit toward other merchandise.

half-tone: A black-and-white photograph prepared for printing.

hard goods, hard lines: In housewares, major appliances.

high design: Stylish, contemporary products. Similar to **high fashion**.

hold (hold slip, on hold): To put an item aside, without a layaway arrangement, for a customer to pick up at a later date. The "on-hold slip" is a form used to tag the merchandise.

hot item: Merchandise that is currently popular and selling quickly.

hot stamping: A method of printing the store name or logo on boxes and bags using a foil imprinting machine.

in the black, in the red: Terms referring to whether a store's financial reports show a profit (in the black) or a loss (in the red).

insufficient funds: See **bounced check**.

inventory: (1) The merchandise a store has on hand to sell; (2) a physical inventory is a tally of every item in the store, a merchandise census. Inventory can be referred to at its retail or wholesale (cost) value.

inventory turns: A mathematical calculation of how many times a store's merchandise stock is sold and replaced in a given period. An "inventory turn" equals sales divided by inventory value. Annual sales of $200,000 at retail, with an inventory averaging $100,000 at retail, means the store is getting two inventory turns. The higher the number of turns, the more efficiently the store's inventory dollars are being used.

invoice: A bill for merchandise or services.

job lot: A grouping of assorted items of merchandise, purchased as a unit.

KD (knocked down): Merchandise sold unassembled, especially furniture.

keystone: 100 percent markup of the wholesale price (e.g., an item wholesaling for $50 would sell for $100 retail at keystone markup).

L/C: See **letter of credit**.

LLC (Limited Liability Corporation): A corporation in which the responsibility of the shareholders is limited to the amount each has invested in the company.

landed cost: On imported merchandise, the wholesale cost, including shipping.

layaway: Holding merchandise for a customer to purchase at a later date, usually with a down payment paid at the time it is put on layaway. Sometimes customers make partial payments on a layaway item before paying off the total price.

layout: The allocation of merchandise and fixtures on the floor plan of the store.

lead time: The time between when an order is placed and when it arrives.

leaning on the trade: Solving cash flow problems by delaying payment to vendors—in essence, borrowing money from them without their permission.

lease terms: A **shell** is four walls, roof, and dirt floor, with no wiring or plumbing; a **half-shell** adds doors, wallboard, and concrete floor, and possibly heat and plumbing. **Key** or **turnkey** means a finished space ready to decorate. **Common area maintenance** refers to paying for the upkeep of sections of the mall or shopping center shared by all tenants. **Will divide to suit** means the landlord will pay for structural changes in the space. An **escalator clause** raises the rent as the building owner's costs, such as real estate taxes, increase. See also **net lease; triple net.**

leased department: A department within a store under separate ownership but operated as part of the rest of the store.

leasehold improvements: Major improvements made by the tenant to a leased space. Leasehold improvements are considered assets and can be depreciated.

letter of credit (L/C): In importing, a system of international credit that is, in effect, a short-term loan from a bank to an internationally recognized bank, assuring a foreign supplier it will be paid for a shipment.

leverage: Using borrowed funds to generate a return from a business venture. A highly leveraged store has a great deal of borrowed debt.

licensed product: Merchandise for which a licensing fee has been paid to the individual or company owning the rights to that image. The cost of Winnie the Pooh bookends, for example, includes a licensing fee

to Disney, which owns the rights to classic Winnie the Pooh merchandise in the United States.

lien: A claim made on a property or business as security for a debt.

lifestyle merchandise: Goods selected because they reflect certain living habits; often used to refer to affordable, contemporary merchandise.

limited partnership: A business format in which the partners are investors only, with liability limited to the amount of their investment. They are prohibited from participating in the operation and management of the business.

line of credit: A loan preapproved for a set amount, to be drawn on as needed.

liquidity: The ease with which assets can be converted into cash.

list price: The manufacturer's suggested retail price.

logo: A symbolic representation of the business, or the business name written in a certain typestyle.

loss leaders: Goods advertised at low markup in order to attract customers into the store.

lower of cost or market: A method of valuing inventory as conservatively as possible. *Cost* refers to the amount actually paid for the goods when purchased, whereas *market* is the value if purchasing the goods at the time of the valuation.

margin: The difference between the total cost of an item and its retail price. Also called the gross margin. See also **markup.**

markdown: The difference between the original retail price and a reduced price. Vendors occasionally offer a markdown allowance on older merchandise in order to get a new order.

markon: See **markup.**

markup: The amount added to the wholesale price to make up the retail price.

Markup can be looked at two ways: some people say an item purchased for $50 and sold for $100 has a 100 percent markup (or markon); others call this a 50 percent markup (or margin).

mass merchandisers: Big stores aimed at a broad segment of the population, usually featuring large quantities of each item and low prices.

massing: Displaying large quantities of a single item.

megastores: Giant stores, often discount operations.

merchandising: Buying and displaying goods for sale.

middleman: A distributor who buys merchandise from one or more sources and sells it at a profit to a retailer, who will add more markup before selling it to the consumer.

minimum order: The lowest dollar amount a vendor will accept for a wholesale order without adding a small order penalty. The purpose of setting a minimum order is to make sure all orders are large enough to be worthwhile for the vendor and to encourage retailers to order enough product to give the line a fair representation.

minimum wage: The lowest hourly salary allowed by state or federal law, whichever is higher.

NA: Abbreviation for "not available," "not applicable."

NR: Abbreviation for "not received."

NSF: Abbreviation for "not sufficient funds." See also **bounced check**.

net: (1) The lowest possible amount. In wholesale pricing, the net is the price after any deductions are taken; (2) in financial statements, the net profit is the gross profit less all operating expenses; (3) on invoices, "net" refers to when the entire amount is due (e.g., "net 30" means the invoice is payable thirty days after the invoice date).

net lease: A rental agreement in which the retailer pays for some other costs, such as taxes, insurance, and maintenance, in addition to the base rent. See also **triple net lease**.

net/net: The wholesale price after all discounts have been taken.

niche store: A shop aimed at a small, focused segment of the market, preferably one that is unserved or underserved by the existing competition.

notes payable: Outstanding loans, debts.

OH: Abbreviation for "on hand" (in stock).

OS: Abbreviation for "out of stock."

OTB: Abbreviation for "open to buy."

occupancy cost: The total amount paid to the landlord to lease a commercial space, including such items as rent, utilities, and a percentage of sales.

off-price retailing: Buying merchandise, often closeouts, at lower than usual wholesale prices in order to sell the goods at attractive prices. Most discount stores buy merchandise at normal wholesale prices and set low prices by taking less than usual markup.

offset: Compensation for the cost of a display fixture, usually given in merchandise. "Offset at retail" means the free goods are valued at their suggested retail price. "Offset at wholesale" means the free merchandise is valued at wholesale and often fully equals the cost of the display.

on the water: En route from overseas.

open account: An established relationship with a vendor allowing merchandise to be shipped to the retailer on credit.

open order: A purchase order that has not been shipped.

open rate: The higher advertising rate paid by a one-time advertiser in a magazine or newspaper.

open stock: Merchandise sold by the piece rather than by the set.

open to buy: The budgeted amount available for new merchandise to arrive during a certain time period for a specific department. For example, June's "open to buy" in jewelry might be $5,000. This figure is based on that department's starting inventory and projected sales for that month. Sometimes abbreviated as OTB.

opportunity cost: Taking into account the fact that money used to purchase certain inventory could have been used for some other purpose.

overhead: The costs involved in operating a store, such as payroll, rent, and utilities.

overtime: Hours worked in excess of forty hours during a seven-day period.

P & L (profit and loss statement): A financial statement showing the store's income and expenses. Same as an income statement.

PLU (price look up): A computerized method of checking prices by programming code numbers or bar codes into a point-of-sale cash register system.

PO: Abbreviation for *purchase order*.

POP (point of purchase): Selling materials, such as a display or sign, provided by the vendor to help sell a certain product.

POS system (point of sale system or terminal): A computerized, or automated, cash register system that compiles data about merchandise sold and also sometimes information about customers.

PWP (purchase with purchase): An item offered at a discount with the purchase of another product.

packing slip, packing list: A receipt listing merchandise included in a shipment. Often shows what merchandise has been back ordered or canceled. Packing lists can usually be distinguished from invoices by the fact that they do not show the total amount owed at the bottom of the page.

partnership: A legal form of business in which two or more individuals assume responsibility for the assets and liabilities of a business, reporting the taxable income of the business as their personal income.

perceived value: The price of an item believed by the purchaser to be the fair market price.

percentage of sales: Rent based in part on the store's total sales.

perpetual inventory: A current inventory dollar value arrived at by continuously adding purchases to the starting inventory and subtracting the cost of goods sold.

physical inventory: See **inventory**.

plan-o-gram: A suggested layout from a vendor for a line of merchandise, usually based on the use of a section of slatwall, shelving, or pegboard.

points: The percentage of profit margin in a retail price. An item with a 45 percent markup at retail is said to make the store 45 points.

positioning: How you want your store to be perceived by your customers, especially in relation to your competitors.

prepaid: (1) Merchandise paid for before being shipped, either at the time the order is placed or when it is ready to ship; (2) an order for which transportation costs have been paid by the shipper, sometimes to be reimbursed by the recipient as part of the invoice total.

press release: A notification of coming events or new products sent to the media in the hope of free publicity.

price code: A symbol on a price tag encoded with the name of the vendor, date of arrival, or other pertinent data.

price gun: A hand-held printer and dispenser of self-adhesive price tags.

price point: A specific price or general price category. For example, a store might want to have a good selection of toys at the $5 price point.

private label: Merchandise manufactured for different stores but custom labeled with each store's name and logo.

pro forma invoice: An invoice to be paid in advance when the merchandise is ready to be shipped. Same as *prepayment*.

product life cycle: A theory that products go through a predictable cycle of popularity, from introduction to market saturation to decline.

program order: A dated purchase order with multiple ship dates. As the later dates approach, portions of the order may be canceled or increased depending on needs.

promotion: An advertising program, such as a 20 percent off promotion on cookbooks.

proof: A copy of an ad or other printed material provided for correction before going to press.

proprietary credit card program: In-house charge accounts for customers, with special credit cards featuring the store name.

public relations, PR: Communication with the public through unpaid media coverage.

purchase order: A listing of products being ordered, stating the item numbers, quantity desired, a brief product description, payment terms, special specifications for delivery, and the quoted wholesale prices.

purchase order number: A code number assigned to a purchase order by the store, and sometimes also by the sales rep or the vendor (e.g., the date the order is written can be used as a purchase order number to distinguish that order from others written with the same vendor at other times).

quick ratio: See **acid test ratio**.

RA number (return authorization number): A code number indicating that the vendor has agreed to take back the merchandise being returned.

ROG (receipt of goods): An invoice term used to determine the date due, as in "net 30 ROG," which means the bill must be paid thirty days after the goods are received by the store.

ROI (return on investment): The financial gain from a business in relation to the amount invested in it. Calculated by dividing the net income by the total assets.

RTA (ready to assemble): Merchandise sold knocked down, or unassembled.

rack jobber: A wholesale supplier who visits a store regularly to take inventories of certain merchandise and replenish the stock.

rate card: A price list for advertising rates, often including information about the audience that the advertising will reach.

receivables: Money owed to the store, for example, by customers buying on credit. Receivables are considered assets.

reconciliation: (1) Cash register reconciliation: making sure the daily total of cash, checks, and charges matches the register's totals; (2) bank statement reconciliation: the balancing of the store's checking account.

references: Companies with a history of selling to the store on credit, willing to share credit history with other suppliers.

remainders: Discontinued items sold by suppliers at a discount, especially books.

resale number: A state-issued identification number that allows a store to buy merchandise to resell without paying sales tax on it; also used to report and pay sales tax collected from customers. The resale number is assigned when the *seller's permit* is issued.

restocking charge: A fee charged by some suppliers for taking back authorized returns of merchandise, usually 10 to 25 percent of the wholesale price.

retail price: The price of an item when offered to the consumer, based on the wholesale price of the item plus markup. See also **SRP**.

retailing: The business of buying goods at

wholesale and selling the merchandise at a higher price to the ultimate consumer.

S Corporation: A subchapter S corporation, in which the shareholders report the corporation's profits as if they were partners rather than shareholders.

SKU (stock-keeping unit): Items of merchandise of the same style, color, and size. A store with a total of seventy-five clocks but just ten different styles, would be said to stock ten SKUs in that category.

SRP (suggested retail price): The price recommended by the manufacturer.

sales floor, selling area: The space in a store devoted to displaying and selling merchandise.

sales per square foot: A figure arrived at by dividing annual sales at retail by the number of square feet of selling space in the store.

sales representative, sales rep: A salesperson, usually working on commission, presenting one or more wholesale lines of merchandise to store buyers for their consideration.

seasonal merchandise: Goods that don't sell equally well all year round because they relate to a particular holiday or season.

secondary market: The reselling of merchandise already purchased at retail. Some collectibles, such as figurines, are sold on the secondary market for more than their original retail price.

sell-through: How well an item or line sells in the store. Complete sell-through in a short period of time is ideal.

seller's permit: See **resale number**.

service merchandiser: An outside vendor that does inventories and reorders for a store on a periodic basis. Similar to a rack jobber.

shelf life: The length of time an item can remain on display without deteriorating.

ship date: The date on which merchandise ordered is to be shipped.

short, shortage, short shipment: Items missing from a shipment that are listed on the invoice and packing list as having being sent.

show special: A reduced price or special terms offered on orders written during the course of a trade show in order to create urgency in ordering.

showroom: A permanent wholesale display of merchandise.

shrinkage: A decrease in inventory levels due to shoplifting, employee theft, donations, breakage, and other causes. Shrinkage accounts for the difference between the physical inventory and the dollar value of the perpetual inventory.

shrink wrap: A cellophane used for wrapping products and gift baskets that shrinks to fit when heated with a hot air gun.

silent partner: An investor who does not participate in the day-to-day operation of the business.

slatwall: A sturdy surface covering with regularly spaced horizontal grooves designed to hold hooks, shelves, and other merchandise display fixtures.

slick: See **ad slicks**.

smart card: A magnetically encoded card that deducts coupon-like specials from the customer's total when checking out; serves as a check cashing card and encodes purchase information for the store's database. Also called a *fidelity card*.

softgoods: In housewares and department stores, merchandise made of fabric, such as clothing, linens, and towels.

sole proprietorship: A business owned by one individual, or in some states a husband and wife, with the taxable income reported as personal income, and all liability assumed by the owner(s).

souvenir: To personalize an item with the

name of the location. A sand dollar paperweight, for example, might be souvenired with "Florida."

special events: Activities set up to attract customers to a store or shopping center.

spiff: An extra incentive paid to the salesperson for selling a certain product or to a wholesale buyer for ordering a certain line. Also known as *push money.*

spot: A radio or TV commercial. A 30 spot is 30 seconds long.

square footage: The area of a store, measured by multiplying the length by the width.

statement: (1) A vendor's monthly recap of current invoices and credits; (2) a display of merchandise large enough to catch the customer's attention, as in "you won't be able to sell these if you don't order enough to make a statement." Also referred to as *telling a story.*

stock room: An area for unpacking and storing merchandise.

stock rotation: Moving older stock to the front in order to sell it first.

stockouts: When a supplier, or a store, is sold out of an item.

strip mall: A shopping center with an outside entrance for each store.

styleout: A product assortment recommended by the vendor.

subs, substitutions: Vendors' choices of items to send when those ordered are not available. It is often worthwhile to specify "no subs" if you do not wish to accept any items other than the ones ordered.

tag line: (1) A slogan that sums up a store's identity; (2) the last few seconds added to a vendor-supplied radio or TV spot, describing the store or promoting an event.

target market: The primary group of consumers to whom a vendor or retailer aims products, services, or advertising.

tear sheets: Copies of printed ads torn out of the newspaper or magazine, usually by the publisher; often required when substantiating claims for advertising allowances.

tender: The mode of payment used by a customer, such as cash, check, or charge. A *split tender* is the use of a check for part of the sale and cash for the remainder.

terms: Provisions stating how and when a vendor is to be paid (e.g., COD, net 30, pro forma).

third-party checks: Checks made out to someone else and then signed over to the store, for example a customer's paycheck endorsed payable to the retailer. Not accepted by most stores.

till: The money in the cash register drawer.

tonnage: A very large amount of merchandise, sometimes displayed "stacked out" in its cartons, a technique called a *bulk stack.*

trade: (1) "Open to the trade only" refers to a wholesale show open only to qualified buyers, not the public; (2) taking something out in trade: see **tradeout;** (3) carriage trade: well-to-do customers.

trade goods: Merchandise, usually from the Orient, available through many different importers (not exclusive to one company).

trade show: A market open to qualified wholesale buyers.

trademark: A company's nationally registered logo or name for a product or business.

tradeout: Swapping goods or services for advertising (e.g., getting radio spots in exchange for providing prizes for an on-air promotion).

transshipping: Reselling merchandise to another store, usually one not able (or authorized) to purchase the goods directly from the supplier. A discounter, for example, might get merchandise transshipped by a store that purportedly ordered the goods to sell at full price. See also **gray marketeer.**

trend: Changes in customer buying habits, such as the trend toward home entertaining. Also used to refer to goods whose popularity may be extreme but transient.

triple net, net net net lease: A rental agreement whereby the tenant pays rent plus all the location's operating and structural expenses, including building maintenance and repairs.

trunk show: A collection of merchandise, often clothes or jewelry, presented by the designer, manufacturer, or sales representative in the store.

turnkey: See **lease terms**.

turnover, turns: See **inventory turns**.

UPC (Universal Product Code): See **bar code**.

value-added merchandising: Enhancing the shopping experience by offering customers an item or service for free or at a low price. Value-added promotions include gift with purchase and purchase with purchase.

vendor: A supplier of merchandise, usually a manufacturer, importer, or distributor.

venture capitalists: Individuals or groups of investors who finance a business in exchange for a percentage of the profits. Venture capitalists, unlike limited partners, may get involved in running the business.

vesting: The time period after which an employee owns the full amount of the money accrued in his or her pension fund. When employees leave without being fully vested, a portion of their fund may revert to the others still in the plan.

visual merchandising: Creating the impulse to buy by displaying merchandise attractively, often accompanied by appropriate signage.

wholesale price: Lower-than-retail price paid by a store for supplies or merchandise purchased in quantity.

wholesaler, jobber, distributor: A supplier who sells merchandise, usually as a middleman, at wholesale to a store.

zoned coverage: Advertising that appears only in certain zones of a newspaper's circulation.

BIBLIOGRAPHY

Advertising and Marketing Checklists. 77 Proven Checklists to Save Time and Boost Advertising Effectiveness. 2d ed. Ron Kaatz. Lincolnwood, Ill.: NTC Business Books, 1994.

The Advertising Handbook for Small Business: Make a Big Impact with a Small Business Budget. 2d ed. Dell Dennison and Linda Tobey. North Vancouver, B.C.: Self-Counsel Press, 1994.

Applied Visual Merchandising. 2d ed. Kenneth H. Mills and Judith E. Paul. Englewood Cliffs, N.J.: Prentice Hall, 1988.

Basic Retailing. 2d ed. Irving Burstiner. Homewood, Ill.: Richard D. Irwin, 1991.

Ben and Jerry's: The Inside Scoop. How Two Real Guys Built a Business with a Social Conscience and a Sense of Humor. Fred "Chico" Lager. New York: Crown, 1994.

Body and Soul: Profits with Principles—The Amazing Success Story of Anita Roddick and The Body Shop. Anita Roddick. New York: Crown, 1994.

Bookkeeping Made Simple. Louis W. Fields. Revised by Richard R. Gallagher. Garden City, N.Y.: Doubleday, 1990.

The Business Planning Guide: Creating a Plan for Success in Your Own Business. 7th ed. David H. Bangs, Jr. Chicago: Upstart Publishing Company, 1995.

Buying and Selling a Business. Robert F. Klueger. New York: Wiley, 1988.

Buying and Selling a Small Business. Michael Coltman. North Vancouver, B.C.: Self-Counsel Press, 1994.

Clicking: 16 Trends to Future Fit Your Life, Your Works, and Your Business. Faith Popcorn and Lys Marigold. New York: HarperCollins, 1996.

Competing with the Retail Giants. Kenneth Stone. New York: Wiley, 1995.

The Complete Franchise Book: What You Must Know (and Are Rarely Told) About Buying or Starting Your Own Franchise. 2d ed. Dennis L. Foster. Rocklin, Calif.: Prima Publishing Co., 1994.

The Complete Idiot's Guide to Managing People. Arthur M. Pell. New York: Alpha Books/Simon & Schuster, 1995.

Customers for Life: How to Turn That One-Time Buyer into a Lifetime Customer. Carl Sewell and Paul B. Brown. New York: Currency Doubleday, 1990.

Delivering Knock Your Socks Off Service. Ron Zemke and Kristin Anderson. New York: American Management Association, 1991.

Developing a Personnel Manual: A Step-by-Step Approach for Your Company. Lin Grensing-Pophal. North Vancouver, B.C.: Self-Counsel Press, 1993.

Diary of a Small Business Owner: A Personal Account of How I Built a Profitable Business. Anita F. Brattina. New York: American Management Association, 1996.

Do-It-Yourself Advertising: How to Produce Great Ads, Brochures, Catalogs, Direct Mail, and Much More. Fred E. Hahn. New York: Wiley, 1993.

The Do-It-Yourself Business Book. Gustav Berle. New York: Wiley, 1989.

The Ecology of Commerce: A Declaration of Sustainability. Paul Hawken. New York: HarperBusiness, 1993.

The Entrepreneur and Small Business Problem Solver. 2d ed. William A. Cohen. New York: Wiley, 1990.

The Entrepreneur's Guide to Building a Better Business Plan. A Step-by-Step Approach. Harold J. McLaughlin. New York: Wiley, 1992.

Free Money for Small Businesses and Entrepreneurs. 4th ed. Laurie Blum. New York: Wiley, 1995.

The Great Game of Business: Unlocking the Power and Profitability of Open-Book Management. Jack Stack, with Bo Burlingham. New York: Currency Doubleday, 1992.

Great Store Design: Winners from the Institute of Store Planners/Visual Merchandising + Store Design Annual Competition. Rockport, Mass.: Rockport Publishers, 1994.

Growing a Business. Paul Hawken. New York: Simon & Schuster, 1988.

Guerrilla Advertising: Cost-Effective Tactics for Small-Business Success. Jay Conrad Levinson. Boston: Houghton Mifflin, 1994.

Guerrilla Financing: Alternative Techniques to Finance Any Small Business. Bruce Blechman and Jay Conrad Levinson. Boston: Houghton Mifflin, 1991.

Guerrilla Marketing Weapons: 100 Affordable Marketing Methods for Maximizing Profits from Your Small Business. Jay Conrad Levinson. New York: Penguin, 1990.

How to Buy and Manage a Franchise. Joseph Mancuso and Donald Boroian. New York: Simon & Schuster, 1993.

How to Open a Franchise Business. 21st Century Entrepreneur Series. Mike Powers. New York: Avon Books, 1995.

How to Open Your Own Store: Everything You Need to Know to Succeed in the Retail Marketplace. 21st Century Entrepreneur Series. Michael Antoniak. New York: Avon Books, 1994.

How to Run a Small Business. 7th ed. J. K. Lasser. New York: McGraw-Hill/ Simon & Schuster, 1994.

How to Start and Run Your Own Retail Business: Expert Advice from a Leading Business Consultant and Entrepreneur. Irving Burstiner. New York: Citadel Press, 1994.

How to Start, Run, and Stay in Business: The Nuts-and-Bolts Guide to Turning Your Business Dream into a Reality. Gregory F. Kishel and Patricia Gunter Kishel. New York: Wiley, 1993.

How to Write a Business Plan. 4th ed. Mike McKeever. Nolo Press Self-Help Law Series. Berkeley, Calif.: Nolo Press, 1992.

Inc. Yourself: How to Profit by Setting Up Your Own Corporation. 8th ed. Judith H. McQuown. New York: HarperBusiness, 1995.

The Interiors Book of Shops and Restaurants. Editors of *Interiors Magazine.* New York: Whitney Library of Design, 1981.

It's Not My Department: How to Get the Service You Want, Exactly the Way You Want It! Peter Glen. New York: Morrow, 1990.

Jane Applegate's Strategies for Small Business Success. Jane Applegate. New York: Plume/Penguin Books, 1995.

Keeping the Books: Basic Recordkeeping and Accounting for the Small Business. 2d ed. Linda Pinson and Jerry Jinnett. Dover, N.H.: Upstart Publishing Company, 1993.

Leadership Is an Art. Max DePree. Garden City, N.Y.: Doubleday, 1989.

Life and Work: A Manager's Search for Meaning. James A. Autry. New York: Morrow, 1994.

"Like No Other Store in the World": The Inside Story of Bloomingdale's. Mark Steven. New York: Thomas Y. Crowell, 1979.

Made in America: Sam Walton. My Story. Sam Walton and John Huey. New York: Bantam Books, 1993.

Making More Money Retailing: Low Cost Ideas for Successful Merchandising and Boosting Profits from Your Retail Store. Barbara Lamesis and Susan Ratliff. Phoenix, Ariz.: Marketing Methods Press, 1994.

Mary Kay on People Management. Mary Kay Ash. New York: Warner Books, 1984.

Minding the Store: A Memoir. Stanley Marcus. Boston: Little, Brown, 1974.

The Nordstrom Way: The Inside Story of American's #1 Customer Service Company. Robert Spector and Patrick D. McCarthy. New York: Wiley, 1995.

Ogilvy on Advertising. David Ogilvy. New York: Crown Publishers, 1983.

1,001 Ideas to Create Retail Excitement. Edgar A. Falk. Englewood Cliffs, N.J.: Prentice Hall, 1994.

1,001 Ways to Reward Employees. Bob Nelson. New York: Workman Publishing, 1994.

Our Wildest Dreams: Women Entrepreneurs Making Money, Having Fun, Doing Good. A Whole New Definition of Success and an Entirely New Paradigm of Working Life. Joline Godfrey. New York: HarperCollins, 1992.

The Popcorn Report: Faith Popcorn on the Future of Your Company, Your World, Your Life. Faith Popcorn. New York: HarperCollins, 1992.

Price Wars: How to Win the Battle for Your Customer! Thomas J. Winninger. Edina, Minn.: St. Thomas Press, 1994.

The Pursuit of WOW! Every Person's Guide to Topsy Turvy Times. Tom Peters. New York: Vintage Books, 1994.

Quest for the Best. Stanley Marcus. New York: Viking, 1979.

The Republic of Tea: Letters to a Young Zentrepreneur. How an Idea Becomes a Business. Mel Ziegler, Bill Rosenzweig, and Patricia Ziegler. New York: Currency Doubleday, 1992.

The Retail Store: Design and Construction. 2d ed. William R. Green. New York: Van Nostrand Reinhold, 1991.

Retail Store Planning and Design Manual. 2d ed. Michael J. Lopez. New York: Wiley, 1995.

SBA Hotline Answer Book: Answers to the 200 Most Commonly Asked Questions of the Small Business Administration. Gustav Berle. New York: Wiley, 1992.

Show Windows: 75 Years of the Art of Display. Barry James Wood. New York: Congdon & Weed, 1982.

The Simple Art of Greatness: Building, Managing and Motivating a Kick-Ass Workforce. James X. Mullen. New York: Viking, 1995.

Small Store Success. Ruth Pittman. Holbrook, Mass.: Bob Adams, 1990.

Small Store Survival: Success Strategies for Retailers. Arthur Andersen LLP. New York: Wiley, 1997.

Small Time Operator: How to Start Your Own Small Business, Keep Your Books, Pay Your Taxes, and Stay Out of Trouble! 20th ed. Bernard Kamoroff. Laytonville, Calif.: Bell Springs Publishing, 1995.

The Soul of a Business: Managing for Profit and the Common Good. Tom Chappell. New York: Bantam Books, 1993.

Start and Run a Profitable Retail Business: A Step-by-Step Business Plan. 3d ed. Michael M. Coltman. Self-Counsel Business Series. North Vancouver, B.C.: Self-Counsel Press, 1993.

The Store Owner's Guide to Practical Recordkeeping. Robert C. Ragan and M. Zafar Iqbal. Chicago: Contemporary Books, 1992.

Store Planning/Design. Lawrence J. Israel. New York: Wiley, 1994.

Store Windows. Number 8. Martin M. Pegler. New York: Retail Reporting Corp., 1995. (Note: Earlier editions of this annual are called *Store Windows That Sell.*)

Storefronts and Facades. Number 5. Martin M. Pegler. New York: Retail Reporting Corp., 1995.

Stores of the Year. Number 9. Martin M. Pegler. New York: Retail Reporting Corp., 1995.

Succeeding in Small Business: The 101 Toughest Problems and How to Solve Them. Jane Applegate. New York: Plume Books/Penguin, 1992.

The Successful Business Plan: Secrets and Strategies. 2d ed. Rhonda M. Abrams. Successful Business Library. Grants Pass, Ore.: Oasis Press/PSI Research, 1993.

Successful Retailing: Your Step-by-Step Guide to Avoiding the Pitfalls and Finding Profit as an Independent Retailer. 2d ed. Paula Wardell. Dover, N.H.: Upstart Press, 1993.

Up Against the Wal-Marts: How Your Business Can Prosper in the Shadow of the Retail Giants. Don Taylor and Jeanne Smalling Archer. New York: American Management Association, 1994.

Winning in Retailing. James A. Rasmus and Gerald D. Rasmus. Carlisle, Pa.: RDA Publishing Group, 1994.

Writing a Convincing Business Plan. Arthur R. DeThomas and William B. Fredenberger. Barron's Business Library. Hauppauge, N.Y.: Barron's, 1995.

Your Own Shop: How to Open and Operate a Successful Retail Business. Ruth Jacobsen. Blue Ridge Summit, Pa.: Liberty Hall Press, 1991.

INDEX

Entries in italics indicate sample forms to copy.